WILL BRITAIN SURVIVE BEYOND 2020?

DAVID MELDING

Sefydliad Materion Cymreig
Institute of Welsh Affairs

The Institute of Welsh Affairs exists to promote quality research and
informed debate affecting the cultural, social, political and economic
well-being of Wales. IWA is an independent organisation owing no
allegiance to any political or economic interest group. Our only
interest is in seeing Wales flourish as a country in which to work
and live. We are funded by a range of organisations and individuals.
For more information about the Institute, its publications, and how
to join, either as an individual or corporate supporter, contact:

IWA - Institute of Welsh Affairs
4 Cathedral Road
Cardiff
CF11 9LJ

tel   029 2066 0820
fax   029 2023 3741
email   wales@iwa.org.uk
web   www.iwa.org.uk

They saw the passing of certain values which at their best were very high and at their worst very human; they did not realise that life consists in change, that nothing can stand still, that today's shrines are only fit for tomorrow's cattle..

George Dangerfield, *The Strange Death of Liberal England*

To my
Mother and Father

Contents

Acknowledgements

Many people have combined tact and firm judgement to improve these essays, but three friends stand out for their stamina: Richard Wyn Jones, Greg Walker and Lee Waters. Without their encouragement and criticism, I doubt this collection would have been published. My personal assistant, Sarah Sharpe, cheerfully worked on the manuscripts as they slowly negotiated the troubled seas of composition. David Wills checked many of my hunches and half recollections on the internet. Without John Osmond's sympathetic and skilful editing this book would have been much weakened.

My initial hope had been to provide a Tory interpretation of the history of the Welsh nation within the British state. Ambition withered to a series of essays which explore what strike me as some of the significant themes in that wonderful history.

David Melding

Prologue

Charles III approached his investiture as King of Scotland with a mixture of resolve and optimism. His much grander coronation at Westminster Abbey had been a triumph that seemed to imbue the resurrected English state with a sense of almost immutable presence. Charles would be the last dual monarch of England and Scotland, but he felt a deep satisfaction in the Scottish Parliament's decision, announced that morning, to proclaim his second son heir to the Scottish throne. The House of Windsor had made up handsomely for the loss of Wales to republicanism.

Introduction

When I studied Soviet politics as an undergraduate in the early 1980s, the reading list contained one item of ideological relief, a small dose it then seemed of political science fiction, namely Andrei Amalrik's 1969 collection of essays *Will the Soviet Union Survive Until 1984?*[1] In retrospect the signature essay seems explosive and prescient; not so then when few took the piece seriously. Yet only seven years after Amalrik's prediction, in the wake of Europe's third great national awakening, the Soviet Union did collapse.

Will Britain ride out this storm of nationalism as it did the previous two when the monarchical empires of continental Europe convulsed in 1848 and collapsed in 1918? This time the Celtic nations of Britain seem more receptive to the forces of nationalism. Previously, as the Scottish commentator Michael Fry has observed of Scotland, 'she just never would have considered herself submerged, let alone oppressed'.[2] Likewise, perhaps more so, Wales.

The autumn of 1989 was a dramatic turning point for eastern Europe, and in Britain too it was a year of uncommon weight as the Thatcher administration marked its 10th anniversary with the resignation of the Chancellor and the demotion of the Foreign Secretary. In Scotland the introduction of the poll tax was met with widespread antipathy and the idea of devolution was resurrected as a prophylactic against Conservative rule. If in 1989 the question 'Will Britain Survive Beyond 2020?' would have sounded to many bizarre, it is now commonplace with historians as diverse as Norman Davies and Eric Hobsbawn[3] joining the debate on the viability of Britain. Nothing marks the transformation of Britain so vividly as the minority SNP government in Scotland and the Labour-Plaid Cymru coalition in Wales, both elected in 2007. Labour's devolution champions did not predict this outcome within just 10 years of the establishment of the devolved institutions! They had sounded the trumpet of devolution to rally their Celtic redoubts, not to see them shaken to their foundations like the walls of Jericho.

Nationalism is not inevitably monotheistic. It is possible to describe the UK as a particularly successful multinational state because its citizens have largely accepted the proposition that they are Welsh or Scottish or

English *and* British. True the English have tended to view Britishness as synonymous with Englishness. But for the Celtic nations this dual national identity has had more vitality. Furthermore, a duality exists within each national identity. Although British national identity has been associated mostly with political institutions and symbols, it has had a cultural dimension too. Similarly, while Scotland since 1707 and Wales since 1407 have been weak political entities, but much stronger cultural ones, political impulses have still occasionally stirred the Celtic nations. For Britishness to remain coherent it must now accommodate the explicit political character of Wales, Scotland, Northern Ireland and perhaps sooner than we think, England. A great but dormant truth is reasserting itself. The Home Nations are sovereign entities. At the moment they choose to be part of the British state. Long may it continue. But let no one be fooled that this allegiance is inevitable. Britain might not survive beyond 2020.

The best way to preserve Britain as a multinational state is to accept that the UK can no longer be based on tacit consent but requires a new settlement. This settlement will need to be federal in character so that the sovereignties of the Home Nations and the UK state can be recognised in their respective jurisdictions. Because British politicians and constitutional theorists have rarely been forced to think in this way, at least not since the Irish crisis that ended in 1921, a sense of despair seems to have fallen on those keen to preserve Britain.

However, an international debate has raged on the durability of multinational states since the collapse of the Russian and Yugoslav federations in the early 1990s. Concepts often ignored by political philosophers, like nationalism and federalism, have received much closer attention. Simeon and Conway, for example, have concluded that 'it is hard to see any form of successful accommodation of multiple nations within a single state that does not include federalism'.[4] A consensus seems to be forming among western political philosophers that liberal multinational states continue to offer the best basis for a stable international order. In an important recent work, the Canadian political theorist Wayne Norman has written 'I am concerned with *how we ought to act, and what sorts of institutions we ought to give ourselves, when we live in societies where nationalism is current...* At the heart of this book is a plea for the continued existence of flourishing, peaceful, democratic multinational states'.[5]

I want to spend a few moments outlining my own development as a nationalist. In 1987, as a member of the Conservative Research Department, I was asked to write a pamphlet on the Conservative Party and the Welsh nation. The pamphlet is long forgotten, but it did mark a new beginning for me as I grappled with my own national identity. Until then my Welshness was merely an accidental entity that had no vivid cultural dimension. Britain, I thought, was a state and not a nation, and I therefore was nationless. The English too seemed to have moved beyond nationalism to the higher, Hegelian, life of the state.

However, I became addicted to reading Welsh history. And the more I read the more I appreciated the coherence of the Welsh nation, and my membership of it. In the 1980s, I also visited Czech friends several times. In Prague I caught some of the infectious enthusiasm the Czechs have for small nation nationalism. The thought of Thomas Masaryk fascinated me and strengthened my sense of Welshness. Throughout this personal renaissance my attachment to Britain never weakened, but I recognised that it too was of a profoundly national character. (How else, in retrospect, can we make sense of the Thatcher administration's battles with the European Union in the 1980s?)

Although now accepting, indeed enjoying, a dual national identity, I still considered the spheres of Welshness and Britishness distinct and not overlapping. My Welshness was in essence cultural, my Britishness political. So I thought even in 1997 when voting 'No' to devolution, although I was profoundly shaken by the vote in Scotland which had already declared the Britain of 1707-1997 null and void. Today, I believe that the Home Nations should have their political sovereignty properly recognised; but I want these same sovereign nations to recommit themselves to the British state, and I believe that a new and fuller British nationalism will then flourish.

References
1. Andrei Amalrik, *Will the Soviet Union Survive Until 1984?* (London 1970).
2. Michael Fry, *The Union* (Edinburgh 2006) p.310.
3. Norman Davies, *The Isles A History* (London 1999) p. 778; and Eric Hobsbawn's remarks quoted in the *Western Mail* 2nd October 2002.
4. Richard Simeon and Daniel-Patrick Conway, 'Federalism in the management of conflict in multinational societies' in *Multinational Democracies* by Gagnon and Tully, Eds. (Cambridge 2001) p. 364.
5. Wayne Norman, *Negotiating Nationalism* (Oxford 2006) pp x-xi.

Chapter 1

Wales and the Idea of Britain

*...so strangely does myth plus legend
plus history weave its meander.*

David Jones, *The Myth of Arthur*

The Roman Influence

When that remarkable man, Publius Aelius Hadrianus, commissioned the wall that would forever bear his name, he knew that the *Imperium* had limits. An unsettling thought, and one set to impinge increasingly on Roman minds. Not that in AD 122 the end of the western Empire could have been reasonably anticipated. Indeed for a while Hadrian's Wall served as a base for expansion into what is today called Scotland. The wall itself was the most stunning military construction yet built in Europe. It would not be remotely matched in Britain until Edward I anchored his dreadnought castles in north west Wales over 1,000 years later. Like all fortifications it was meant to deter and defend.

Hadrian's Wall, in the spheres of mind and matter, divided Britannia. The western limits of Romano-Britannia owed more to geography than politics. Europe's north west peninsula had been inundated by the post Ice Age flood some 6,000 years before Claudius set foot on the land of the Catuvellauni in AD 43. Romans, men of the tideless Mediterranean, feared the ripping tides that tear at Britain. One risky nautical adventure was enough: Ireland was left to the mysteries of the 'Ocean'. Ireland and northern Scotland thus became the only parts of the Celtic civilisation to survive undisturbed into the early Middle Ages.

During what we choose to call its 'La Tene' phase (roughly 500 BC – AD 100) Celtic culture rooted itself firmly in Britain and Ireland. It appears not to have been accompanied by large-scale migration. Rather, adventurous traders and warriors, most of them young men, settled and eventually established themselves as an élite over the indigenous population. They brought many tangible gifts – from chariots and coins to iron tools and roads – but it was in the realm of ideas that the Celtic influence proved indelible.

The Celts were perhaps the first civilisation to universalise the concept of immortality. Eternal life was not the preserve of gods and kings. Not that the Celts conceived of an after-life but instead saw existence as a constant crossing between this and the other world. Gods were ancestors and heroes rather than creators and judges. These ancestor gods existed in great profusion, anticipating the cult of saints, and were often venerated in triune form, anticipating perhaps the Trinity.

Optimism in religion was matched by a playful exuberance in art which is rich, symbolic and beautifully patterned. The 'La Tene' style still flourishes today. Celtic culture had come into contact with the Mediterranean world and this produced 'an artistic synthesis which is among the most exquisite of the creations of mankind' to quote the historian John Davies.[1] The achievements of our ancestors in the Neolithic and early Iron Age should not be overlooked – man built his first stone monuments, the megaliths, here on the edge of Europe. However, their lives remain largely hidden in pre-history. The poet David Jones was surely right in regarding the first great civilisation north of the Alps to be the bedrock of the *Matter of Britain*.

At its zenith in about 300 BC the Celtic civilisation stretched from Ireland in the west to Anatolia in the east (in time the Galatians would receive a letter from St. Paul). It encompassed most of the Iberian peninsula and extended into northern Italy. With Greece and Rome, it was one of Europe's three great civilisations and then the most vigorous. What the Celts lacked was a strong civic culture, and this proved a severe impediment as soon as Roman interest moved beyond trade to military conquest.

No doubt had the Celts been left undisturbed they would have developed centralised states, but even the most advanced Celtic settlements, present in Britain at the time of Caesar's reconnaissance in 55 BC, were no more than proto-urban. Yet these settlements were as large as medieval towns. The failure to develop a centralised bureaucracy meant that the Celts fought good battles but bad wars. Rome was sacked in 390 BC, ensuring future Roman antipathy, and Delphi in 278 BC.

The Greeks proved more forgiving and it is from them that we have received antiquity's most measured account of the Celtic civilisation as well as the very name 'Keltoi'. Despite its vast territorial range, it is impossible to speak of a Celtic empire. It was a glorious, vivid culture and it grew on one of the strongest branches of the Aryan family of languages.

There is little consensus about the depth of Roman influence in the Empire's most remote province. The historian Norman Davies believes that 'Roman Britain left no lasting legacy of note'[2] and he points out that unlike Gaul and Spain, a Romance language did not develop in Britannia. He even describes the Roman period as a cul-de-sac in the evolution of the Isles. Davies has done much to remind a largely English audience of the significance of Celtic culture, but he sweeps too much aside when he argues that the only substantial item in the Roman legacy was Christianity.

Hugh Kearney's pioneering work *The British Isles: A History of Four Nations* offers the opposite interpretation and considers the Roman influence on Britannia to be so powerful 'that it is only by a great effort of the imagination that we see the need to go beyond the lasting monuments of Roman rule to the scattered relics of the Celtic societies which everywhere in Britain preceded it'.[3]

The territorial extent of Roman rule is much easier to determine than its lasting influence. Southern Britannia, roughly the area south of a line drawn from the Thames estuary to the Severn channel, experienced settled civil administration. Northern Britannia was also deeply penetrated; but large pockets of Celtic influence remained in upland areas such as Yorkshire, and this necessitated a much heavier military presence and extensive fortification. The highland zones to the west and north were merely under military control. We can see in outline by AD 400 the four units that would one day constitute the Home Nations. However, the development of nations is not an inevitable and teleological process, and these stems could have produced alternative ramifications (Britain would be divided quite differently in the Viking period).

Even in the south, the most Romanised part of Britannia, the population remained overwhelmingly Celtic. While the towns were a powerful Romanising force, and a Romano-Celtic élite enjoyed a bilingual culture, the bulk of the population lived on the land and was much less amenable to assimilation. Nevertheless, the urban culture brought to Britannia by the Romans has always inspired those who think about the *Matter of Britain*. Civic life, especially when infused with Christianity, struck many as a divine gift almost comparable to the discovery of fire.

Until very recently, children in primary schools were taught that the post-Roman phase of British history constituted the Dark Ages. The Welsh nationalist writer H.W.J. Edwards argued, in a book entitled *Sons of the Romans*, that nationalism was rooted not in the ideology of the French Revolution but far deeper in the past when church and state combined to form a single civic entity.[4] Glanmor Williams noted that even at the eve of the Reformation the Welsh 'were intensely proud of their ancient and particular history; not least because, emphasizing as it did their alleged connections with Rome, its empire, civilization and church, it conferred upon them immense moral superiority over their Saxon neighbours who, for so long, had been unlettered heathen barbarians'.[5] In Wales, a British foundation myth flourished in Tudor times that stretched back to Brutus of Troy and claimed that the Celtic church was founded by Joseph of Arimathea.

Yet what must have most struck the Celts who lived through the occupation was the military nature of Roman rule. Between AD 48-79 thirteen campaigns were conducted in what is now Wales, and three legions were kept in the military zone of Britannia (based at Caerleon, Chester and York). This amounted to one of the heaviest, and most expensive, military deployments in the Empire. The economic returns made this expenditure worthwhile because Britannia's mineral resources were extensive. So lucrative was Britannia, that the Province's governorship was accorded particularly high status. Unsurprisingly, civic life outside southern Britannia was essentially an epiphenomenon of military occupation. Here, Roman rule was always more fragile than in Gaul or Iberia. Even so, the town of Caerwent, with perhaps some 3,000 inhabitants, was the largest to develop in Wales before the Industrial Revolution.

When the Romans introduced Christianity to Britannia in the fourth Century the greatest event in our cultural history occurred, or more accurately started. Today some 70 per cent of the British population identify themselves as Christian (a remarkable cultural phenomenon) while retaining little urgency to practice the faith. The Celtic church, in so far as the term is coherent, was a later development and should not be confused with Romano-British Christianity which was unequivocally part of the imperial structure of the late Roman Empire. Bishops appear in Britannia just one year after the Edict of Milan, which granted Christianity its imperial recognition, and they played an active part in church affairs.[6] The presence of British bishops is recorded at the Council of Rimini in 359.

With official sanction, the Church spread throughout the Roman Empire in the latter part of the fourth Century and attracted the patronage of the powerful and ambitious. In Britannia Christianity spread in urban and rural areas and became strong enough to survive into the post-Roman era. Even so, its influence was far from pervasive and Celtic deities still attracted the devotion of many people. Celtic religion was essentially humanist and accessible, which marked it out sharply from the cold and aloof state religion of pagan Rome. Christianity seems to have had little difficulty in appealing to these aspects of the Celtic imagination: it was personal in that God had become man, and optimistic in believing that it was the will of God that everyone should receive salvation.

Against this background one of the Church's most optimistic thinkers emerges, the Romano-Celtic monk Pelagius. Writing in Rome when the city was menaced by the Goths in 409-410, and when Romano-Britannia was leaving the imperial orbit, Pelagius challenged the very notion of original sin, 'If sin is natural, it is not voluntary: if it is voluntary, it is not inborn'.[7] Man could, then, choose good by virtue of his God given nature. This optimistic stance came up against the bleak pre-destination implicit in Augustine's doctrine of Grace. The debate raged on for twenty years or so and the Augustinian doctrine, although much modified by the Church, won out. However, Pelagius has worn better than Augustine in ultimately backing free will and universal salvation against pre-destination to damnation for all but the elect. Britannia and Gaul were deeply influenced by Pelagius' thought, and the British bishops twice had to call on the services of the great St. Germanus of Auxerre to root out the heresy.

Romano-Britannia did not suddenly collapse in 410. A Romano-British culture survived for some time independent of Rome. The Empire in the west came to an end gradually but decisively in the fifth Century. A 'new' Rome emerged at Constantinople and the eastern Empire turned Greek and survived until 1453. Could a similar evolution have occurred in Britannia and resulted in a Celtic Byzantium? There is a hint of this fanciful vision of a new Rome in some depictions of what was lost as the pressure from the Germanic barbarians increased inexorably in the next two centuries. But it is a fantasy: there was little appetite amongst the British aristocracy to recreate the mechanisms of centralised government. The imperial vacuum was filled by local potentates.

The Celts had survived the arrival and departure of the *Imperium*. Soon the forces that brought the *Imperium* to an end would impinge heavily on the Isles. A new epoch had begun. In his epic poem *The Anathemata* David Jones laments this time of destruction, as one of 'bridges broken down'.[8]

Change and Chance

In one flat if seismic sentence the *Anglo-Saxon Chronicles* record, 'And in their days Hengest and Horsa, invited by Vortigern, king of the Britons, sought out Britain in the landing-place which is named Ebba's Creek, at first to help the Britons, but later they fought against them'.[9] The British-Welsh tradition came to view such enormity as the consequence of treachery not idle folly.

If Arthur represents light and hope in Celtic legend, Vortigern is the dark *Matter of Britain*. According to one Welsh tale he was ostracised and spent the rest of his life forlornly wandering the earth – a common fate for traitors in European legends. Vortigern's perfidy depicts in epic form an event which took some two centuries to unfold. German mercenaries were used in Britannia in the late Roman period and this practice was probably continued by various British kings after the Roman withdrawal. While the Romano-British remained the paramount force throughout Britannia in the 5th Century, the Celtic élites faced an array of formidable challenges. Although a sense of unity lingered, an insular concept of sovereignty did not develop – the Roman province of Britannia had not become its own *Imperium*. Rather the vague hope of a restoration of Roman authority motivated many to keep up the old ways. At the start of the 6th Century it was a fragile and vulnerable Britannia that faced the climacteric phenomenon of German migration.

Now we enter the age of rebus in which all manner of things were made. This stuff of Britain will always remain recondite – a catacomb not a cathedral. In exploring these subterranean passages of the *Matter of Britain* we must proceed tentatively and delicately, but proceed we must. Not everything is elusive. The sense of loss that emerges from British texts (steadily becoming Welsh) is plangent. In his *De Excidio Britanniae* (Concerning the Fall of Britain) the Romano-Celtic monk Gildas rants and raves about the enervating sins of his fellow Britons. Written around 540, it was the predictable response of a Celtic Christian whose imagination was dominated by the divine force of Providence. Only sin could account for the fact that the civil and Christian Britons were being overwhelmed by the non-urban and pagan Germans.

Plague, poverty and pagans were the three tails of the whip wheeled by Christ as fearsome judge or Pantocrator. The Venerable Bede, writing nearly two centuries later, modified this Christian interpretation slightly by emphasising the virtue of the now godly Saxons as servants of the

12

Almighty. If victory brought the Saxons a sense of manifest destiny, defeat left the Celts the hope of salvation, and this was made legend if not flesh in the figure of Arthur. The Celts held fast to the idea of Britain even as much of Britannia fell into Saxon hands. David Jones captures this spirit of loss and hope,

> All the efficacious asylums
> *in Wallia vel in Marchia Walliae*
> > *ogofau* of, that cavern for
> > Cronos, Owain, Arthur.
> *Terra Walliae!*
> > Buarth Meibion Arthur!
> > Enclosure of the Children of Troy![10]

The guilt-ridden anguish of Gildas is understandable, but it obscures the dynamic at work in western Europe between 400-700. Waves of barbarians overwhelmed much of the former western Empire, but these German tribes were not uniform in character. Those destined to settle in France, Spain and Italy had been in prolonged contact with Rome. They adopted many Roman practices, such as urban life, and came to speak the daughter languages of Latin.

German migration to Britain did not follow this continental pattern. The northern German tribes – we will now use the tag 'Saxons' – were much less Romanised and not inclined to settle in towns. This would be the only significant German migration not to produce a Romance language. Unlike their Frankish and Gothic cousins, it took the Saxons a very long time to win their conquests. Indeed, Britain was not entirely conquered at all, and this had the consequence of dividing the land into a Celtic west, a Teutonic east, and a Gaelic north.

Celtic-British kingdoms disappear from history gradually: Elmet in Yorkshire c. 650, Cornwall c. 838, and Strathclyde c. 1000. Aneirin's long poem *Y Gododdin* commemorates the British attack on Catterick in north Yorkshire which, if it had succeeded, might have hindered the alliance between the Anglian kingdoms of Bernicia and Deira.[11] The British forces gathered at Dineidyn (probably Edinburgh) and were led by the Gododdin king Mynyddawg Mwynfawr. Only one warrior survived, we are told, but before defeat they killed many of the enemy. As Aneirin laments 'Though they went to churches to do penance/The inescapable meeting with death came to them'.[12] Even in the 10th

Century, when hope of restoring a Celtic Britain was forlorn, a polemical poem *Armes Prydein* (The Prophecy of Britain) sees the English being vanquished by a Celtic alliance from Wales, Ireland, Brittany, Cornwall and the Old North.[13]

While a Celtic Britannia now only existed in myth and legend, the land of western Britain had become *Cymru* by the end of the 8th Century. The early medieval Celtic culture that now developed in Wales was in advance of most European experience. The unifying effects of language, literature and law started to produce the sinews of nationhood. However, Wales was a triptych rather than a single composition. Yet it is true that in the reigns of Rhodri ap Merfyn, Hywel ap Cadell, Maredudd ab Owain, and Gruffudd ap Llywelyn we can see strong intimations of political unity.

The consolidation of statelets into larger political units was a European phenomenon, but the process was a fragile one. This phenomenon was not like a *Risorgimento* powered by a sense of national consciousness. While the claims made by some political theorists that nationalism was not conceptually possible until the Reformation (or even the French Revolution) can hardly convince those with an appreciation of medieval history, seeing the history of Wales, England and Scotland pre-1066 as fundamentally a process of nation-building is highly unsatisfactory. If the *Matter of Britain* lay dormant, half remembered and often distorted in tales of a Romano–British past, the *Matter of Wales* could not yet cohere. This was true also for England, and very much so for Scotland. That astonishing Judeo formula – *gens, rex, ecclesia* – never quite fell within the reach of the medieval mind. There existed not a Welsh people (rather, as in England, peoples), nor a Welsh ruler capable of founding a dynasty, nor a Welsh church with metropolitan authority. What did exist was a land recognised by Celt and Saxon alike to be *Cymru*. Offa's Dyke, a boundary even more significant than Hadrian's Wall, is the suitably monumental recognition of this wonderful fact.

It is not easy for our post-Enlightenment minds to apprehend the imaginative force that Christianity exerted on the lives of our ancestors. Had the Christian Celts been able to conceive of something as abstract as *nationalism* it may have strengthened their undoubted sense of patriotism. Nevertheless, it would not have replaced their belief that man's principal purpose was to make himself fit for eternal existence with God. Even those historians who argue that the influence of Rome on Britain was limited, acknowledge the enduring significance of

14

Christianity. Traditional Celtic religious practices were synthesised successfully into the new faith. This partly explains why Christianity not only survived the end of the western Empire, but continued to grow in Britain.

By the 6th Century there were small monasteries all over Wales. The Church in Celtic lands was monastic in its organisation, but it is not possible to speak of a Celtic church in the sense of a distinct and separate development. Christianity in Wales was part of the universal Church which accepted papal authority. However, this was not yet the age of the centralised, imperial papacy, and a considerable diversity of style existed throughout the Church. It is true that the Pelagian heresy – which reflected some ancient Celtic beliefs – did take root in Britain, but it was contained by the bishops. The monophysite heresy, the belief that Christ was God but not God-man, which was by far the most fissiparous force in the Church at this time, did not spread west; and in any event it would have been profoundly out of sympathy with the Celtic tradition. The view that the Church in Celtic lands was proto-Protestant is the implausible argument of Reformation propagandists.

Augustine of Canterbury is often portrayed by historians sympathetic to the Celtic cause as a proud, petulant and pedantic man. This is almost certainly unfair. It is the case that Augustine's arrival in Kent marks one of the most momentous events in British history. Yet it nearly failed to happen at all. When in Gaul the hesitant and inexperienced Augustine thought of turning back for Rome with his small band of monks. Pope Gregory the Great stiffened Augustine's resolve and what Catholic historians call the Church's first mission started in 597. Gregory could have used Celts to evangelise the Saxons, and indeed Irish monks had already converted some of the Picts and would soon spread the Gospel to Northumbria. But this course was not followed, no doubt in part because of the continuing conflict between the Britons and the Saxons. The papal mission inevitably created some tension between the Celtic bishops and Augustine and his successors at Canterbury.

Welsh bishops did not formally accept the authority of Canterbury until the 12th Century, but no one could deny that Gregory saw Britain as one province to be governed by archbishoprics in London (soon moved to Canterbury) and York. Despite the fanciful inventions of Gerald of Wales, Wales never achieved this metropolitan status and Scotland received its first archbishopric and formal mark of autonomy as late as 1472.

It is not surprising that some historians have seen a rift opening up between the Celtic bishops and Rome as a consequence of Augustine's mission. The Synod of Whitby (664) is cited as the most compelling evidence of this fact. While the view of Rome on the dating of Easter won out, Whitby was more about authority than the clash of competing cultures. What united the Church – whether in Rome or Wales – was the common practice of the sacraments, liturgy and mass. Nevertheless, a powerful idea now started to enter the English imagination – that of a special bond with Rome which marked the manifest destiny of England. The Anglo-Saxon Chronicles record that in 605, just a year after Augustine's death, 'Æthelfrith led his army to Chester and there killed a countless number of Welsh; and thus was fulfilled Augustine's prophecy which he spoke: "If the Welsh do not want peace with us, they shall perish at the hands of the Saxons"'.[14]

Papal favour and a sense of destiny soon produced a belief in the lordship of English kings over Britain. There are several references to English overlordship in the Anglo-Saxon Chronicles and, while we may discount these accounts somewhat as naturally unsympathetic to the Celts, they describe an underlying reality which reflected a European phenomenon, the growth of feudalism. The entry for 926 in the Worcester Manuscript provides a vivid insight into the early-medieval mind:

> Here fiery rays appeared in the northern part of the sky. And Sihtric perished and King Athelstan succeeded to the kingdom of Northumbria; and he governed all the kings who were in this island: first Hywel, king of the West Welsh, and Constantine, king of Scots, and Owain, king of Gwent, and Ealdred, Ealdwulf's offspring, from Bamburgh. And they confirmed peace with pledges and with oaths in a place which is named Rivers' Meeting on 12 July; and they forbade all devil-worship and then parted in concord.[15]

This acceptance of overlordship did not imply a loss of independence. What might appear to us as an act of humble submission can more coherently be viewed as an acceptance by the paramount power of the native rulers in Scotland and Wales.

By 700 the forces at work in the post-Roman era had produced a negative outcome: Britain would not be Celtic. It remained an open question whether it might be Saxon. The received historical interpretation, that the period 500 – 1066 saw the establishment of Saxon hegemony, has only recently been assailed. In any exploration of the *Matter of Britain* attention must be given to the Scandinavian connection. From the late 8th Century, Norwegian and Danish migration began and it accelerated in the middle of the 9ᵗʰ Century (the Swedes went east and founded Rus).

The existing social structures in England, Scotland, Ireland and Wales were tested and largely transformed by military exigencies into semi-feudal orders. Under Alfred the Great (reigned 871-99) and Edgar (reigned 959-75) the emerging Saxon realm under the lordship of Wessex became more centralised. The shire system, established by Edgar, was a military structure.

The Church also started to change the theory of kingship and its practical capabilities. Saxon kings from Offa had drawn on the resources of the Church to add authority to the concept of kingship, which was seen increasingly as sacred. The Church provided later Saxon rulers with a formidable bureaucracy capable of formulating law, keeping accounts, and regulating trade. The Domesday Book would consolidate existing practice. This did not directly threaten the Celtic lands, but it was becoming clear that *Angelcynn*, as Alfred referred to the land of the English folk, was the most powerful force shaping the *Matter of Britain*.

While Britain could still have moved into the Scandinavian orbit, or become a less centralised political entity with a patchwork of Celtic, Saxon and Norse kingdoms, the dynamic towards unity in England was strong. This is seen in the reign of Cnut (1016-35) who, while Norse, saw himself as the legitimate English king. In 1066, with Harold's victory over the Norsemen, came at last the prospect of the *Matter of Britain* cohering into the kingdoms of England, Scotland and Wales. Of course the price of this outcome for Scotland and Wales would be the Saxon overlordship of Britain. But had not Providence been leading in this direction for 450 years? Within 450 hours of Harold's victory at Stamford Bridge came the emphatic answer. While the workings of Providence are inscrutable, those of the Normans would require little interpretation.

Rhuddlan
Even as Harold Godwinsson drove Gruffudd ap Llywelyn back into Wales in 1063, the wheel of fortune had started to turn against the

soon-to-be king. In the history of England, Gruffudd's incursions mark little more than Harold's emergence as the premier earl of Saxon England. The event carries altogether greater weight in Welsh history. Gruffudd's hegemony over Wales did not survive his murder, at the hands of his own disappointed and defeated men, later that year.

In a European context, the absence of a unified Welsh kingship in the eleventh Century is unremarkable. But the British arena was about to become peculiar and more demanding than at any time since the Roman conquest. However, as things stood in 1063, Welsh independence did not seem threatened. Far back in the 7th Century the Saxons had attempted to drive into south Wales and so control both sides of the Severn sea. They were conclusively repelled by the men of Gwent, one of the most important events in the history of Wales according to John Davies. While Wales remained a volatile political entity capable of occasional unity under a strong prince, in Gwynedd the prospect of a more permanent Celtic realm could be glimpsed. It was Gwynedd that had preserved in its purest form the idea of Britain. Gwynfor Evans wrote that 'Wales remained the principal if not sole heir of *Romanitas* in the island' of Britain in the early medieval period.[16] David Jones' poetic eye saw the Romano dragon emerge as the emblem of Wales, a "red rampin' griffin" and 'Caesar from his stern-post flew the same'.[17]

The annihilation of Saxon England threatened also to repudiate the idea of Britain. Although he bravely defeated the Norse, Harold succumbed to their offspring the Normans after undergoing for a second time that most terrible of Providence's ordeals: test by battle. A new epoch had been ordained and England ceased to be an independent kingdom. Welsh and Scottish independence was immediately menaced by Norman incursions. In Gwent, where the Saxons had failed on the banks of the Wye, the Normans succeeded with disturbing alacrity. By 1090 the fate of Wales seemed bleak, but relations between Norman England and Scotland stabilised. The Normans regarded the Scottish kingdom as a realm worthy of recognition, while Wales was seen as lacking the stability brought about by a strong ruling dynasty.

Nevertheless, the cultural animosity the Normans felt towards the Saxons did not pollute the Norman-Welsh relationship. The Welsh and Norman aristocracies often had cordial relations and sometimes intermarried. Even the *Matter of Britain*, now pretty much under sole Welsh guardianship, in time came to interest the Normans. True it received a more utilitarian treatment in the hands of the Normans than it did in the minds of the Welsh. Even Arthur, that most elusive hero of Welsh legend, was pressed into more practical Norman service. Yet that the *Matter of Britain* became a potent force in Norman England during the 12th Century indicated the power of this idea on the medieval imagination. While Norman arms subdued much of Britain, strangely no new ideology weakened the idea of Britain.

The Normans quickly conquered England and held extensive territories in France, Spain, Italy and the Levant, but Wales largely remained in the hands of her native rulers. Of course, by 1093 the reality of a loose Norman overlordship could not be denied. Yet in the God-ordained temporal hierarchy of medieval Christendom, such suzerainty did not imply humiliation. Overlordship was already part of Welsh political life.

Nevertheless, Norman hegemony did differ in one vital respect from that of the Saxons. The Normans penetrated and colonised lands in Wales. In the vales and lower valleys of south and west Wales these incursions were carried out by hungry younger sons and lesser lords; while along the March, great barons enjoyed the status of petit sovereigns. It would be no accident that in English regnal politics the Marcher lords would be a potent threat to the power of the Crown.

Meanwhile, the Royal eye rarely fell on Wales and instead wandered across the channel to ogle more desirable territory in France. This mixture of indifference towards Welsh traditions and fear of Marcher power could make the Crown an ally of the native Welsh princes. Between 1170 and 1270 a more or less stable relationship prevailed between the Welsh princes and the Norman-Angevin kings. Its most remarkable outcome was the Treaty of Montgomery in 1267 which the historian John Davies observes 'was a great achievement, for the treaty was a recognition of the fact that Llywelyn had established the basic constituents of a Welsh polity'.[18]

In 1100 Wales was very far from a shrunken Britannia. It had created a new world with the melodious words of the Welsh language. The most magical creation emerged in Dyfed where an unknown author of genius produced the redaction of the *Four Branches of the Mabinogi* with which we are familiar. In the 19th Century Charlotte Guest added seven other tales to *Pedair Cainc y Mabinogi* and entitled her translation *The Mabinogion*. These medieval tales stand today as one of the canons of

European literature. John Updike captured the marvel of *The Mabinogion* when saying that the tales:

> were concerned with how things *were*, in that pre-time when names were bestowed and giants engendered races, a pre-time still in our own fibres... The old tales drink from the spring wherein fact has not yet been filtered from fancy, and remind us that any narrator begins by believing that he has something marvellous to tell.[19]

The Welsh were confident in speech and becoming more familiar with the written word. Inevitably many tales and poems were lost, but thankfully the world we see in *The Mabinogion* owes its chance preservation to the *White Book of Rhydderch* and the *Red Book of Hergest*. Both manuscripts were written in the 1300s after the end of independence, and it is significant that the Welsh language was practically unaffected by the forces of anglicisation that so totally transformed Welsh law and politics. Scotland experienced the reverse outcome and saw an anglicized Scottish-Norman élite establish an independent but English-speaking kingdom.

While the Norman-English could do little to silence Welsh speech, the glorious hero of that oral tradition, Arthur, was captured and turned to a grand Norman purpose. The critic Peter Ackroyd, in his book *Albion*, asks how Arthur 'became the central figure or figment of the English imagination whose creative life has stretched into the twenty-first century with no sign of abatement?'[20] We should start our answer with Geoffrey of Monmouth. In the late 1130s Geoffrey produced his *History of the Kings of Britain*. According to the historian R.R. Davies, at this point the Normans were not much concerned with the *Matter of Britain*, as their imagination led them more readily to Northern France, but Geoffrey's work 'posed a profound political challenge'.[21] Arthur had waged his battles, real or mythological, against the Saxons and this made him a potential ally of the Normans. However, Arthur had led the Britons, and the Britons (now Welsh) were still very much present and playfully rejuvenating the legend.

Arthur appears in the story of *Culhwch and Olwen*, written down well before Geoffrey's *Historia*, and the world it depicts is an undoubtedly Celtic one. After Geoffrey's imaginative treatment, the Arthurian legend presented the Normans with a challenge and an opportunity. The challenge was how to respond to the prophecy that Arthur would return and claim his rightful inheritance as King of Britain, symbolically represented by the Crown in London? In a world where relics and symbols played a powerful role, even influencing dynastic politics, this prophecy was taken seriously. But if this challenge could be met, then the opportunity of establishing a British monarchy might be grasped. The Britons – through what was now Welsh historical lore – had brought into the Middle Ages the concept that the island of Britain was an irreducible unit.[22]

Before we briefly consider the Norman response to the challenge of Arthur, it should be noted that the option of ignoring the legend or debunking it was not pursued, such was the imaginative power of Arthur and the *Matter of Britain*. Like the Tudors later, the Normans grabbed the Arthurian legend and used it as a means of legitimising a rather tenuous claim to the throne. The right of conquest had to be sublimated and absorbed into a grander purpose. The legend had a ready market once its ownership was prised away from the troublesome Welsh. This was done easily enough by repeating the old canard-cum–censure conceived first by Gildas, and elaborated by the Venerable Bede, that the Britons had through perfidy lost the favour of God and the right to rule Britannia.

Arthur was literally kidnapped in 1278 when his 'remains' and those of Guinevere were disinterred and then re-buried before the great alter at Glastonbury in the presence of Edward I. As he entered his final battle against the Welsh, Edward had assumed the magical mantle of Arthur. A few years later the Chronicles at Bury St. Edmunds observed that 'England, Scotland and Wales are under his sway. He has thereby acquired the former monarchy of the whole of Britain, for so long fragmented and truncated'.[23] As John Davies so pungently puts it, 'Arthur was received into the Valhalla of his enemies'.[24] Even today Arthur is firmly in the English embrace. Peter Ackroyd states that the:

> story of Arthur has always been striated with sensations of loss and of transitoriness, which may well account for its central place within the English imagination; the native sensibility is touched with melancholy, as we have seen, and the sad fate of Arthur and his kingdom corresponds to that national mood.[25]

Welsh independence in ecclesiastical matters was strong, although the Catholic Church in Wales had lost the innovation it had shown in the age of the Saints. Its achievements in no way matched those of the Welsh language and its literature. In Wales the Church had to respond to a transformation that the historian Glanmor Williams considered 'not incomparable in scale and magnitude to that later brought about by the Protestant Reformation or the Methodist Revival'.[26]

The great era of papal reform had started and it would see consistent canon law promulgated and the diocesan system established, together with fixed parishes. Meanwhile, in France, monasticism was receiving a near miraculous rejuvenation. The Normans were keen agents of church reform, and in Wales its principal aim was to obtain the explicit obedience of the bishops to Canterbury. This did not require the elimination of Welsh customs and practices, but it did necessitate the ecclesiastical equivalent of overlordship.

However, care should be taken to correctly calibrate the significance of this development as national churches were not present in Christendom at this time. Even Canterbury had to bow to Rome, and for many church reformers as well as defenders of local customs, a strong papacy offered a welcome counterweight to royal interference in church affairs. Yet this word of caution does not vitiate the fact that the Church and its monasteries became as important as the burgh and castle to Norman control of England and parts of Wales. It is true that in general church reform was a European force and it would have impinged at some point on Wales, but in practice it often provided a spiritual justification for the political ambitions of the Normans.

By the middle of the 12th Century all of the Welsh dioceses had acknowledged the authority of Canterbury. This did not end aspirations to establish a Welsh province of the Church. All over Europe, as the diocesan map that would last until the late 19th Century was being formed, arguments were being advanced for the granting of metropolitan status. In Wales the cause was taken up by Giraldus Cambrensis (Gerald of Wales). Between 1199-1204 Gerald visited Rome on several occasions to press the case for an archbishopric at St. David's. Pope Innocent III, the greatest medieval pope and the most influential since Gregory the Great, was sympathetic and accepted the distinctiveness of Wales. Innocent was quite prepared to take on the vested interests of kings and princes, but he interfered little in the temporal affairs of rulers unless the vital interests of the Church were at stake. While a case could be made for a Welsh province, it was not considered essential to the fabric of the Church. Put simply, in Rome the political aspects of the Welsh claim were considered stronger than the ecclesiastical. A similar judgement had already been passed on the call for metropolitan status to be granted to St. Andrews in Scotland. The Scottish experience at the hands of the papacy is instructive. Although denied metropolitan status, the Scottish church was recognised as the 'special daughter' of Rome, which was a not so subtle reminder to England that this status could develop into autonomy.[27]

In the person of Gerald we can see an interesting dichotomy. Part Welsh, part Norman, he had a sense of not belonging to either people, a confusion that tends to produce either a radical or disturbed mind. His sensibilities were distinctly ambivalent in that he saw the *usefulness* of many Norman reforms, but resented the rough treatment of such an old and noble people as the Welsh. John Davies calls Gerald 'the first non-Welsh-speaking Welshman, and he gave vent to his frustrations which would not be wholly irrelevant three quarters of a millennium after his time'.[28]

This sense of ambivalence towards Norman reforms pervaded much of Welsh life in the 12th and 13th Centuries. Initially the Norman Benedictine monasteries were a colonial phenomenon; but the succeeding wave of Cistercian foundations became more Welsh in character, reflecting the native respect for asceticism that stretched back to the age of the Saints. Parts of both the Creed and the Bible were translated into Welsh. And Welsh princes saw the value of establishing religious houses such as the great Strata Florida.

Ambivalent, too, was the Welsh reaction to the influence of Norman law. Welsh customary law had received a masterful expression in the *Laws of Hywel Dda*, which was made possible by the rich and flexible capacity of the Welsh language. Here we can find intimations of concepts that could have developed into a code of criminal law, but essentially the *Laws* met the needs of a sophisticated but non-feudal society. The promulgation of more formal and centralised codes of law – both by Church and State – took place across Europe. R.R. Davies notes the popularity of Norman legal innovations such as jury verdict and the abolition of blood-feud compensation. He concludes that 'powerful as were royal fiat and statute in the promotion of English law in the British Isles, its victory was ultimately that of popular appeal and demand'.[29]

The 13th Century is proof, if such is needed, that medieval Europe was not a static and intellectually inert society. In fact the pace of change was rapid and its ramifications extensive. Christianity would receive its greatest theological expression, and soundest philosophical defence, in the work of St. Thomas Aquinas. Roger Bacon re-discovered the scientific method. France and England emerged as powerful national communities. And the papacy stood at the apogee of its strength and exerted more political power than any international body has done since.

These great forces re-shaped Europe and anticipated the modern era. Those on the periphery of Europe – the Welsh, Irish and Scots; the Scandinavians and Slavs – faced serious challenges in the wake of such fundamental change. And for the Welsh, Irish and Scots, the changes were magnified by the actions of the Norman-English. In 1200 Wales was largely independent, a society still capable of developing political institutions. But time waits neither for man nor nation, and compared to the situation facing Wales in 1063 the prospects for coherent native rule were less propitious. Even so, the most probable outcome remained a semi-independent Welsh kingship that had accommodated Norman-English suzerainty. In essence this was the outcome in Scotland, and indeed Scottish independence increased in the 14th Century. But in Wales the outcome was Rhuddlan, the extinction of an independent political life which was as total as the oblivion that later fell on the Greeks with the fall of Byzantium.

It started in France. In 1203 King John lost all his French territories save Gascony and a couple of redoubts. The Angevin Empire, the Norman *Imperium*, came to an abrupt end. Some time elapsed before the finality of this denouement was accepted in England, but its consequences were immediate. England was no longer part of Outremer; it had in a real sense re-gained its independence. Norman barons in England *became* English, having mostly lost their lands in France. Magna Carta was their contract with the *English* Crown.

It was a new world. Yet Norman blood still coursed through these English veins. Just like the Hanoverians some 600 years later, having lost one empire they set about acquiring another. The new *Imperium* would of necessity be insular, *British*. At hand was the *Matter of Britain*, which transmitted the faint but persistent pulse of a unified Britannia. The Celts had failed to establish an insular *Imperium* when the Romans left; it now fell to the English to take up the idea of Britain. This profound ideological shift can be seen in the Treaty of Woodstock which made explicit Gwynedd's status as a fief of the English Crown. This was not mere overlordship, but potentially direct control. Welsh princes ceased to enjoy the protection of the English king in return for their allegiance, but held on sufferance the Crown's property.

It was a much extended boundary and at first it proved impossible to sustain. As Henry III's power waned, Llywelyn made great advances in Wales and eventually forced the King to come to terms through the Treaty of Montgomery in 1267. It seemed that Wales had again established itself as *de facto* a Principality with the potential to develop into a coherent political entity. But ominously, the English Crown had not lost its appetite for a British monarchy, or more dangerously an English monarchy over Britain.

Wales was no puny entity. Its territory had been defined for some 600 years. In terms of literature and language Wales had contributed magnificently to European culture. And Wales was a martial society that produced some of the most ferocious warriors in Europe. Many a Norman expedition had met with disaster in the mountainous fastness of Wales. However blind are the powerful forces that help shape national destinies, the vital factor in understanding the calamity that fell on Wales in 1282 is the person of Edward I. John Davies has argued that Edward was the *only* medieval English king who had the capacity to subjugate Wales. It took great anger, justified or not, to move him, and he must have realised what the financial consequences of conquest would be. His newly strengthened English realm completed the grim task with skill.

Llywelyn the Last and his hapless brother Dafydd proved brave, but also naïve and maladroit in the face of Edward's terrible majesty. Edward paid the price for the Principality, and it was vast. Edwardian Wales was the most fortified territory in Europe. English ambitions in Scotland could not be pressed and this gave the Scottish kingdom valuable time to prepare its defences. Edward had to abandon his burning desire to lead a crusade to save the Holy Land. According to R.R. Davies, a British solution to the government of the Isles was lost once Edward I conquered Wales. The *Matter of Britain* may have been in English hands, but the failure to acknowledge the plurality of Britain meant that it could never be used creatively. It became a dull and inert concept, and one incapable of generating solutions to the harder problems that faced England, Wales and Scotland. The Statute of

Rhuddlan (1284) was the formal means by which Edward annexed Llywelyn's Principality and made it part of his realm.

Renaissance

What marks 1282 as a unique event in British history, wrote David Jones, is that it saw the end of 'a line of mediaeval princes that stemmed straight from Roman Britain'.[30] Welsh literature had long celebrated this foundation myth, but even our most accomplished modern epic poet acknowledged that the '*princeps Walliae* who died that day, at unequal odds with his overlord, the King of England, had dominion over a small, somewhat loosely knit society'.[31]

Loss is an elusive concept, especially when it leaps forward into the world of what-might-have-been. What we can say is that if the genius of Welsh life had never found a full political projection, it now lost the opportunity to generate one. Perhaps the most mournful aspect of Owain Glyn Dŵr's rebellion some 120 years later was the very vividness of the state it imagined, but only fleetingly achieved. An independent Wales could have survived under less exacting circumstances (although with borders much truncated compared to those first accepted by Offa and still largely valid today). But unlike most small states in continental Europe – one thinks, for example, of the Swiss Confederation, founded in 1291 - Wales had a dominant power between it and any potential ally. Britain was already a land set apart where the counter-balancing forces of Emperor, Pope and Prince were if not entirely absent, then diluted. And England was a unified realm, at least when in political repose. This condition eluded France and Spain until the eve of the Reformation, and Germany and Italy until modernity.

Politics apart, however, Wales suffered little loss elsewhere in its national life. She remained powerfully coherent in the concepts of land, language and literature that generate a nation's theory of mind.

When Wales lost the last, scant vestiges of her medieval independence, Europe consisted of realms rather than nations, although there were some extraordinary exceptions like Venice and Switzerland. It was during the 14th and 15th Centuries that the two great tributaries of the modern nation-state began to flow. In both the Renaissance and the early intimations of the Reformation we can see the forces that would sweep away the medieval world. But man's capacity to imagine the nation was narrow when Llywelyn lost his throne, and this explains the lack of crisis in the worlds of language and literature in Wales. Even the world of politics continued much the same after the Conquest. Native élites, a few princlings apart, survived with alacrity as constables of castles or stewards of royal estates. Most of the time in medieval society, local government was the whole of government.

Yet something had been lost and the bards certainly knew it: although what continued to ache most in the muse was an elusive memory of Britain, a Celtic Britain. As the opening line of *Branwen, Daughter of Llŷr*, the greatest of the Four Branches of the Mabinogi, declares: 'Bendigeidfran son of Llŷr was crowned king over this Island and exalted with the crown of London'. While the surviving manuscripts of the Mabinogi date from after the Conquest, the tales themselves were probably first recorded in the second half of the 11th Century. This was just before the arrival of the Normans, an event that ended the era of stable Celtic-Saxon co-existence. These magnificent tales celebrate an earlier Celtic mythical age of ancestor-heroes. They are full of magic cauldrons, which bring dead warriors back to speechless life, and severed heads that talk incessantly. And, of course, they brought prophecies like what would happen to London if one of the Three Happy Concealments was ever disclosed.[32] The Black Death struck in 1348.

If we can say that the Mabinogi exuberantly creates a mythical past, the poetry of Dafydd ap Gwilym looks around at the ever present glory of man-in-nature. Like Gerald of Wales, Dafydd's imagination was stimulated by two cultures. While Gerald was an Anglo-Norman with a deep appreciation of Welsh culture, in Dafydd this combination was reversed. Dafydd was born in 1320, roughly equidistant in time between Petrarch and Chaucer, and in whose company he is justifiably placed. His uncle was the Norman-serving constable of Newcastle Emlyn and responsible for Dafydd's abundant knowledge of European sources.

Dafydd travelled extensively around Wales and seems to have been equally at ease in the homes of the uchelwyr (gentry) and in the proliferating Anglo-Norman boroughs. His mastery of the cynghanedd amounted to a recreation of the form. In introducing such themes as courtly love, man-in-nature, and subjective feelings, he was a genius who transcended his time. In his figurative techniques, inventive vocabulary and use of innuendo, Dafydd's work did more for the literary integrity of the language than anything before the translation of the Bible. Although he celebrated God and His creation, it is man – usually Dafydd himself – who is at the heart of his poetry, and this permitted profound psychological insights, as we see in the treatment of loss and death in the *Ruin*:

> You ruined shack with open gable-end,
> between the mountain and the pasture,
> it would seem grievous to all those
> who saw you once a hospitable home
> and see you now, with ridge-pole broken,
> beneath your roof of laths, a dark and shattered house.
> Yet once, inside your joyful walls
> there was a time – a stabbing rebuke –
> when there was greater merriment within
> than you now, unsightly hovel …[33]

That this cannot be read as an allegory of the loss of Welsh independence irritated the likes of Gwynfor Evans. He wrote, 'Dafydd ap Gwilym was an exception among the poets in his lack of interest in politics and in the future of the nation'.[34] A more charitable judgement is that politics played a small part in national life at this time and Dafydd simply delighted in the larger part that was left. The beauty of the landscape and the joys of the language interested him more than the sometimes ugly behaviour of the conquistadors. Dafydd was the greatest of the bards, those poets who wandered around Wales now that the princely courts had vanished. The striking literary renaissance that started in the 14th Century can hardly be said to have been made possible by the loss of independence, but nor can we say that political upheaval stymied Welsh cultural life. As Dafydd Johnston puts it: 'With the aid of hindsight the loss of political independence can therefore be seen to have been ultimately beneficial to Welsh poetry in the later Middle Ages'.[35]

According to one observer, in the 14th Century English became 'the language, not of a conquered, but of a conquering people'.[36] During the second half of the century, English became the language of law and politics. Henry IV was the first king since the 11th Century to speak English as his mother tongue. A little later, in 1474, William Caxton printed the first book in English (the *Recuyell of the Historyes of Troye*), and thereafter English started to acquire the power brought about by standardisation.

In Wales, bilingualism became increasingly common among the gentry and merchants, but Welsh remained unchallenged as the language of the community, the Englishries naturally apart. The language was under greater threat from the technical innovations of the Renaissance. Printing rapidly reduced the cost of books and undermined the oral tradition; it was in the literary sphere the equivalent of the Norman Conquest. While the Welsh literary tradition was strong, if a little archaic (reflecting the language itself), it was not a mere backwater, and its currents flowed into English and European literature and 'had a liberating effect on the European imagination'.[37] Welsh was one of the great literary languages of Europe and 'one of the dialects of the revelation of God'.[38] For some 250,000 people on the edge of Europe in the late Middle Ages, this was an achievement of the first rank.

It is one thing to acknowledge that a pattern of life survived, quite another to accept with equanimity the bereavement that followed the death of Gwynedd. Something noble and essential had been lost. David Jones felt this deeply, but he was consoled by the thought that had Welsh 'dynastic resistance collapsed only two centuries earlier than it did, I doubt very much whether there would now be a dominion of Wales any more than there is a dominion of Strathclyde or of Dumnonia'.[39] With the deaths of Llywelyn and Dafydd the whole Welsh aristocracy sunk into oblivion, an extinction as significant as that of the Saxon aristocracy after their defeat at Hastings. But what is more notable, the sinking of a ship or that it completed so many heroic voyages? Enough had been transported into the later Middle Ages to allow Wales to survive the storm of Anglo-Norman colonisation. Perhaps David Jones had something of this in mind when he wrote,

> And the thewed bodies
> the true-hearted men so beautiful
>   between perpendiculars
> and over-all.
>   Timber of foundation
> chosen as stoutest and topping them
> forechosen and ringed
>   in the dark arbour-lands.[40]

Unionists too often gloss over 1282 and the subsequent Edwardian revolution. The significance of the event is smothered by an implausible argument that progress towards a unitary Britain was inevitable. Some even suggest that in calling his new domain the Principality of Wales, Edward inadvertently did a service to the Welsh nation in protecting it from further diminution at the hands of the Marcher lords. Edward was certainly irritated by the quasi-royal powers exercised by Marcher lords in much of south and west Wales. In his subtle and succinct study of the lordship of Gower, Robert Bartlett observes 'even here, in the militarised borderlands far from Westminster, Edward I's government tested how far it could go, searching out limits and precedents, always pushing its most powerful card – the question "by what warrant?"'[41]

Edward's pious and legalistic mind would have made him a great pope, and it is only in the papacy in the 13th Century that we see an institution acquiring comparable authority to that in England being created by the Crown. Vindictiveness was not part of Edward's character: the story told to schoolchildren in Wales, that Edward promised to anoint a prince of Wales who spoke no English, and so invested his baby-son, is poor history but better fable. His 'rights' established, Edward had no desire to traduce the Welsh gentry, far less snuff out Welsh culture. Edward's remarkable success in strengthening the authority of the Crown put England on the path to statehood. On that march the concept of Britain was little more than a straggling baggage train. It was a lame Wales that found a birth on board and somehow turned it into a bandwagon.

While annexation did not lead to a policy of assimilation, Wales became little more than a colony of the English Crown. Plenty of opportunities existed for service. The Welsh gentry flourished in the 14th Century and lesser mortals found a ready market for their well developed martial arts. As R.R. Davies puts it:

> The Welsh were the Gurkhas of the English armies of the Middle Ages; and, like the Gurkhas, they had often seen more of the world, through the necessity of service, than had many of their allegedly worldly wise neighbours.[42]

The English State that these men served started to take shape in the 14th Century. It is true that the English Crown's success in Wales was not matched in Scotland, and greater still was the failure to make real the English claim to the French throne in the Hundred Years War. Yet, these wars created powerful forces. English kings were not inclined to be content with anything less than a strong crown at the centre of a sovereign, centralised government. At the same time, the vast sums needed to sustain English military strength also created the chance for Parliament to grow in influence. In turn Parliament gave the aristocracy renewed power when seigniorial authority was in decline. Of course the relationship between a strong crown and an ambitious Parliament was a tense one, but when in equilibrium these forces started to generate the dynamic of a modern state.

Edward I's victory in 1282 was a conquest not a settlement; 1400 became a revolt not a renaissance. Owain Glyn Dŵr saw himself as the warrior of legend prophesied to restore Welsh independence. What happened on 16th September 1400 when Owain had himself proclaimed Prince of Wales was the start of a national revolt that can 'only be explained in terms of long-cherished dreams and aspirations'.[43] It was the most vivid event in the medieval history of Wales, and its scope and imagination drew on a wide range of experiences.

Wales was a disinherited nation with an élite destined to serve the official half-life of deputies to often absent English office holders. The Welsh warrior class was under-employed in the relative peace that prevailed in the late 14th Century. And the economic forces that had in England caused the astonishing Peasants' Revolt also prevailed in Wales. A wise and authoritative king could have managed these dissonances and treated the Welsh élites with tact. However, in 1399 Richard II was deposed and shortly afterwards murdered, his legitimate heir past over, and the throne usurped by Henry Bolingbroke. These were turbulent times for England. The Welsh revolt had a popular cause, an able leader, and most important of all happenstance. This was not enough in the face of strengthening Lancastrian rule and the foresight of Edward I in making Wales the most encastellated territory in Europe. By 1407 the revolt was effectively over, but not before it had expressed the idea of Welsh statehood.

Owain had a vision of what an independent Wales would look like in a wider British entity. Two documents arc key, the Tripartite Indenture[44] of 1405 and the Pennal letter to the king of France. In the Tripartite Indenture Owain formed an alliance with Henry Percy (Earl of Northumberland) and Edmund Mortimer (Owain's son-in-law). The objective of the Treaty was astonishing:

> If it appears to the three lords with the passage of time that they are indeed the persons of whom the Prophet speaks, between

whom the governance of Greater Britain ought to be divided and partitioned, then they will strive, communally and individually, to the best of their abilities to ensure that this is effected.[45]

While Owain's revolt was inextricably linked to the wider upheaval in English politics, it was not overwhelmed or marginalised by these forces. Remarkably, the portion of Britain allocated to Owain extended beyond Wales and as far as the Trent. Such an enlarged Wales was of course fanciful but it did recall Welsh prophetic teaching and the 'Three Realms of Britain'. Gwynfor Evans had little time for such 'paranoic and completely unrealistic dreams', which he believed made the Welsh 'ready prey to the ravages of Britishness which went from strength to strength after the Battle of Bosworth and the triumph of the Tudors'.[46]

What is more significant than the geographic extent of the Wales envisaged by Owain at his most exuberant, is the idea he had of a Welsh state. The Pennal letter (1406) sets out the details of a sophisticated structure that drew on the latest developments in European thought. Owain sought to deepen his alliance with France by transferring the obedience of the Principality to the Avignonese popes. He called for St. David's to be accorded metropolitan status, echoing the claims of Gerald of Wales, and to have jurisdiction over the three other Welsh sees and five English bishoprics (Exeter, Bath, Hereford, Worcester, and Coventry and Lichfield). The roots of this fantastic claim lay deep in Welsh ecclesiastical mythology and by voicing them Owain's 'Ecclesiastical Wales was to be even more extensive than the political Wales of the Tripartite Indenture'.[47]

More realistic, although also full of ambition, was Owain's desire to found two universities in Wales (Scotland would gain its first university, St. Andrews, in 1413). Owain's genius went far beyond the battlefield. In his political vision we see a plausible Welsh state. The proposals contained in the Pennal letter demonstrate the extensive support he received from the gentry and clergy in Wales.

As Owain asserted his claims of sovereign authority by calling Wales' first parliament in 1404, Henry IV was beginning to accept the new limits on royal power. In 1407 the Commons won precedence over the Lords on the question of taxation. By 1414 Henry V had accepted that the king could not amend a Commons Bill (merely approve or reject it). Here we see in faint outline the separation of powers between executive and legislative functions.

A series of discriminatory measures followed Owain Glyn Dŵr's revolt and gave added weight to the established practice of considering the Welsh as second class subjects of the king. Welshmen were excluded from the higher reaches of political life in the English realm. In practice, this oppression was hard to sustain in Wales, particularly as the 15th Century became a period of turmoil in English regnal politics. Even so, the psychological trauma caused by this ideology was very real and served to limit the English vision for the governance of Britain. Edmund Burke, in his sublime speech on *Conciliation with America* exposed the folly of this discrimination against the Welsh when considering the situation of the American colonists in 1775:

> Sir, during that state of things, parliament was not idle. They attempted to subdue the fierce spirit of the Welsh by all sorts of rigorous laws ... They disarmed the Welsh by statute, as you attempted (but still with more question on the legality) to disarm New England by an instruction. They made an act to drag offenders from Wales into England for trial, as you have done (but with more hardship) with regard to America ...They made acts to restrain trade, as you do; and they prevented the Welsh from the use of fairs and markets, as you do the Americans from fisheries and foreign ports. In short, when the statute-book was not quite so much swelled as it is now, you find no less than fifteen acts of penal regulation on the subject of Wales.[48]

This institutionalised malice existed in theory, if rarely in practice, until the Acts of Union. It is little wonder that the Welsh considered the Tudors to be the fulfilment of the ancient prophecy that had ultimately failed to consecrate Owain Glyn Dŵr.

It has been said, a little harshly, that the Tudors were Welsh in the sense that the Windsors are German.[49] As the Tudor dynasty consolidated its rule and drew Wales into a more regularised union, all sorts of fancies took flight about a Cambrio-British renaissance. Henry VII, for a long while exiled in still independent Brittany, was the hero-returned who had landed at Milford Haven (a stone's throw from his birthplace at Pembroke Castle) and progressed through Wales on his way to Bosworth Field and glorious victory over the usurpers of the crown of

London. He named his heir Arthur. And he welcomed Welshmen into his service. At last the prophecy was realised and a Welsh prince took possession of the monarchy of Britain. The valiant Welsh had held out long enough to see Britannia restored. As the Venetian ambassador observed, 'The Welsh may now be said to have recovered their former independence for the most wise and fortunate Henry VII is a Welshman'.[50] Here is the great narrative of the Welsh gentry and its shaky premise was fully accepted by Gwynfor Evans, although with starkly different deductions:

> The Welsh believed that they had won a glorious victory on Bosworth Field by setting a man of Welsh descent on the throne of England. This victory came close to costing the Welsh nation its life. The future would show that this victory was the most catastrophic defeat the Welsh had in all the thousands of years of their history. A military victory: a spiritual defeat. But for this victory the Welsh nation today would probably be living in dignified freedom, making its contribution to world civilisation, and living with at least as much economic prosperity and social justice as any one of the countries of Scandinavia.[51]

The truth was altogether more anodyne. There is little evidence that Henry VII cared much about his Welsh origins, but he did find Celtic legend useful as a unifying force. His exile in Brittany was involuntary (for a while he was little more than a captive) and his 'glorious' landing in west Wales had been preceded by an abortive attempt to land in Dorset. Memories of the hero's triumphant march through Wales were, like so many products of that malleable sense, moulded by later events rather than those of the time (Henry was in fact received with caution, sometimes indifference). And in naming his son Arthur, Henry VII was inspired by a myth now firmly under English ownership.

The role of the Tudor dynasty was less significant than that of the developing English state in determining the fate of Wales. Henry re-established strong, stable government after the turmoil of the Wars of the Roses. The forces at play in state development could now flow more strongly, but these forces were already present and active. Even the admission of Welshmen into higher political service was already practice in the reign of Edward IV. In fact, the policies of Henry VII and Edward IV bear close comparison. Internally, England again was one of the strongest realms in Europe and its strength and very character as a modern state would be redoubled during the course of the Reformation.

But myths matter. In the *Matter of Britain* we see a myth capable of producing very concrete outcomes. In seeing the Tudor dynasty as a line that sprung, however improbably, from Cadwaladr, the last 'true' king of Britain, the Welsh gentry remained more Welsh than English for several generations. Indeed, it is possible to argue that these myths 'shaped a concept of Welsh nationhood that survived because of – rather than in spite of – the imposition of English statehood upon the Welsh people'.[52]

The so called Acts of Union (1536 and 1543) were no more a settlement than the Conquest of 1282; Wales was not negotiating as a realm far less a state. However, in entering the English state, the Welsh gentry found common cause with the Crown against the now debilitated Marcher aristocracy. The Acts of Union themselves were part of a wider process to end the remaining seigniorial authority of the aristocracy and the ecclesiastical autonomy of the Church. And the resources of the state would bring entirely unforeseen benefits such as the use of Welsh as a language of religion.

Even in the political absorption of Wales into England, theory was following practice. Surprisingly, the new structures of government recognised the distinctiveness of Wales. Wales had its own circuit of courts – the Great Sessions of Wales operated efficiently until their abolition in 1830. The Act of Union 1543 also recognised the Council of Wales. These institutions no more implied the political autonomy of Wales than did Edward's investiture of a Prince of Wales in 1301, but they represented some accommodation with Welsh distinctiveness. While this official recognition was limited and hardly passionate, it was also accompanied by an indifference to Welsh culture that allowed great scope for national advancement. While official business in Wales had to be conducted in English, there was no policy of coercion to suppress the Welsh language. A new generation of patriotic Welsh humanists, full of intellectual vitality, emerged during the later Tudor period and rather than help in a 'process of structural and psychological violence'[53] against the nation's cultural inheritance, as Gwynfor Evans claimed, set about a rejuvenation of the Welsh language with great celerity.

The early stages of the Reformation caused as much bemusement in

Wales as they did in England. The late medieval Church stood in need of reform, but the revolution brought about by the 'new learning' amounted to Europe's greatest ideological upheaval before the French Revolution. It was also peculiarly personal. Jaroslav Pelikan argues that not 'since Augustine had the spiritual odyssey of one man and the spiritual exigency of Western Christendom coincided as they did now'.[54] Yet few in Henry VIII's realm were troubled by Luther's existential uncertainty (*how do I know that I am saved?*) and instead retained a calm belief in the efficacy of the sacraments.

However, the Reformation was about to sweep across England and Wales as a consequence of an altogether more earthy personal crisis. Henry was not a natural Protestant: the tactile, communal and sacerdotal Church suited his character and excused his proclivities with the minimum of fuss. He wanted to reform Church structure, but little of its dogma, in a policy some have called 'Catholicism without the pope'. In asserting royal supremacy in ecclesiastical matters, Henry created a state that was sovereign and the source of all authority temporal and spiritual. This was an ideology of caesaro-papalism in the Byzantine tradition and it created what one writer calls a 'simple' political space to replace 'complex' ones.[55] Henry's realm truly became an *Imperium*, a constitutional entity sufficient of itself.

With the exceptions of Whitland, the rejuvenated Neath and the great Strata Florida, all Welsh monasteries were dissolved in 1536. What was 'the greatest act of land nationalization in the history of England and Wales'[56] had surprisingly little impact on Welsh society, for despite their past achievements the monasteries were a 'sadly dwindling asset'.[57] The loss of fine architecture and many powerful works of art was severe, more so in Wales as these higher cultural achievements were rare. And much of what by chance survived the dissolutions was later destroyed in the frenzy of iconoclasm that occurred in the reign of Edward VI. By 1536 the houses of religion played little part in the intellectual life of Wales and its expression in language and literature. It is fair to say here that the dissolution of the monasteries was more than offset by the translation of the Bible, and the transformation of Welsh into a religious language, which became urgent to reformers intent on preaching the gospel. Nevertheless, the Reformation left religious life in Wales diminished and the eventual Elizabethan settlement lacked the emotional power of the Old Religion or the Lutheran zeal of the 'new learning'. In time this void would be filled by the more passionate practices of Methodism.

While there may have been little enthusiasm among the people for the new religion, Welsh intellectuals soon realised that the Reformation brought exciting opportunities for personal advancement and national regeneration. Elizabeth I tended to appoint Welshmen to Welsh bishoprics and expected them to be resident and active in improving the quality of the clergy. Richard Davies, in his influential 'Epistol at y Cembru' (letter to the Welsh Nation) of 1567 returned to the *Matter of Britain* to establish a Celtic justification for the Reformation. He argued that the reformed Church was not a heretical novelty but the Church of the Apostles restored to its pristine glory. This pure Church had been brought to Britain by Joseph of Arimathea, but thereafter became tainted by the papal superstition which 'Augustine of Canterbury had brought to England as the emissary of Rome'.[58]

As well as preserving the monarchy of Britain, the Welsh also brought to the new Rome of the Tudor *Imperium* the true Church militant. Generations of Welsh intellectuals, more comfortable now in their status, drew inspiration from this myth. Such ideology was heady stuff and it seems quite risible to modern readers. However, the 16th Century was still an age mostly devoid of critical scholarship and Davies' grand narrative seemed to make sense to those seeking a coherent interpretation of utterly momentous events.

Even given the emphasis on preaching in the reformed churches of Europe, the translation of the Bible and other core liturgical texts into Welsh was not in anyway inevitable. While Parliament passed an Act in 1563 for the production of a Welsh Bible, it was a cool and pragmatic decision. Yet it still defined English-Welsh relations for nearly three centuries: united in religion, divergent in language. It both preserved the most important conduit of national experience and allowed it to flow freely in the English-British state.

This accounts in part for the strong cultural nationalism of Wales lacking a sharp political edge; most of the national revivals of the 19th Century were initially a reaction to linguistic oppression. In William Morgan Wales found a true Renaissance linguist of genius.[59] He was a gifted scholar who worked with great skill from Hebrew and Greek texts. As well as superb erudition, Morgan had the ability to write like a literary angel. John Davies compares the Welsh Bible in its literary significance to Luther's Bible and the Authorised Bible in England. Indeed, as he says, 'it could be argued that it was more central, for as

German and English were languages of state they had secular means to maintain their unity, purity and dignity'.[60]

When William Morgan's translation appeared in 1588, Welsh was one of the first non-state languages to have a vernacular Bible. It must be doubted that this would have happened had Henry VIII and his heirs remained Catholic. While the Counter Reformation reformed religious institutions and emphasised the importance of preaching, the zeal to produce vernacular translations of the Bible was less keen in a Church that remained sacerdotal in character.

The Tudor exploitation of Celtic-British foundation myths reached its apogee in John Dee's claim that a *British Empire* (he seems the first to use the expression) was justified by the conquests of Arthur and Prince Madoc. Dee presented Elizabeth with evidence of her title to an Atlantic *Imperium* in 1578. The Madoc myth was particularly potent, and tales of the 12th Century prince's journey to North America were common until the early 19th Century. In the 1780s stories started to circulate in North America about a tribe of Welsh-speaking Indians, the linguistic progeny of Madoc! When giving his full Presidential authority to the Lewis-Clark Expedition into the American mid-west, Thomas Jefferson was lampooned by John Quincy Adams 'for telling prodigies' about such things as Indians descended from 'Welchmen'. What one historian has said about the impact of the Lewis-Clark Expedition on the construction of the American nation can stand also as a judgement on Tudor policy and its use of Welsh myths. Its importance 'lay on the level of imagination: it was drama, it was the enactment of a myth that embodied the future'.[61] We come to a profound truth, as Gwyn Alf Williams observed since 'at least the 10th century, the century of Hywel Dda and his One Law for One Wales, this tiny and marginal people the Welsh have survived by anchoring themselves in variant forms of Britishness".[62]

By 1588, the year of the Armada and the publication of the Welsh Bible, a vivid Welsh identity had existed for a thousand years. This awesome achievement was in part inspired by the *idea of Britain*. Now that *idea* was set to become the *practice of Britain*. And with the discovery and colonisation of the Americas, the *Matter of Britain* would not be found on the edge of Europe but at the centre of the World. Let's finish with David Jones' amazing Britannia, a brilliant penny piece:

We *are* a water-maid
fetch us a looking-glass!
a comb of narwhal ivory, a trident
and a bower anchor –
and the Tower lion
nor twisk his lasher.

Here is our regnant hand:
this ring you see upon it were gave us long since by a'
ancient fisher; 'tis indulgenced till there be no more sea:
kiss it.
No, no, on y'r marrow-bones – though you hooked behe –
moth, you shall kneel!

This bollard here
where keels tie, come from all quarters of a boisterous world,
hand us to it to sit upon.[63]

References

1. John Davies, *A History of Wales*, Penguin Books (1994) p20.
2. Norman Davies, *The Isles: A History*, Macmillan (1999) p118.
3. Hugh Kearney, *The British Isles: A History of Four Nations*, Cambridge (1989) p19.
4. H.W.J. Edwards, *Sons of the Romans: The Tory as Nationalist*, Christopher Davies (1975).
5. Glanmor Williams, *Wales and the Reformation*, University of Wales Press (1999) p1.
6. Peter Salway, 'Roman Britain', in Kenneth O. Morgan (ed), *The Oxford Illustrated History of Britain*, Oxford (1984) p42.
7. Jaroslav Pelikan, *The Emergence of the Catholic Tradition* (100-600), University of Chicago Press (1971) p315.
8. David Jones, *The Anathemata*, Faber and Faber (1952 reprinted 1972) p113.
9. *The Anglo-Saxon Chronicles*, Phoenix Press, London (2000) p12.
10. *Anathemata*, p55.
11. Meic Stephens (ed), *The Oxford Companion to the Literature of Wales*, Oxford (1986) p216.
12. Quoted in Dafydd Johnston, *The Literature of Wales*, University of Wales (1994) p7.
13. Ibid, p9.
14. *Anglo-Saxon Chronicles*, p23.
15. Ibid, p107.
16. Gwynfor Evans, *Land of My Fathers*, p42.
17. *Anathemata*, p154.
18. Davies, *A History of Wales*, p148.
19. John Updike, Preface, *The Mabinogion*, Everyman (2000), p xiii.
20. Peter Ackroyd, *Albion*, London (2002), p107.
21. R.R. Davies, *The First English Empire*, Oxford (2000), p39.
22. Ibid, p44.
23. Ibid. p33.
24. Davies, *A History of Wales*, p133.
25. Ackroyd, p110.
26. Williams, *Wales and the Reformation*, p6.
27. Michael Lynch, *Scotland: A New History*, London (1991), p100.
28. Davies, *History of Wales*, p131.
29. *The First English Empire*, p159.
30. David Jones, *Epoch and Artist*, Faber and Faber, p41.
31. Ibid.
32. *The Mabinogion*, p36.
33. Dafydd ap Gwilym, *Selected Poems*, Penguin (1985) p186.
34. Evans, p250.
35. Johnston, p34.
36. Quoted in Ackroyd, p102.
37. Ibid p96.
38. Davies, p174.

39. *Epoch and Artist*, p42.
40. *The Anathemata*, p175.
41. Robert Bartlett, *The Hanged Man*, Princeton (2004) p93.
42. R.R. Davies, *The Revolt of Owain Glyn Dŵr*, Oxford (1995) p24.
43. Ibid p154.
44. The Tripartite Indenture has only survived in a secondary source; but the historian RR Davies (*Ibid*. p166) considers the source reasonably accurate.
45. *Owain Glyn Dŵr*, p167.
46. Evans p143.
47. *Owain Glyn Dŵr*, p172.
48. The works of the Rt. Hon. Edmund Burke, London (1801) Vol III, p85.
49. Actually, I am saying this; but I draw inspiration from John Davies 'It may be doubted whether Elizabeth I had more interest in the cradle of her line at Penmynydd than Elizabeth II has in the cradle of hers at Saxe-Coburg' (*History of Wales* p275).
50. Gwyn A. Williams, *The Welsh in Their History*, London (1982) p18.
51. Evans, pp281-2.
52. J. Gwynfor Jones, *Early Modern Wales 1525-1640*, Macmillan (1994) p209.
53. Evans, p295.
54. Jaroslav Pelikan, *Reformation of Church and Dogma* (1300-1700) Chicago (1984) p127.
55. William T. Cavanagh, *Killing for the telephone company: why the nation state is not the keeper of the common good*, in Modern Theology, April, 2004, pp243-274.
56. Williams, *Wales and the Reformation*, p105.
57. Ibid p104.
58. Ibid p245.
59. Ibid p349.
60. Davies p244.
61. Merrill D. Peterson, *Thomas Jefferson and the New Nation*, Oxford (1970) pp766-7.
62. Gwyn A. Williams, pp16-17.
63. *The Anathemata*, p145.

Chapter 2

Wales and the Practice of Britain

*Are not the people of America
as much Englishmen as the Welsh?*

Edmund Burke, *On Conciliation with America*

A problem facing Welsh conservatism is that in defending most things British it has tended to overlook many things Welsh. Not, of course, in the nation's polite and contained cultural dimension; but in the sense of Welshness being a vital and pungent force in British history. Welsh Conservatives must start to reappraise, or frankly apprehend for the first time, the Welsh tradition and see it not as a weak branch of British history but one of its tap roots.

While it was possible for patriotic Welshmen to pretend that the Tudors really were Welsh, the truth was that the great visions of Glyn Dŵr had disappeared and Wales was a profoundly diminished political entity by 1536. When Scotland was drawn into the British state-building project, a much wider constitutional space was created. While England and Wales could not in all probability have generated the modern idea of Britain, Scotland's inclusion in the Union transformed the situation. The idea of Britain allowed Scotland and Wales to participate in a state that was not narrowly dominated by England. The success of the British state in the 18th and 19th Centuries confirmed Welsh and Scottish loyalties, although significant dissonances occurred – the Blue Books controversy in Wales, for example. It was not until well into the 20th Century that these basic loyalties were questioned to any notable degree.

Towards a New Britannia

By 1558 the *idea* of Britain had endured for a thousand years, but its *practice* began in earnest during the reign of Elizabeth I. Although the Tudors and Stuarts tinkered with the ideology of Britain, it was the suddenly much aggravated demands of state-formation that created the terrain on which a British state could be built. The creative energy of the medieval mind was more readily deployed in the religious sphere than the political, and this was something of an impediment to the *Matter of Britain* and limited its development.

It would be an exaggeration to describe medieval politics as static, yet it was a slow-moving world where the basic boundaries were considered set and ordained by God. The Almighty played an active part in political life and His actions were mediated by the Church. The Reformation brought a dynamic theory of sovereignty which adapted this world view radically. Protestants believed that the monarch was personally ordained by God and consequently political institutions no longer laboured under the incubus of an autonomous and universal Church. It was now feasible for the *Matter of Britain* to cohere and become an *Imperium*: a state simple, absolute and complete both temporally and spiritually.

In England the heat generated by such sudden ideological change created a brilliant but brittle state. Elizabeth established a national Church that sought humane middle ground between the fierce poles of *true* religion – whether Protestant or Catholic. This compromise allowed space for constructive statecraft and it also spared Britain close involvement in the wars of religion which flared up regularly on the Continent until the Treaty of Westphalia in 1648.

Yet, while the altar ceased to dominate the state, the throne did not. In the reigns of Elizabeth, Charles II, and Anne, succession crises threatened the relative calm of Britain's moderate Reformation. And while the Civil War and Interregnum ultimately failed to establish an alternative to monarchy as the executive authority, by 1689 Parliament had established itself as the sovereign body of state. However, it was not until the hands of the dull Hanoverians gripped orb and sceptre in the early 18th Century that the Elizabethan state's achievements became irreversible.

Wales played little part in these great questions of state. Welshmen were viewed as neither English nor foreign, a theme explored with humour by Shakespeare in *Henry V*. The Bard probably had a good Welsh actor (or a gifted mimic) on his books for the character of Fluellen, constantly mutating Bs to Ps, is drawn with great affection. We can still recognise the caricature today in Fluellen's long-winded eloquence:

> Captain MacMorris, I beseech you now, will you vouchsafe me, look you, a few disputations with you, as partly touching or concerning the disciplines of the war, the Roman wars, in the way of argument, look you, and friendly communication? Partly to satisfy my opinion and partly for the satisfaction, look you, of my mind. As touching the direction of the military discipline, that is the point.[1]

Shakespeare's audience must have been well acquainted with the melodious cadences and diction of the Welsh accent, otherwise Fluellen could hardly have succeeded as the play's principal comic character. But Fluellen also stands as a symbol of Wales, the most distinctive Celtic nation in Britain.

To many nationalists this is the central tragedy of Welsh history – the most culturally separate part of Britain most closely shared the political and economic fortunes of England. But it is perhaps better viewed as paradox rather than tragedy because the Welsh often seemed to consent to this tacit union. It was certainly not meek deference. Wales penetrated the English political domain and exacted a price for its peaceful participation. The Bard has Fluellen centre stage on the eve of the Battle of Agincourt, then England's greatest military victory, and he clearly sees England and Wales enjoying a common political destiny following the evaporation of Owain Glyn Dŵr's rebellion. But the two nations are not made one flesh. In a discreet bow to the Tudor cause, Shakespeare has Henry affirm 'I am Welsh' because he was born in Monmouth[2] and Fluellen replies enthusiastically, 'All the water in Wye cannot wash your majesty's Welsh plood out of your pody'.[3]

During the second half of the 16th Century the Catholic Church revived strongly and a Counter Reformation both limited the spread of Protestantism and absorbed some of its more positive aspects. Several Welshmen were prominent in this process. Gruffydd Robert, former Archdeacon of Anglesey, became a key advisor to that saintly colossus of the Church, Cardinal Borromeo; Morgan Phillips and Owen Lewis helped found one of the Catholic Church's greatest seminaries, Douai University; and more sinisterly, Hugh Owen became the 'intelligencer-in-Chief' to the Spanish monarchy.[4]

The Welsh cause became a theme in Spanish propaganda which promised that once Elizabeth was deposed the Welsh would be 'lords as they were before' in keeping with the dignity of 'such valorous and noble people of truth and antiquity'.[5] Nevertheless most of Elizabeth's Welsh subjects remained instinctively loyal to the Crown, and the Welsh gentry, unsurprisingly, considered the actual connection to England more beneficial than a potential one to Spain. With the Armada vanquished and the Welsh Bible published in 1588, serendipity had given England and Wales perhaps their greatest achievements of the age in the same glorious year.

A few exiled and exotic Catholics excepted, Welsh intellectuals did not hunger for a national politics but rather for the word of God in Welsh to spiritually feed the people. Some three hundred years later, when industrialisation was transforming society as fundamentally as the Reformation had done, the Welsh élite again reaffirmed this choice by placing the spiritual realm ahead of the political, when they called for the disestablishment of the Anglican Church. And the Welsh were not alone in placing religious values ahead of political ones. The Scots made a similar choice in 1707 when they preserved their Church but not their Parliament.

Wales emerged from the 16th Century with its national integrity, at least culturally, largely intact. While the nation's political aspirations fell far short of those expressed by Glyn Dŵr, they were still robust enough to ensure the creation of a jurisdiction, *England and Wales*, that did not turn the Welsh nation into an English province. The accession of James I in 1603 gave a further boost to the concept of an over-arching Britishness that might create institutions capable of attracting loyalty beyond England. James has good claim to be considered the most intellectual of British monarchs. In a seminal speech to Parliament in 1604 he set out a clear case for a deeper union:

> ... little Kingdoms are now in process of time, by the ordinance of God, joined into great Monarchies, whereby they are become powerful within themselves to defend themselves from all outward invasions ...

> And hath not the union of Wales to England added a greater strength thereto? Which though it was a great Principality, was nothing comparable in greatness and power to the ancient and famous Kingdom of Scotland ... Hath not God first united these two Kingdoms both in Language, Religion, and similitude of manners?[6]

Wales was perhaps an anomaly, a point of interest like Brittany in France. It was Scotland that drove the need for a wider concept of the state – one that was not English. James believed that a 'perfect' union was possible that still respected local customs and national differences. He was not advocating an English monarchy over Britain, but a new united realm centred on him as king. This must have pleased the Welsh gentry and strengthened their traditional loyalty to the Crown. As James told Parliament in 1607 'Irish, Scottish, Welsh and English, divers in Nation, yet all walking as subjects and servants within my Court...'.[7] James was ahead of his time in calling for a British state, but the ideological case he first advanced eventually won the day in 1707. Still the unification of the crowns in 1603 was a key event, as the historian John Davies states:

Unlike the Bretons, who were incorporated into the state and the nation of the French, the Welsh henceforth could feel that they were partners in a state which represented the union of the three nations. It was difficult for them to consider themselves to be both Welsh and English, but to be Welsh and British was acceptable, particularly in view of the central role of the concept of Britain in the Welsh national myth.[8]

By the end of James' reign Welsh Members of Parliament were much more active and confident. Their period of 'apprenticeship'[9] had ended. Sir John Herbert (of Neath Abbey) had even risen to Second Secretary of State and was a strong advocate of James' programme to create a 'perfect' union with Scotland.[10]

Despite deeper involvement in parliamentary affairs, the Welsh gentry largely supported Charles I's attempts to rule without Parliament. However, as Charles' rule became less secure in the late 1630s and early 1640s, the Welsh gentry became at best tepid supporters of the royalist cause. Such indifference could not secure neutrality, and in practice 'the support Charles received from Wales was central to his ability to resist the Parliamentary forces for four years and more'.[11] This fact was not lost on the Commonwealth government that ruled between 1649-1660. Overall, the Welsh gentry negotiated these turbulent times with alacrity and were well placed at the Restoration in 1660 to enjoy an era of unparalleled influence and status.

While the gentry prospered, the Welsh literary tradition reached a milestone that also threatened to be a terminus: the age of the wandering bards was coming to its end. At about the same time, the poet Henry Vaughan, the self-styled 'Silurist', consciously moved away from the Welsh tradition and saw himself as 'the first poet of a "civilizing" poetry in English'.[12] In the cultural life of Wales, English was set to become a much more potent threat, but one largely contained until well into the 19th Century.

The historian J. Gwynfor Jones has aptly observed that 'the Tudor inheritance in the 17th century was expounded and interpreted essentially against a background of ancient British traditions, there emerged a growing sense of national consciousness among the politically articulate'.[13] Jones questions the central assertion of naïve nationalism that the Welsh gentry betrayed the *gwerin*. Rather than being the start of the élite's cultural alienation from the Welsh people, the Tudor settlement and its development under the Stuarts 'assisted in creating and preserving a sense of "British" identity among the politically articulate, and shaped a concept of Welsh nationhood that survived because of – rather than in spite of – the imposition of English statehood upon the Welsh people'.[14] Wales, then, avoided cultural and political extinction. While these pre-democratic times provide few measures of popular consent, there were no uprisings of any great note in Wales during this crucial period.

The deposition of James II in 1688 was an event of similar political magnitude to the Civil War. Instead of declaring the troublesome concept of absolutism null and void, Parliament appropriated the theory from the king and considered itself sovereign. Perversely, this created the conditions for strong executive control within Parliament. Today at the state opening of Parliament the monarch is locked out of the House of Commons, but the executive is present in the chamber with all the absolute power that the Stuart's had yearned for.

Parliamentary sovereignty, full and absolute in theory, regularly constrained in practice, would confuse constitutional thought for 300 years. Its first victim was the Scottish Parliament, abolished in 1707. While the Scottish Act of Union preserved much of what was essential to Scottish nationhood, it made Britain a unitary parliamentary state. Britishness was again a useful balm, although less significant to the Scottish national myth. Queen Anne hoped, however, that her English and Scottish subjects would 'have hearts disposed to become one people'.[15] A British state had been created at a time when the nascent British Empire enjoyed a real prospect of expansion. However, Britain was some way off its high imperial age, and initially the Scots found the lucrative prospects of a large free market more attractive. If forming a state out of the *Matter of Britain* had been a formidable task, that of forging a British nation would be doubly daunting.

Britain: An Emerging Nation

A British national identity started to develop in the 18th Century. In one respect, modern critics of Britishness are correct to call this process a construct, as it was initiated by political events – most notably the 1707 Act of Union. But Britain was already a complicated cultural space and according to Linda Colley 'was like the Christian doctrine of the

Trinity, both three and one, and altogether something of a mystery'.[16]

Those politicians who promoted British identity succeeded in part because they did not see it as a novel ideology but as a practice rooted in past experience and capable of variation in Wales, Scotland and England. There was some robust resistance in Scotland and England, but much less in Wales, to the growth of Britishness, and this continued in popular culture until the Napoleonic wars.

What has to be explained is not so much the passive acceptance of a British identity by the bulk of the population, but rather the active support the concept eventually received. Here some powerful factors were key accelerators. The industrial revolution, stimulated by Britain's free market, created such wealth and power that Britain quickly became the world's pre-eminent power. Culturally Britain drifted further away from the Continent, propelled both by a fear of the French and a disdain for anything Catholic. And critically, Britain responded to the blast for *Reform* that became the political symphony of the Enlightenment. In the ferment of such change, Britishness seemed to offer stability by enhancing the forces of the modern world.

In her masterly work *Britons: Forging the Nation 1707-1837*, Linda Colley concludes that, 'War played a vital part in the invention of a British nation after 1707, but it could never have been so influential without other factors, and in particular without the impact of religion. It was their common investment in Protestantism that first allowed the English, the Welsh and the Scots to become fused together...'.[17]

Norman Davies places more emphasis on the economic transformation which followed the 'creation of a united free trade area managed by the common government and legislature in London'. A unified British economy started to develop after 1707 and when 'industrialization began a few decades later, it gave rise to British industry; and when a working class came into being to work the industry, it was a British working class'.[18]

Of course, there is no difficulty in seeing these powerful forces as complementary and interactive. Success in war (usually against France) confirmed faith in Protestantism and created more opportunities for economic success. Nevertheless, the industrial revolution that was well underway by the late 18th Century did hit the *Matter of Britain* like an asteroid, although the transmuting dust only settled in the 19th Century. Even Britain's biggest political setback of the age, the loss of the 13 American colonies, became a fillip to her growing enterprise culture as restrictive mercantilist policies were abandoned and Britain embarked on a new age of free (or freer) international trade.

Throughout the 18th Century Wales remained rural, underdeveloped and sparsely populated. There were pockets of industrial activity and mineral exploitation, but such activities had little impact on most of the population who were engaged in some form of agriculture or related activities. Yet the production of an efficient steam engine in the 1760s meant that coal would soon be king and its presence the main factor in determining the location of heavy industry. The fecund south Wales coalfield soon made Wales one of the vital organs of British economic development. And the local availability of coal allowed ironworks to develop at the heads of the south Wales Valleys.

John Davies has observed that the 'revolution which was afoot in Merthyr in 1801' would ensure that 'the majority of the people of Wales were sucked into the pattern of life which was pioneered there'.[19] That this utterly novel 'pattern of life' required vast sums of capital, way beyond the means of local entrepreneurs, has led some to assert that the industrial revolution was imposed on the Welsh. However, we should avoid the conclusion that industrialisation was somehow uniquely alien to the Welsh character. This was a new phenomenon and no less alien in its initial stages to people in England and Scotland. And there was ample evidence of innovation and enterprise in Wales, albeit sporadic. Sir Humphrey Mackworth, the English-born squire of Neath, did much to improve standards in the copper industry in the early 1700s and his coalmines were perhaps the most advanced of their time. He is best remembered today for imposing on his workforce the discipline of a regular working week. Another example of indigenous enterprise was the development of the north Wales slate industry, mostly the work of local landowners such as Richard Pennant.

While scientific discoveries promised a new economic order, the massive productivity gains that were imminent would be won by the skills of labour as much as by the carbon of capital. The puddling, or stirring, of iron increased productivity fifteen-fold and it became known as the Welsh method. Skilled Welsh ironworkers and coal miners were much in demand in the newly independent American republic. Crucially, as industrialisation swept across south Wales it provided work for the surplus rural population which was increasing rapidly in Wales as in much of Europe. Mass migration, which amounted to a diaspora in Ireland, could have dealt a serious blow to the Welsh language. Instead, internal migration created an overwhelmingly Welsh-speaking industrial population in the 19th Century. Industrialisation made Wales a more integrated and coherent national space. In the socio-economic sphere it can be seen as analogous to the political reforms of the Tudor settlement.

As Deuteronomy records, man cannot live by bread alone, and the breath of the numinous continued to pass over the *Matter of Britain*. During the reigns of the Hanoverian kings (1714-1837) Wales experienced a religious transformation every bit as radical as the industrial revolution. The Anglican Church had lost much of the vitality gained earlier by a Welsh liturgy and a conscientious and resident episcopate. Hanoverian bishops tended to be urbane and intelligent, but also absent and spiritually passionless. It is not surprising that amidst this ecclesiastical latitudinarianism a force for reform emerged.

While Methodism would become the main pillar of Nonconformity in the 19th Century, it started within the Anglican Church and indeed remained there for many years. At the heart of Methodism was a primitive but powerful call for personal repentance as the means to salvation. Preachers like Howel Harris and Daniel Rowland described in great detail that the wages of sin were not death, but exquisite and eternal agony in Hell. There was more than a tinge of sadomasochism in this dismal eschatology, but it must be remembered that its central purpose was to secure for the ungodly the joy of salvation by making them repent. The more humane aspects of the Methodist tradition found sublime expression in hymns written above all by Charles and John Wesley, and in Wales by William Williams Pantycelyn. This hymnody constitutes Methodism's most enduring contribution to Western Christianity.

The heroes of Welsh Methodism were of such ability and zeal, if not always emotional stability, that a distinctive national character was stamped on the movement. This is not to say that it found an immediate response either from the intelligentsia of Old Dissent or from the population at large. Even in the 1790s the Welsh were still predominantly Anglican. This would quickly change as Methodists responded to the demands of the industrial revolution with Darwinian élan.

Yet it would be another generation before Methodism found a strong political voice, and at first Methodists appeared to possess a deference to authority and established order that was distinctly Tory. As Gwyn Alf Williams observed, 'the Methodist was apolitical and quietist, the Independent or Baptist a "politician". This is why the complex phenomenon embraced in the catchphrase "the radicalising of the Methodists" was so central to nineteenth-century Welsh politics'.[20]

Certainly, some prominent Old Dissenters, themselves moving away from Trinitarianism, did not much like the Methodist Revival and its call for emotion rather than reason to spark man's relationship with God. Iolo Morganwg was famously grumpy about the 'Methodistical' advance and Iolo's beautiful hymns contain none of the spiritual anxiety of William Williams. Instead, he glories in the Haghia Sophia, the divine wisdom:

> From reason to reason, from gift to gift,
> Forward we go to every truth,
> To pure learning in the word of our God,
> In that alone we shall live.[21]

Iolo's use of reason in apprehending the divine was destined to resonate better in a more agnostic age. His contemporaries were increasingly being won over by those who, later, would be christened Calvinist Methodists. The long delayed split from the Anglican Church occurred in 1811 and an era of arch Nonconformity began. By the middle of the 19th Century this denomination so characterised Welsh religious experience that it was practically the national church. Wales became more fervently Protestant, a condition demonstrated in the ferocious opposition to Catholic emancipation in the late 1820s.

For all its future force in Welsh society, Methodism was not the most influential religious movement of the 18th Century. In one area above all others Wales led the world, and this was in the provision of basic literacy through church schools. Griffith Jones, an Anglican priest, devised a system of circulating schools in the 1730s. The idea was not new, but the application and dedication of Jones was key to the success of these temporary schools. They concentrated solely on a simple but intensive curriculum aimed at making children and adults alike literate in their mother tongue (at this time, naturally, usually Welsh). So striking were the results that news reached far and wide (Catherine the

Great was one admirer). Wales was one of the few countries to have a literate majority by the second half of the 18th Century. Although the context of this education was totally religious, Gwyn Alf Williams wisely observed that the Welsh 'learned to read during the Atlantic Revolution, that great tide of revolutionary aspiration and ambition which swept the entire Atlantic basin'.[22]

At the heart of the newly created British state was a 'Parliament of unique stature and power – it had no match in Europe and it overshadowed the monarchy. The Welsh and English had already begun to display a deep reverence for parliamentary sovereignty, and as the 18th Century progressed the Scots increasingly joined the cult. While the theory of parliamentary sovereignty would do Britain no favours when handling the American crisis, its longer-term influence was more positive.

Britons felt confident that parliamentary government guaranteed both their freedom and the nation's Protestant inheritance. Parliament was crucial in generating Britain's theory of self. By the second half of the century calls for parliamentary reform were heard with increasing frequency, but it was a mark of Parliament's essential legitimacy that the cry was *reform*, not *revolution*. Even when the 1832 Reform Act failed to satisfy the radicals, the demands of the Chartists still focused on the reform not abolition of Parliament.

Reform, a most volatile force in autocratic states, came to represent the spirit of Britishness and, when given appropriate direction, it became a constructive force for modernisation. The great cause of the age – the abolition of slavery – was eventually championed by the British state, after protracted parliamentary battles, and it gave many Britons a further sense of confidence and purpose in a rapidly changing world. While James I had a vision of a Britishness which focused on the king, 18th Century politicians increasingly gave up such Jacobite notions and concentrated on the role of Parliament in building the British state and its empire. Hanoverian monarchs lost most of the Crown's former executive authority, and only awkwardly managed to come to terms with their new and more symbolic role in national life.

Parliamentary representation was controlled by the aristocracy and higher gentry. This pattern prevailed in Wales, although usually in the Tory rather than Whig cause. Welsh MPs did not constitute a national block and they rarely acted with the zeal of some of their Tudor and Stuart predecessors. Welsh representation in Parliament had lost its earlier excitement and novelty, becoming more a matter of family prestige. This is not to say that political preferment for Welsh members was difficult to secure, rather that it was rarely sought.

In fact, the English élites proved accommodating in the new British state and were rarely hostile to the Welsh or Scottish gentry but rather admitted them into the ruling élite. This can be seen in the Williams Wynn dynasty which became a quintessential part of the British establishment. Many have poured particular scorn on the gentry of this period, seeing their behaviour as the final betrayal of national politics. The problem with this view, even after allowing for the inevitable hyperbole, is that while there could certainly be national causes at this time, there was no Welsh, English or Scottish national politics. Britannia ruled the national wave!

Placated by ease and privilege, the gentry now played little part in debating and developing political ideas in Wales. A few Tory Jacobites, espousing the Stuart cause in private boozy dinners, can hardly be compared to the likes of John Dee or John Herbert and their contributions to Cambro-British political thought. Instead, the world of political ideas in Wales became dominated by a small intelligentsia, usually with roots in the tradition of religious Dissent.

Cowbridge, today considered the home of instinctive if sleepy conservatism, was in the 18th Century a centre of fervent and radical debate. Here the values of the Enlightenment found a ready response, and Glamorgan became 'a nursery of the democratic intellect'[23] which was starting to question the values of the ancièn regime. Two figures stand out, Richard Price and Iolo Morganwg, and though both radicals they treated their Welshness and Britishness in very different ways.

Dr. Richard Price was born in Llangeinor, near Bridgend. A rationalist in the classical mould, Price was a Dissenting minister who spent most of his career in London where he became famous for his radical sermons and pamphlets. This was the Dr. Price who provoked Edmund Burke to write *Reflections on the Revolution in France*, the classical expression of conservatism. But the radical controversialist was the lesser Price. John Davies has awarded Price the supreme accolade of being 'the most original thinker ever born in Wales'.[24] And this is not cheap praise, for Price was one of the most gifted mathematicians, moral philosophers, and economists of the age. His pioneering work on actuarial calculations stimulated the development of the insurance industry, and his analysis of the National Debt was groundbreaking. Although a radical, Price was very much part of the establishment, and he influenced some of the most powerful politicians of the day such as William Pitt the Younger and, in America, Alexander Hamilton. Unsurprisingly, Price won recognition and status in his own time, and he still appears today in standard reference books on philosophy and political thought.

In *Reflections*, Burke famously condemned Price for being one of those radicals prepared to condone massacres and assassinations as 'a trivial price for obtaining a revolution'.[25] In fact, Price died before the period of Terror started in France, but it is fair to say that Burke was far the more prescient on the likely outcome of the Revolution. Yet Price was hardly alone in optimistically welcoming the Revolution as a rational response to the injustices of absolute monarchy. In contrast, in their responses to the American crisis, Burke and Price shared a measure of agreement. Both urged restraint on the British government and held that the Americans had some justified grievances. Burke predictably wanted to preserve the British connection with America, but perhaps surprisingly so did Price – although he envisaged a looser empire based on common interest. Here Price was much more prescient than Burke. Price advocated a free association of states with a common council for the whole empire or with the Crown as the institution representing imperial union.[26]

These astonishing ideas were expressed a full century before the Victorian campaign for imperial union. The crucial difference between Burke and Price is found in their attitudes towards Parliament. While a sincere and eloquent advocate of the rights of Americans, Burke's plea for restraint bounced back after hitting the wall of parliamentary sovereignty. Burke had to acknowledge that however imprudent, Parliament had the right to pass legislation for the colonies with or without their consent. Price was under no such incubus. He believed that sovereignty was drawn from the people not a parliament or king. The American colonies had the right therefore to pass their own domestic laws and to determine taxation.

In addition to his powerful impact on British political thought, Richard

Price also influenced American politics through his advocacy of federalism. In his *Observations on the Importance of the American Revolution* Price urged the newly independent colonies to establish a strong federal authority. Like Alexander Hamilton who later took up this cause in the *Federalist Papers*, the motivation was to recognise the need for central co-operation between otherwise independent states. It is not possible, of course, to see in Price's federal concepts a formula that could have been simply applied to Britain, but his ability to understand how different jurisdictions might be accommodated within a state was innovative.

The famous battle between Burke and Price on the lessons of the French Revolution has been described as 'perhaps the last real discussion of the fundamentals of politics in our country'[27] and after 1792 'the debate increasingly became a more direct struggle to capture the allegiance of metropolitan and provincial artisans'.[28] This leads us on to the remarkable contribution made by Iolo Morganwg to Welsh ideas.

While Price was a Welshman who thought radically about British and international politics, Iolo Morganwg started to explore Welsh political experience. Although Iolo was no stranger to London and its radical salons, and he was in close contact with the Gwyneddigion, a London Welsh society that welcomed the French Revolution, his genius was always more readily applied to Welsh history and culture – its interpretation, and more controversially its invention. The distinguished historian Prys Morgan points out that Iolo was one of the first Welsh thinkers to criticise the Acts of Union. Iolo also condemned the gentry, descendents of the princes, for colluding with the English who were intent, he thought, on the destruction of the Welsh language. As Prys Morgan remarks, Iolo 'believed that … something had to be done to discover for the Welsh a history that was more independent, more grand and sublime, than the subservient history handed out to the Welsh by English writers'.[29] Accordingly, Morgan writes, Iolo should 'be considered the true spiritual father of modern Welsh nationalism'.[30]

This tribute is richly deserved, although Iolo's methods were not always fastidious. As well as providing a striking interpretation of Welsh history, Iolo also used his creative talents to manufacture evidence where it was absent. While this may have been something of a moral proclivity, it is hardly unprecedented in history and it was strongly evident in the Romantic movement of which Iolo was part. The most notorious forger, some would say sublime, was the Scottish poet James Macpherson who 'discovered' the poems of 'Ossian'. The English critic Peter Ackroyd has written that Macpherson's 'forged words forged – in another sense – a new reality'.[31] This was true also of Iolo's work.

Iolo's most inspired creation was the discovery – the utter invention – of the last druids and their apparently unbroken tradition. He claimed that the druids had survived only in Glamorgan, yet were on the point of extinction, and that he now possessed their secrets. Iolo went about reviving the tradition and convened a meeting of the *Gorsedd Beirdd Ynys Prydain* (Assembly of the Bards of the Isle of Britain) at Primrose Hill, London in 1792.

That the first Gorsedd met in London reflects both the influence of the London Welsh and also Iolo's belief that London was the heart of the old Brythonic World.[32] The Gorsedd was loosely connected to the embryonic Eisteddfod in 1819, but the Gorsedd's elaborate pageantry – perhaps Iolo's most exuberant creation – was not adopted until 1858.

Iolo was inspired by the 'rational' religion of the French Revolution which had created equally rich and bizarre ceremonies. Nevertheless, as an example of nation-building the Gorsedd was an act of towering genius. All traditions have a whiff of the bogus at the beginning, but they cannot last and inspire the imagination of future generations unless they contain an inner truth. The Welsh literary tradition *was* magnificent, and Welsh history *had* too often passed through the prism of unsympathetic English historiography. Iolo gave the Welsh that most wonderful psychological gift, self-confidence. He stands with Pugin, who physically and spiritually re-built Parliament, and Disraeli, who re-invented the monarchy and clothed it in a glorious symbolism. All were nation builders and made the slightly bogus beautiful.

The call for reform, both parliamentary and social, was advanced with energy and eloquence in the 1790s, and it focused on the more revolutionary themes of human rights and popular sovereignty. However, as the decade wore on it became increasingly difficult to draw simple inspiration from the French Revolution as it descended first into Terror, and then Dictatorship under Napoleon.

Events across the Channel seemed to vindicate Burke and his defence of the old order. Once the Napoleonic wars started, Britons were inclined to think more about the preservation of the state rather than what type of state they wanted to preserve. The older radical tradition, epitomized in the work of Richard Price, became more fashionable as it had always been suspicious of the language of human rights and had emphasised instead that prudent reform was needed to preserve order and authority. Victory in 1815 reinforced British self-confidence and gave many Britons a sense of destiny, a belief that the British nation had a unique mission.

Yet, despite possessing a strong measure of national unity, the British state also contained a deep inner tension. The élite had a profound fear of Jacobinism – the ideology that had emerged from the French Revolution and which sought fundamental political and social change. The British people, steadily becoming an industrial working class, were not much tempted by Jacobinism, but they did want greater recognition of their contribution to the state.

The 1832 Reform Act gave Britain one of the most advanced constitutions in Europe (although it was far from democratic) and it silenced the reactionary diehards who insisted that *reform* really meant *revolution*. Two of the most significant extra-parliamentary events of the 1830s took place in Wales, and they were both closely related to the Reform debate. The Merthyr uprising of 1831 followed the rejection of the Reform Bill by the House of Lords and the agitation was at least partly started by radically minded industrialists. It soon got out of hand and for four days order completely broke down and the authorities had no control over the town. The people had moved from being a supporters club for the ironmasters and their political aspirations, to a mob demanding a better system that would recognise their interests. There was a touch of the ineffable, almost millenarian about the uprising, as if the people could not yet speak coherently only act forcefully. As Gwyn Alf Williams put it, with no lack of eloquence, the people 'found no adequate vocabulary; there probably was none to find'.[33] The authorities did try to negotiate, in part a tactic to defuse the situation, but they found it difficult to establish what the people wanted. As Gwyn Alf Williams put it with even greater eloquence:

> In the last resort they wanted nothing that those masters could give them, because they wanted everything. They wanted a renovation of all things. They wanted *Reform*.[34]

Here *reform* did have the sound of inarticulate *revolution*. By the late 1830s, the limitations of the Reform Act were quite apparent and its failure to much advance the democratic principle could not be denied. The Chartists were more articulate than Merthyr's rioters. Here the people did find voice, and the most important Chartist demonstration in Britain took place in Newport in 1839. Chartism in south Wales grew out of the Merthyr Rising which echoed around the rapidly industrialising communities of Glamorgan and Monmouthshire.

There is some doubt about what truly motivated the 5,000 demonstrators who marched on Newport.[35] Were they intent on general rebellion, a Merthyr uprising writ large? Or did they limit themselves to the reformist demands of the Charter which focused on the need for a reformed parliament? In Britain if not Newport, the Chartists were the inheritors of the radical tradition which had a faith in British institutions and hence wanted *reform* not *revolution*. Their disciples would play a prominent role on the left of the Liberal Party in the second half of the 19th Century. The firebrands of Merthyr, those who hoisted the red flag for what is thought the first time, inspired the working classes to eventually find voice in a more militant ideology, socialism.

Britain: An Emerging Empire

In the 19th Century Britain became the world's first superpower by combining industrial strength and military force with efficient administration. The Napoleonic wars had threatened to reverse the outcome of the Seven Years War (1756-62) which had given Britain a clear edge over France as the dominant power. In defeating the French in North America, Britain unwittingly allowed American self-confidence to grow as the colonists no longer had to fear Catholic absolutism.

The eventual loss of the 13 colonies, the *first* Empire, had a more positive unintended consequence for the builders of Empire as their attentions turned to the East. Valuable lessons were also learned on how to conduct more constructive relations with other British-settler colonies. What is more commonly understood to have been the British Empire – control over extensive territories in Asia, Africa, the Caribbean and the Middle East, was, at least in its formal imperialist projection, a 19th Century phenomenon.

It is an exaggeration to say that Britishness was synonymous with

Empire because British nation-building started so much earlier. British imperialism centred on the belief that the British state was achieving a higher level of civilisation which created a moral duty to lead the world, an ideological narrative that had a powerful hold on those shaping foreign policy. This sense of destiny was strengthened by forces at home that were creating new social, economic and financial orders.

As the industrial revolution accelerated it produced the greatest change in how humans live since agriculture allowed fixed settlements to replace hunter-gather communities some 10,000 years before. Britain did not exclusively 'invent' or 'discover' these astonishing processes - they existed in embryo all over the world. The industrial revolution would have started elsewhere if not in Britain; but in Britain a combination of circumstances allowed industrialisation to take off. Modern life had begun. It began in Britain.

The enthusiastic contribution of many Scots to the imperial project is frequently acknowledged. Wales was not short of the imperial spirit either. As the historian K.O. Morgan observes 'Despite its radical tradition, Wales was much attracted to imperialism… Mafeking was celebrated with the same wild frenzy from Bangor to Aberdare'.[36]

One Welshman, John Rowlands, led an extraordinary life even for the times. Born to poor, Welsh-speaking parents, Rowlands spent much of his early life in the St. Asaph workhouse where it seems he was harshly treated and often beaten. A resourceful youth, he ran away and eventually worked his way to New Orleans in 1859. There his fortunes improved, and John Rowlands became Henry Morton Stanley after being adopted by a kindly cotton-broker of that name. He served both in the Confederate Army and, albeit after capture, in the US Artillery. Intelligent and hardworking, Stanley took advantage of the growing appetite for journalism and became an excellent newspaper correspondent. In 1869 he was ordered by the *New York Herald* to 'find Livingstone!' As Thomas Pakenham has written with neo-Victorian condescension, 'Stanley became the *New York Herald's* model foreign correspondent: a cocky American manner concealing a bleeding Welsh heart within'.[37] He quickly became convinced of Britain's duty to civilise Africa. Despite receiving extensive popular support in Britain through a series of books and lectures, he was never taken to heart by the establishment. As he wrote, 'I do not understand Englishmen at all. Either they suspect me of some self-interest, or they do not believe me

... for trying to kindle them to action I am called ... a hare-brained fellow totally unused to business'.[38] He was driven into the less compassionate hands of King Leopold of the Belgians, an event that did nothing to improve the lot of Congolese. After a frenetic career in Africa, Stanley ended up a Unionist MP. His life was as eventful as that of Cecil Rhodes; and both men had psyches as smooth and untroubled as the Victoria Falls.

While Stanley lived a life of peripatetic adventure abroad, most of his fellow countrymen could only imagine such exploits from the safety of their own homes. But this did not prevent them from taking a certain pride in the imperial mission. The Welsh had always felt a vague ancestral connection to London and the idea that the Crown of Britannia was located there. Now London was becoming the world's first global city, influencing or controlling a vast portion of the world's trade and finance. And there in great majesty sat Victoria – not the English monarch, not now merely the British monarch, but an Empress reigning over a quarter of the world.

The apogée of the imperial age came in 1897 when Queen Victoria celebrated her Diamond Jubilee. According to Lawrence James, 'The Jubilee was more than a display of imperial muscle; the Queen was at the heart of the empire and it was loyalty to her which helped give it a sense of cohesion ... Her genuine, maternal care for her subjects ... was widely publicised'.[39] It was in the second half of the 19th Century that a conscious and coherent dual nationalism took root among the Welsh and the Scots. The English could not remain aloof altogether, but they tended to see Englishness and Britishness as synonymous. The Irish for the most part did not identify as British even in the high imperial age, instead they set their hearts on a sort of dominion status where they would be linked to the British Empire but not the British state, or at least not fully so.

However sublime the idea of empire may have been in the popular imagination, its creation and maintenance was contingent on very material processes. And by the 1880s it was clear that Britain had serious industrial rivals who were unlikely to allow British dominance to continue indefinitely. The British Empire would have a short but vivid life. Industrialisation and its effects remained long after the imperial mission fizzled out during the First World War.

Nowhere was the industrial revolution more intense than in Wales. In 1800 Wales had a population of about 600,000 and 80 per cent lived on the land. By 1914 two and a half million people lived in Wales, 80 per cent of them in urban settlements. In the first decade of the 20th Century Wales was second only to the USA as a country of net immigration. By 1890 the Cardiff-Barry ports exported more tonnage than anywhere else in the world. It was mostly coal. Although industrialisation utterly transformed south Wales, coal had no rival and this created a very narrow industrial base. Later some nationalist thinkers, most notably Saunders Lewis, would view industrialisation as an alienating process, creating a force that undermined the 'true' Wales. But it is difficult to see how the values of the older, rural Wales could have survived at all had not internal migration to industrial communities been possible. Wales avoided mass emigration, unlike Ireland, because it could absorb a rapidly growing population. Nevertheless, a new Wales was created, and though no less Welsh in its early stages at least, it created a more radical dynamic. As Gwyn Alf Williams asserted:

> … if Wales had not been industrialised during the nineteenth century, its people would probably have suffered the same fate as the southern Irish. Since the Welsh were so much fewer, any recognisable entity which could be called 'Wales' would have disappeared in that century, its people blown away by the winds of the world. It is against this massive growth of an industrial Wales of British-imperial character that every other Welsh phenomenon must be set.[40]

And Williams saw a tension between two 'ideas' of Wales. What 'has come to be thought of as "traditional", Nonconformist, Welsh-speaking, radical Wales in particular, that Wales which created so many of the characteristic Welsh institutions, notably the educational, was in some sense a by-product of this industrialisation, in other senses a reaction against it'.[41] The railways which made a National Eisteddfod possible, also brought the English-speaking world a lot closer to Wales.

With an economy so heavily reliant on international trade, there was little support for the Conservative policy of tariff reform. Rather, as K.O. Morgan states 'Wales was a stronghold of free trade'.[42] The Conservative Party's promotion of protectionist policies was mostly a response to the emergence of strong international competitors, notably Germany and the USA. It was combined with a more elevated if ethereal desire for imperial unity (indeed some Conservative politicians advocated an Empire-state). Some historians argue that the Conservative Party's rejection of free trade was a more significant factor than its opposition to disestablishing the Anglican Church in turning the Welsh electorate away from the Tory cause. It certainly influenced voting behaviour in several elections and united a wide range of interests in Wales. As Morgan notes, the 'South Wales chambers of commerce vied with the Miners' Federation in their denunciation of Hicks-Beach's [the Conservative 'Chancellor of the Exchequer] export duty on coal in 1901 as a menace to coal exports'.[43]

The religious heart of the Liberal ascendancy was Nonconformity. This was not an inevitable outcome. The Old Dissent was more radical than much of bourgeois liberalism, and in the 18th Century many saw Methodism as a reactionary force trading collective political action for individual spiritual consolation. However, by the middle of the 19th Century the Liberal Party was using the forces of Nonconformity in the battles for further reform of the state.

The conversion of Wales into a Nonconformist nation perhaps limited the potential for the growth of a national party in Wales analogous to the Irish Parliamentary party. Instead, despite having a cultural distinctiveness far deeper than that between Ireland and England, Wales was largely content for political questions to remain a matter for Britain as a whole, an attitude that prevailed also in Scotland. Ireland, of course, had only joined the Union in 1801 and then reluctantly, and had always been alienated by the concept of a Protestant state. The fact that the British élite could not deliver Catholic emancipation for a further 28 years made Ireland's place in the Union highly irregular.

One event could conceivably have disturbed Welsh acceptance of the British connection. What has become known as the 'Treachery of the Blue Books' occurred in 1847, with the publication of a report on the state of education in Wales by a House of Commons commission. A Welsh born radical MP, William Williams, proposed the commission, and three commissioners were dispatched to Wales to conduct the inquiry. The young commissioners could not speak Welsh and they had little experience of teaching outside élite public schools. Unsurprisingly, the commission exaggerated the weaknesses of education in Wales. While able and sincere, the commissioners were heavily reliant on translators and on the frequently jaundiced views of Anglican clergymen who rather resented the spread of Nonconformity and its role in educating the working classes. Although flawed, the 1,252-page report was mostly a 'conscientious description of the schools offering education to the working class children of Wales'.[44] About ten pages wandered into questions of morality and sexual mores, and this is what caught the attention of commentators in London.

The commissioners were capable of praise, noting for example the general benevolence of the Welsh which made 'murders, burglaries, personal violence, rapes, forgeries, or any felonies on a large scale' so rare. However, this did not stop a heavy judgement falling on the Welsh, because 'there are, perhaps, few countries where the standard of minor morals is lower'. The assessment of sexual behaviour was even more damning. 'The want of chastity results frequently from the practice of "bundling", or courtship on beds, during the night – a practice still widely prevailing. It is also said to be much increased by night prayer-meetings, and the intercourse which ensues in returning home'.[45]

The implied combination of Nonconformity and fornication naturally caused uproar, but its longer term effect was to generate a deep seated inferiority complex amongst the Liberal élite. It was the old calumny first articulated centuries earlier by Gildas, then amplified by Bede and made common currency by the Normans. Quite simply, the Welsh were more sinful than the English. The commissioners' views on the Welsh language were also strangely ambivalent. On the one hand, Welsh was acknowledged to be flexible enough to express every idea of theology but, on the other hand, utterly deficient for secular subjects. Such a contradictory assessment did not stop an emphatic verdict:

> The Welsh language is a vast drawback to Wales, and a manifold barrier to the moral progress and commercial prosperity of the people. It is not easy to over-estimate its evil effects. It is the language of the Cymri, and anterior to that of the ancient Britons. It dissevers the people from intercourse which would greatly advance their civilisation, and bars the access of improving knowledge to their minds. As a proof of this, there is no Welsh literature worthy of the name.[46]

Michael Hechter considers this episode a clear example of cultural denigration. The English élite, he argues, viewed the Welsh like the natives of India and the other colonies, 'the natives are seen to be warm and friendly and in desperate need of English help to set them on their feet'.[47] Gwynfor Evans criticised the Nonconformist élite for their obsessive concentration on the bogus moral judgements that dominated the Report: the 'real treachery – the betrayal of the language and the civilisation of Wales – which gives the Blue Books their lasting importance, caused little agitation'.[48]

The desire to be seen as respectable understandably pervaded Nonconformity. However, by promoting strict sexual ethics, sabbatarianism, temperance, and disestablishment, Nonconformity slowly started to lose touch with the more earthy forces at play in Wales, such as the growth of the labour movement and the development of organised spectator sports. In 1847 the Welsh language still had a fair chance of surviving industrialisation and its consequent transformation of society, but the Blue Books fiasco tipped the balance. A new idea planted itself inside the nation and it undid the Elizabethan compromise of accepting Welsh as the language of everyday life. Whereas the Tudors grasped the challenge of turning Welsh into a language of reformed religion, the Victorians viewed Welsh as intractably anti-modern.

Outside Wales, men of great learning like Matthew Arnold could both praise medieval Welsh literature and yet assert that 'if a Welshman has anything of real importance to say he must say it in English'.[49] Someone as eminent as Hugh Owen, founder of the University of Wales, demonstrated the ambivalence that even Welsh speakers had in relation to the language. Owen never taught his sons Welsh and 'he seems to have shared the belief... that the Welsh Language represented a problem to be solved, rather than a redoubt to be defended'.[50] The Blue Books controversy was not an act of calculated colonial exploitation. Its origins were far too accidental for that. Yet it was a case of the British state at its most English and culturally aggressive. The psychological impact on the Welsh was as vast as that of the Kinsey Report on the wider Anglo-Saxon world a hundred years later when the common prevalence of sexual habits once thought deviant was demonstrated.

Wales was not alone in the UK in losing a sense of self-confidence in its language. In Ireland the Nationalist leader Daniel O'Connell anticipated Matthew Arnold when he said in 1833, 'A diversity of tongues is of no benefit; it was first imposed on mankind as a curse, at the building of Babel. It would be of vast advantage to mankind if all the inhabitants of the earth spoke the same language'.[51] Like the Blue Books' authors,

O'Connell, a gentleman to the core, could not conceive that the masses might be capable of bilingualism. To learn English, the language of the modern world, they would have to give up Irish. As O'Connell observed, 'I am sufficiently utilitarian not to regret its gradual abandonment'.[52] O'Connell was right in predicting the likely development of a common world language, an Esperanto-English. The notion that English represented progress and without it the modern world could not be apprehended was deeply damaging to Celtic culture.

The threat posed by English was acute, but there were still many signs of hope for the Welsh language in the second half of the 19th Century. Publishing in Welsh – books, journals, and newspapers – flourished, although often under the close supervision of Nonconformity. In part this was a consequence of the increase in the number of Welsh speakers, as well as better communications which made distribution viable. The National Eisteddfod attracted large audiences and was key to the popular appreciation of the arts.

Some Welshmen, most prominently Dan Isaac Davies, made the crucial leap to bilingualism as a way of securing the place of Welsh alongside English. He published an influential pamphlet 'Three Million Bilingual Welsh People in a Hundred Years'.[53] This led to some official recognition of Welsh in state schools. Yet significant as these developments undoubtedly were, one can also read in them a sense that the Welsh cultural fastness was being eroded. The sheer ubiquity of Welsh, which had defined the nation for a thousand years or more, was weakening.

This could be seen most clearly in education policy. The 1870 Education Act paved the way for universal elementary education. It would prove to be a key force in the acceleration of anglicisation in this period but it was not the only factor. Nor was the Act designed to harm the Welsh language. In fact it accommodated the teaching of Welsh. What it confirmed, however, was the growing desire of parents to see their children educated through the medium of English. This vital shift in attitude had begun before 1870. It was in the voluntary school sector where the 'Welsh Not' had made its bleak appearance.

English also dominated higher education. The University of Wales, established in 1872, offered its curriculum entirely in English. Interpretations of these powerful events, which changed the linguistic preference of a nation, vary from those who think them an act of calculated malice by the British state, to those who consider them inevitable in a modernising world. Gwynfor Evans first:

> What made 1870 a blacker year than 1282, and even 1536, was the imposing of the English educational system on all the children of the country. Perhaps the nationalism of Wales would have been too strong to allow such an act of barbarism a quarter of a century later; but in 1870 this was only starting to sprout. The most striking manifestation of the death-wish in Wales was its willing acceptance of this hideous system.[54]

Second, a more sanguine Dai Smith:

> The decline of a European glory like the Welsh language is a tragedy, but it is not made less so by pretending that the factors making for the anglicisation of Wales were avoidable. Neither enlightened administration, patriotic fervour nor compulsory Cymricization could have altered the clash between cultures (not nations) that the process of linguistic change represented in Wales.[55]

The extension of the franchise in 1867, and the clear implication that universal suffrage would be the only foundation on which a modern democratic state could be based, meant that the people (the fabled *gwerin*) had the principal responsibility to imagine the nation. What had previously been largely the preserve of élites became a common task. Across Europe, where many national groups (such as the Italians, Slavs and Greeks) had suffered levels of cultural denigration not often overtly experienced in Wales, a similar process began.

The great national revivals of the 19th Century tended to focus on the need for national political institutions precisely because alienation had been a core part of the experience of living in large multinational, monarchic empires. That the Welsh national revival only dimly reflected this call (notably in the Cymru Fydd movement) is in part explained by the tendency of many Welsh people to believe that the nation could prosper within the British state. There was also a feeling that one could coherently identify as both Welsh and British in a sort of *bi*nationalism. Some argued then, and many more do so now, that the British-English state was far from benign, but this view did not capture the popular imagination.

The British state also adapted itself in the later decades of the century to better accommodate national sentiments. This succeeded in Wales and Scotland, but not Ireland. In 1867 the idea of legislating separately for Wales was not accepted in Parliament, but by the 1880s this position had changed radically with the passing of the Welsh Sunday Closing Act. In Scotland an even more striking act of exceptionalism occurred with the re-establishment of the Scottish Office in 1885. These developments were accepted by both major political parties, although instigated largely by the Liberals who succeeded in producing a national programme of some coherence, even if tinged with the quietism of bourgeois respectability. And as K.O. Morgan has observed, by 1914 even 'Unionists no longer questioned the propriety of separate legislation for Wales, and few doubted its claim to national status, at least in its more ceremonial aspects'.[56]

There were other ways to imagine the nation. The establishment of *Y Wladfa* (a Welsh colony) in Patagonia in 1865 was an event of considerable importance. John Davies believes that the 'venture provides evidence of a desire to create political institutions which would protect and foster Welshness – evidence, in fact, of the existence of Welsh nationalism'.[57] Saunders Lewis also believed that the Patagonian venture was an heroic example of national awakening. The colony had an advanced constitution based on universal suffrage, while the administration – commercial, political and judicial – was conducted in Welsh. Unfortunately, this proved too free in every sense for the Argentine government which introduced coercive measures in 1880. Nevertheless, in *Y Wladfa* we see the most clearly developed idea of a Welsh polity since the time of Glyn Dŵr.

In the heartland of industrial south Wales, the Rhondda Valleys, an altogether different vision of Welsh society was imagined a couple of generations later. The radical tradition was generally more comfortable with community rather than class as the generator of political activity. Welsh coal owners often shared the cultural outlook of their workers and this created a certain weakness in Liberalism as it could appear quietist. Trade Union activity, which had seemed set for significant advances in the 1850s, weakened and unions were often seen as English institutions based on individual rather than community interest. But miners in the more assertive areas of the south Wales coalfield began to question this bourgeois Liberal consensus and its belief in class co-operation. In 1912 a remarkable document was published by a group of Tonypandy miners, *The Miners' Next Step*. It questioned both the leadership of the South Wales Miners Federation and the very need to have leaders. These militants distrusted union leaders because they believed a conflict of interest was apparent which prevented real progress. For union leaders progress 'may arrive at such a point that they would not be able to retain their "jobs", or their "jobs" would become so unimportant that from this point of view they would not be worth retaining. The leader then has an interest – a vested interest – in stopping progress'.[58] In this call for direct workers control there was, as Hywel Francis and Dai Smith point out, a rejection of 'consensus society' that had developed previously, and its replacement by 'more divisive, combative tendencies'.[59]

While a Welsh colony or a workers republic were the most vibrant alternatives advanced in this period, mainstream political thought, when reflecting on Celtic distinctiveness, concentrated on the Irish question and its implications for the UK and the Empire. However, Wales and Scotland showed little enthusiasm to emulate Ireland's demand for Home Rule. Instead it was a religious issue that dominated political debate in Wales.

It might appear strange today that the question of disestablishing the Anglican Church in Wales could dominate and define the nature of political activity. True, Wales did superficially look wholly Nonconformist. Something like 5,000 chapels were built in Wales in the 19th Century – one a week! This was the greatest wave of chapel building anywhere in the world. The critic Anthony Jones has described these chapels as 'the national architecture of Wales'.[60] But the Nonconformist élite did not just want to demonstrate their distinctiveness in bricks and mortar. They wanted to change the nature of the constitution by insisting on, at least in Wales, the separation of Church and State.

From this angle the call for disestablishment appears less self-obsessed. Even so, it is difficult to believe that the issue fired the imagination of the average voter in Wales, although it was always a useful tag to demonstrate disdain for everything Tory. It is also an exaggeration to view Welsh Nonconformity as analogous to Catholicism in Ireland. The Anglican Church had experienced a strong renewal of its own in the second half of the 19th Century with the number of communicants doubling – surpassing the growth in Nonconformity. The Oxford Movement, the High Church's mission to the poor, found great success in Cardiff (where one of the Movement's finest churches was built - St. German in Roath) and in other urban areas of south Wales. And it should be noted that when disestablishment did eventually come in 1920, the Church in Wales enjoyed a golden period and transformed itself from the *Eglwys Loegr* of fable into the *Yr Hen Fam*.[61] Although the disestablishment issue did contain profound questions – the Church-State relationship, and that of religious equality – there were times when the controversy 'resembled a formal and unreal pageant, which left the great mass of the population unmoved'.[62] In the ecclesiastical realm at least, Wales had achieved full recognition as Pope Benedict XV had already established Cardiff as an archbishopric in 1916.

In some areas of working class life Nonconformity did not catch the national mood at all. Spectator sports, especially Rugby Union, attracted regular antipathy from the pulpit. The codification and spread of sport as a common recreation is probably the most unambiguously successful achievement of Victorian and Edwardian Britain. While direct physical release was limited to the players themselves, spectators became involved in a quasi-spiritual experience that provided a welcome relief from the hard banality of industrial life.

And as English became the world's language, Association Football became the world's game. Here, as with Rugby Union, Welsh distinctiveness was fully recognised when the Football Association of Wales was established in 1876. With that other glorious amusement, the Monarchy, sport could reflect the ceremonial aspects of nationhood. As Martin Johnes remarks:

> Many of the other symbols of this Welsh nationhood were limited in their appeal but rugby was more embracing and further reaching than Nonconformity, the Welsh language, the Liberal Party or any of the national institutions it created … Wales was being remade by its people into a popular rather than purist nation.[63]

This transformation is perhaps best illustrated by the adoption of the Nonconformist hymnody by Welsh rugby in the 1920s. Somehow the enthusiastic but beery rendition of *Cwm Rhondda* expressed a new reverential harmony between terrace and chapel.

While the Welsh have often revered the 'Crown in London' and its vague Brythonic antecedence, the courtesy title *Prince of Wales* has not created a bond as deep as that provided by the confluence of the English and Scottish monarchies. Until Queen Victoria visited Wales in 1889, the last monarch to spend any time in the Principality was Charles I during the Civil War when Wales was a safe haven. It is true that the Hanoverians were cool to the Scots throughout the 18th Century, but the Scottish tour of George IV in 1822 restored the Royal link and created a craze for things Caledonian. The closest Welsh equivalent was the investiture of the Prince of Wales in 1911, held at Caernarfon, and under the personal supervision of David Lloyd George. Nevertheless, the secondary position of Wales was indicated by the failure of the Court ever to meet in Wales and the lack of a Royal residence. No Welsh order of chivalry existed and Wales was absent from both the Union Jack and Royal Standard. According to Nick Groom, Wales was in a state of 'heraldic invisibility':

> Consequently, in an attempt to achieve greater national recognition, the Welsh petitioned the government in 1897, 1901, 1910, 1935 and 1945 to request that the Welsh dragon be included in the royal arms. Each time they were refused because, in the words of the College of Arms, Wales had never been a kingdom: 'There is no such thing as a Welsh national flag'. The Garter Knight of Arms told the Home Office that, 'There is no more reason to add Wales to the King's style than there would be to add Mercia, Wessex or Northumbria or any other parts of England'.[64]

Of course this was historical nonsense. The Welsh dragon appeared on the armorial bearing and badge of Henry VII, the founder of the Tudor dynasty. The lack of regal recognition since is difficult to justify. After 1921, the province of Northern Ireland had residual recognition on the Royal Standard with the Irish harp, but Wales remained entirely absent. That the people of Wales overlooked such formalities and still strongly identified with the Crown, as seen for instance when Edward VIII visited south Wales in November 1936, is a notable feature of Welsh culture in the early 20th Century.

The World Crisis

The calamity that struck Europe in 1914 soon embroiled Britain and her empire. At first the full menace of the crisis was not grasped as, at home,

Asquith's government continued to grapple with the Irish question which itself was threatening civil war. Few appreciated the strength of the troubled waters ahead and only a deranged mind could have imagined that this storm would last for over 30 years with regular periods of crisis, turmoil and war in Europe.

Once Britain committed to help France, a decision that was inevitable but reluctant, the public responded with the heady enthusiasm of those anticipating a swift and exemplary conflict. Thanatos won a much greater prize. Wales suffered casualties that were on a par with the most patriotic parts of the Empire, some 40,000 killed. By 1918 three of Europe's four emperor-monarchs had been deposed together with the social orders they represented. Despite the constructive efforts of some statesmen at Versailles, the ground was not laid for a new European order. But Wales produced the Great War's greatest leader, David Lloyd George, who symbolised the fulfilment of Welsh nationhood within the British state.

In Lloyd George Wales seemed to find her hero figure, the Arthur of legend. The first man without independent means to become Prime Minister, he demonstrated that Welshmen could reach the highest offices of state. Indeed, Lloyd George re-shaped the state in significant ways, first as Chancellor of the Exchequer and then as a war-time Prime Minister. His 'Peoples Budget' of 1909 established that the primary social purpose of the state was to promote welfare rather than to protect property. In 1916 Lloyd George formed a small War Cabinet to give his government a sense of urgency in prosecuting the war (the model was used by Churchill in the Second World War). After the conflict, the War Cabinet's secretariat became a permanent Cabinet Secretariat which allowed the executive to function with much greater efficiency, something John Grigg described as 'one of Lloyd George's outstanding contributions to the modernisation of the British State'.[65]

Whereas Gladstone became something of an honorary Welshman by marrying a Welsh heiress and living in Wales, Lloyd George was the Welsh-speaking product of the inner nation, although he was capable of criticising aspects of narrow Nonconformist culture. During the war's early stages he urged his countrymen to do more, 'At Crècy and Agincourt, where the British were eminently successful, half the soldiers were Welsh'.[66] While his reference to the Welsh martial tradition was sound, it stretched the point a bit to call such adventures British. Lloyd

George was always a little sensitive to suggestions that Wales was not doing her bit for the war effort. In 1916 a letter appeared in *The Times* which suggested that holding the National Eisteddfod in wartime was a little frivolous, and especially so singing at such events. Lloyd George famously replied that 'The blinds of Britain are not down yet, nor are they likely to be'. And he continued, 'I am glad that I came down from the cares and labour of the War Office of the British Empire to listen and to join with you in singing the old songs which our brave countrymen on the battlefield are singing as a defiance to the enemies of human right'.[67] This captured the mood of the British much more accurately than *The Times'* choleric correspondent. They sang on the battlefield in a more ironical manner. David Jones' masterful *In Parenthesis* observes:

> Riders on pale horses loosed
> and vials irreparably broken
> an' Wat price bleedin' Glory
> Glory
> Glory Hallelujah
> and the Royal Welsh sing:
> Jesu
> lover of me soul ... to *Aberystwyth*.[68]

The poet perceives more than the politician, and David Jones writing in 1937 about his wartime experiences knew that the conflict had not secured a land fit for heroes:

> Give them glass eyes to see
> and synthetic spare parts to walk in the Triumphs, without anyone feeling awkward and O, O, O, it's a lovely war with poppies on the up-platform for a perpetual memorial of his body.[69]

The 1920s became a decade of acute psychological trauma as the permanence of loss shook the nerve of grieving widows and youthful spinsters. One symptom of this pain was the growth in spiritualism which offered the hope of communication with the dead. Yet most could not access such consolation and thought instead about a world that could descend into such an apocalypse. David Jones, in a deeply disturbing image, reminded these broken souls of the reality of the battlefield that had consumed their husbands, lovers, brothers, uncles, children:

> But sweet sister death has gone debauched today and stalks on
> this high ground with strumpet confidence, makes no coy
> veiling of her appetite but leers from you to me with all her
> parts discovered.[70]

Lloyd George emerged from the war with a reputation transformed
from that of gifted Welsh politician to leading British statesman. In the
words of the popular press, he was the man 'who won the war'. His
political stature was such that after the 1918 'coupon' election he led
a coalition in which the Conservatives were by far the largest party.

Lloyd George had worked well with the Conservative Party during the
war and was on good terms with its leaders. The post-war coalition lasted
nearly four years, remarkable given the volatility of the times, and only
collapsed when an economic recession set in and the Irish settlement
extracted a spiteful reaction from Unionist diehards. Unlike many of his
contemporaries, Lloyd George saw the reality of the post-war world. The
old Edwardian order that mitigated democracy with aristocratic guidance
would not return. Although a moderate on the German question, he
knew that public opinion had to be respected and so he moved carefully
to encourage a more constructive climate of conciliation. The Versailles
Treaty troubled Lloyd George because it pandered to the French view
that the full costs of the war could be recovered from Germany and that
German territory ought to be reduced by the maximum extent. Instead,
Lloyd George believed than an enduring peace required the victors to 'act
in the spirit of judges sitting in a cause which does not personally engage
their emotion or interests, and not in a spirit of a savage vendetta'.[71] And
he was especially prescient when commenting that, 'I am strongly averse
to transferring more Germans from German rule to the rule of some
other nation that can possibly be helped'.[72] Lloyd George worked hard
during the rest of his premiership to lessen the severity of the Treaty, but
his time soon ran out and despite the often predicted comeback, he never
held office again. Ultimately, Lloyd George's astute analysis of the
international situation and the grounds upon which a stable European
order could be based did not prevail. It was too soon after such a
cataclysmic conflict for a rational peace. France favoured Germany's
material degradation rather than her moral renewal.

At home another conflict, with a pedigree as old as the Franco-
German animosity, was reaching its end game. In Ireland Lloyd
George's skills did prevail, but perversely at some cost to his

reputation. That the Irish Free State *did* slide into civil war in the early 1920s is an indication of the even greater conflict that could have occurred had Ireland not been partitioned in 1921-2. It has been said a little harshly that Lloyd George succeeded where others had failed in Ireland because in the south he ignored the Protestants and in the north he ignored the Catholics. One historian has passed a fastidious judgement that seems to sum up the establishment's view of Lloyd George's whole career, 'Gifted though he was as a negotiator – and the final outcome owes much to his skill – it is difficult to find much principle in Lloyd George's manoeuvres. He emerges with credit, but a trickster none the less'.[73] Lloyd George probably did not expect Northern Ireland to survive for long. He certainly said so to some of Sinn Fein's leaders. Yet his resolution of the crisis endured for nearly 50 years, although more like an armistice than a settlement.

The possibility of 'Home Rule All Round' always lingered faintly about the Irish crisis. In 1919 a Speaker's Conference was convened to look at the question of devolution in the UK and for a short while a major shift in constitutional thinking seemed to be taking place. However, the Conservatives remained tepid at best on the issue and had little difficulty in encouraging Lloyd George to first settle the Irish question. Consequently the Speaker's Conference was sidelined as Lloyd George grappled with far less effete realities in Ireland. There, unless a compromise was found, the most likely outcome was an Irish republic and a self-declared Ulster dominion. Both would have been disastrous for British prestige and for peace and order in Ireland. Lloyd George's solution, particularly in Ulster, was messy but realistic. It dealt a considerable blow to the cause of devolution or Home Rule, although for Lloyd George this was an unintended consequence.

The south of Ireland had gone well beyond Home Rule and only barely remained a dominion in the British Empire. To orthodox Unionists this simply confirmed the dangers of Home Rule and the risk of fragmentation that it brought to the UK. Ulster became a devolved micro-state whose existence was tolerated by the rest of the UK 'which after 1921 could intensify its development as a union state with a highly centralised form of governance'.[74] Rather than a precedent for devolution to Scotland and Wales, Northern Ireland served as a deterrent. Many have criticised Lloyd George for reneging on Welsh Home Rule, but the truth is that there was little consensus for the measure and the cause petered out in the early 1920s when the splits within Wales anticipated with amazing exactitude those that would occur in the 1970s. Instead, some favoured a more cautious approach. David Davies MP, formerly Lloyd George's parliamentary private secretary, wrote in 1919, 'It has always appeared to me that the establishment of a Welsh Office was a necessary fore-runner of a Welsh legislature'.[75]

Lloyd George is amongst the first rank of British Prime Ministers. In the 20th Century only Churchill and Attlee surpassed him: Churchill by ensuring victory in an even grimmer conflict; and Attlee by forging a consensus for the welfare state. Yet in his range Lloyd George *was* the greatest Prime Minister of the 20th Century. After a period of remarkable innovation as Chancellor of the Exchequer, he succeeded both as a wartime and peacetime premier. At last a Welshman had seized the 'Crown of Britain'. He had briefly flirted with the idea of becoming a 'Prince of Wales' in 1890s when he backed Home Rule, but it was the world of British politics that really attracted him and magnified his great talents. According to J.M. Keynes he emerged from the enchanted woods of Celtic antiquity, and it is fair to say that the English never fully understood him – which probably accounts for his diminished reputation. Nevertheless, Churchill was suitably generous when Lloyd George died in 1945, describing him as 'the greatest Welshman which that unconquerable race has produced since the age of the Tudors'.[76]

In the 1920s Britain and Wales entered an era in which the very fundamentals of national identity were explored. The forces that created such existential questioning had long been present, but they were massively accelerated by the Great War. Britain was no longer the dominant world power despite hanging on to an empire increasingly characterised by worn silk and ostrich feathers rather than the gatling-gun and gunboat. France had become the principal continental power, a position predicated on the maintenance of German war guilt and a string of pro-French satellites around the volatile black hole of Germanic Europe.

Wales suffered severe economic decline as the export market for coal collapsed. In the 1920s and 1930s some 400,000 people left Wales as male unemployment reached a peak of 43 per cent. Meanwhile, the ramifications of industrialisation and anglicisation became fully apparent. Alfred Zimmern, the first professor of International Politics at University College, Aberystwyth (the first, in fact, anywhere) observed:

Firstly, the Wales of today is not a unity. There is not one
Wales; there are three Wales. There is Welsh Wales, there is
industrial, or, as I sometimes think of it, American Wales; and
there is upper-class or English Wales. These three represent
different types and different traditions. They are moving in
different directions, and, if they all three survive, they are not
likely to re-unite.[77]

Despite the economic crisis of the 1920s, industrial Wales still seemed
the nation's most dominant force. This unsettled a group of influential,
intellectual nationalists, such as Saunders Lewis, who were moving
away from the traditional Liberal consensus that had dominated 'Welsh'
Wales. They feared that an Anglo-Welsh Wales would be absorbed by
the English-British state or even, when their paranoia reached its full
extent, that it would be consumed by an international proletariat utterly
devoid of national rootedness. Lewis led a small band and the
Nationalist Party he helped found in 1925 was, according to Dai Smith,
more a cultural group than a political party. Under the direction of
Lewis, Plaid stated that for 'the moral well-being of Wales, and for the
health, moral and physical, of its people, there must be a de-
industrialisation of South Wales' and 'Agriculture should be the main
industry of Wales and the basis of its civilization'.[78]

Reacting to the 1931 census which recorded a further drop in the
number of Welsh speakers, Lewis repudiated the idea of a multicultural
Wales because 'a Welsh-only Wales is alone consistent with the aims
and the philosophy of Welsh nationalism'.[79] Wild and uncompromising
at times, Saunders Lewis was also capable of nuanced thought.
Although attracted to some aspects of continental conservatism (for
instance, the longing for the supposed values of the pre-industrial age),
he was not pro-fascist. Nationalist intellectuals like Lewis were forming
their political ideas when the very viability of capitalism seemed in
question. What may now appear a bizarre over-reaction seemed much
more coherent at the time.

There was something biblical about Lewis, nevertheless. While some
nationalists set their hearts on a Welsh parliament, Lewis wanted to
restore a sort of bucolic European civilisation to Wales. It has been said
of Ludwig Wittgenstein that when offering correspondents advice he
could be dangerously profound, 'his remedies would be all too drastic,
surgical. He would treat you for original sin'.[80] There was more than a

hint of this proclivity in Lewis' remedies for the Welsh nation. Perhaps this is why he is a source of mild embarrassment to many Welsh nationalists today, his strictures seem impracticable. But Lewis posed profound questions about the nature of the nation and the state, and he spoke with a force that could never have been generated by the Liberal tradition (far less Unionist). When addressing the jury in the famous Penrhos bombing range trial, he said:

> '... we hold the conviction that our action was in no wise criminal, and that it was an act forced upon us, that it was done in obedience to conscience and to the moral law, and that the responsibility for any loss due to our act is the responsibility of the English Government...
>
> I shall try to put before you the dilemma and the conflict of obedience in which the Government's cruelty placed the leaders of the crusade against the bombing range, and the limits to the rights of the English State when it transgresses the moral law and acts in violation of the rights of the Welsh nation...
>
> It is part also of the moral law that no state has the right to use any other national entity merely as a means to its own profit, and no state has a right to seek national advantages which would mean genuine harm to any other nation. All that is universal Christian tradition'.[81]

However flawed, such thinking changed the nature of political discourse in Britain. Lewis was drawing on the thought of continental nationalists such as Thomas Masaryk, the founder and philosopher-king of Czechoslovakia, who had done so much to convince President Wilson of the need to recognise national self-determination as a fundamental right. Welsh nationalists could also draw inspiration from the example of the Irish Free State which, with the civil war behind it, had embarked on a highly conservative programme of social and national reconstruction which attempted to blot out the modern world.

Of course it would be decades before the electorate re-considered their basic allegiances. The 1920s had already seen a massive political shift. In 1918 the Liberal Party secured twice as many seats as Labour in Wales. That proportion reversed in 1922 and thereafter the Liberals never again won a majority of Welsh seats. Although the Labour Party contained many Welsh speakers and patriots, it was a much more anglicising force than a Liberalism which had been rooted in an indigenous Welsh Nonconformity.

In 1900 Keir Hardie was returned as a Labour member for Merthyr despite distributing English-only literature in a constituency where 60 per cent of the electorate spoke Welsh as their first language. The trade union movement, which grew significantly in the Great War, also tended to reinforce this process of anglicisation and became an essential force in the organisation of the British state. By 1916 the entire south Wales coalfield was unionised. Labour, like the Liberals and some Conservatives, had flirted with the idea of a looser and more federal UK when trying to find a solution to the Irish crisis. However, by the 1920s Labour was fast becoming a staunch Unionist party as its chances of winning a UK general election grew. As John Davies notes, 'the Labour party lost interest in the issue of Welsh self-government. Indeed, it could be argued that the party's historical role was to consolidate the process of integrating the Welsh into the British system'.[82] The political scientist Barry Jones has asserted even more boldly, 'Labour's electoral strength in Scotland and Wales and that party's belief in a united working class have done more to maintain the unity of Britain than Conservative Unionist ideology and rhetoric'.[83] In the 1930s a new, vigorous and angry proletarian self-consciousness emerged in response to the Depression. The Welsh miners who fought against Franco were, according to Hywel Francis,

> not affected or motivated in any way by a national or nationalist consciousness: not one of the volunteers was, or ever became, a member of the Welsh Nationalist Party (later Plaid Cymru). They did not form a separate ethnic company but served alongside English, Scots, Cypriots and a few Irish, inside the British Battalion...[84]

The later stages of industrialisation accelerated the process of anglicisation. In the 1891 census, 54 per cent of the population were recorded as Welsh speakers. By 1931, the figure was 37 per cent. It took less than two generations for Wales to become a predominantly English-speaking nation.

An influx of English migrants and the insidious view that Welsh was anti-modern combined to deal the final blow to Welsh as a community language. Gwynfor Evans believed that this tragedy, and all will surely agree it was such, resulted from the 'havoc…wrought by what may be called the English revolution, which was planned as deliberately as Mao Tse Tung's cultural revolution'. And, as he also claimed, the establishment's most 'powerful weapons were the English schools which all Welsh children were compelled to attend'.[85]

This angry hyperbole is understandable, but the bleaker truth is that there was no co-ordinated coercion of the Welsh language. The process was largely accidental, the epiphenomenon of a range of forces created by the 'modern' world, not least among them the desire of many Welsh people to acquire an ability to speak English. Later in the 20th Century many European countries became bilingual at no cost to the native language. Alas, Welsh faced the challenge of anglicisation before the dawn of pragmatic bilingualism. The last word on the loss of Welsh as a community language can go to David Jones in a letter to *The Times* in 1958, 'It is by no means a matter for the Welsh only, but concerns all, because the complex and involved heritage of Britain is a shared inheritance which can, in very devious ways, enrich us all'.[86] Like God, or more properly belief in the Almighty, Welsh had a difficult 20th Century. Both ceased to be communal practices and merely held on to the face of the modern world by the fingernails of personal piety.

Nevertheless, anglicisation did not make Wales English but instead created a distinctively English Wales. Dai Smith has argued that 'English-speaking Wales has long had its own life in its own terms. It is not a half-baked, imported substitute and its own history is not best served by dwelling on the contemporary fixation over languages'.[87] This is a little too sanguine, but it is certainly true that Welsh experience did not cease because a majority of the population lost the language.

The 1920s and 1930s saw the emergence of a distinguished school of Anglo-Welsh writers. Caradoc Evans is considered the father of this tradition and, as Dafydd Johnston observes, the 'term "Anglo-Welsh" should not be taken to imply any dilution of Welshness; indeed, it is most fittingly used of those writers who assert their Welsh viewpoint most vigorously'.[88] This was true also in the world of visual art where a concept of Welsh nationhood was re-imagined and transformed to meet the demands of industrial society. While the traditional Welsh-speaking notion of nationhood took a battering in the first half of the 20th Century, it was strong enough to influence the shape of indigenous art that emerged in the south Wales coalfield.

While part of the price paid for a tougher and more resilient 'modern' nationalism was a larger Anglo-Welsh component, it liberated nationalist thought from its more folksy image of bucolic peasants dancing in clogs and pinnies in some sort of pre-industrial Celtic Arcadia. As Peter Lord has noted, 'until the Great War, artists and intellectuals interested in visual culture made no coherent attempt to image the industrial landscape and its people. Indeed, many of them perceived the physical and cultural characteristics of industrial society as inimical to their idea of the nation'.[89] Artists like Evan Walters, Vincent Evans and Cedric Morris produced art of international significance based on limpid interpretations of local, industrial subjects.

The Anglo-Welsh movement, although not yet termed such, was championed in the magazine *The Welsh Outlook* founded by the industrialist David Davies MP in 1914. David Davies (later Lord Davies of Llandinam) was committed to the ideal of collective security in international affairs and through his patronage the Temple of Peace and Health was built in Cathays Park, Cardiff in the classical-modern style. Together with his sisters, Gwendoline and Margaret, David Davies ensured that continental influences infused Welsh art and literature and that Welsh art in general had a wider, international audience.

If the idea of Welsh nationhood was being transformed in the inter-war period, that of the empire was losing its once accidental coherence. Of course, there never really was a single, unified British Empire. One component, the dominions of Australia, Canada, New Zealand and South Africa, was already independent. The enduring cultural ties were strong enough, especially when buttressed by mutual economic interest, to maintain a more or less common foreign policy. However, in 1931 the Statute of Westminster ended all pretence of Westminster's legislative sovereignty over the dominions.

The Imperial empire, essentially the Indian sub-continent, was put on the path to autonomy with the Government of India Act in 1935, yet another federal constitution produced by Britain's unitary parliament. This left only the African and Caribbean dependencies entirely within the empire's orbit.

Since the American crisis in the late 18th Century, a tension had existed between an increasingly democratic homeland, with an ideology of liberty at its heart, and a subservient empire. While independence for the 'white' dominions could look like mere domestic autonomy within the empire, this pretence was difficult to sustain in the case of India (and indeed Eire), as Churchill well realised when conducting his diehard opposition to the Government of India Bill. Yet the steady retreat of empire did not produce a sense of unalloyed loss, much to the chagrin of empire loyalists. Many rediscovered the empire's 'mission' in the process of leading nations to democratic independence. In any event, Britain had lost the power to maintain a world empire by force.

British political theorists reflected on these trends and also on the fate of the now defunct Austro-Hungarian and Ottoman empires. Sir Ernest Barker, perhaps the most distinguished political thinker of the time, believed that multinational states could only survive if they generated a sense of dual loyalty:

> …in the Commonwealth at large, the British, the Australian, the Canadian, and the South African can all wed their different nationalities to a pride in a common culture – a common inheritance of law and language and loyalty – to which they all pay allegiance. It would seem that there may be a double (if not a triple) nationality. A Scotsman, for example, has his own national fund; but he is also a partner in the broader fund of British nationality. He has the two homes of the Scottish and the British nation. If he is satisfied with his double domicile, no question arises. If he should ever resolve to prefer a single home, and to stay there, he will have his way.[90]

This calm and urbane analysis stood in sharp contrast to the views of the ultra-unionist A.V. Dicey who, while permitting a cultural multinationalism, warned that a coherent state could have only one source of sovereignty. Dicey thundered that federalism would be 'the first stage towards a dissolution of the United Kingdom into separate States'.[91]

On the other hand, Barker had no such anxiety about facing new constitutional challenges, because he was confident about the value and resilience of the British state. His voice was a prescient one. As he noted, 'we may say … that Scotland is a nation which is a quasi-State; Great Britain is a State which at the least is a quasi-nation'.[92] He also classified Wales as a quasi-state within the UK. Barker realised in the

1920s, long before most of his contemporaries, that to survive Britishness must have a national character, and the nations of Scotland and Wales must be able to secure some of the attributes of a state.

Britain – empire, state and nation – experienced its greatest inner coherence when facing its greatest external threat. If human civilisation survives the nuclear age, the Second World War will stand to the modern world as the Peloponnesian war stood to the classical. Enlightenment concepts of what is a man and what is a state were smashed apart in the conflict. Yet for Britain this was an Indian summer when national destiny seemed to be re-affirmed. No other European state survived the war feeling so coherent.

The whole Continent had been either occupied by German forces, become allies of the Nazi's, or been forced into humiliating neutrality on German sufferance. Ultimately the narrow English Channel and a sliver of Stalingrad saved Europe from Nazi domination. In time the utter horror of the conflict, and the implications for states incapable of effective defence, would re-shape constitutional thought and bring fresh challenges to a British state that had experienced vindication not oblivion. The war did mark the end of empire, but in another sense also its victory.

Although some 18th Century seers like Richard Price saw the potential for America to outgrow the motherland, few could have imagined what advantages this would bring. Had the USA ended up as sparsely populated as Canada or Australia, the outcome of the war could have been grimly different. The loss of the *first* empire in the 1780s helped save Britain in the 1940s. One can catch a glimpse of the utter vastness of the Anglo-American war effort in the words of a future Chancellor of the Exchequer:

> The coast of Normandy began to take shape through the haze. And then as full light began to come one saw the ships and the planes. It was a sight so paralysing that tears came to my eyes. It was as if every ship that had ever been launched was there, and even as if the sea had yielded up her wrecks. It was as if every plane that had ever been built was there, and, so it seemed in fantasy, as if the dead crews were there too. There had never been since time began such a rendezvous for fighting men: there never will be again.[93]

Later that year, in November 1944 that 'ramshackle, triumphantly unscientific organisation'[94] Mass-Observation recorded some interesting thoughts from Kenneth Redmond in Bridgend. Mass-Observation was dedicated to providing a fuller picture of British life, and one not tainted with metropolitan condescension. Redmond, a Communist Party member, had clearly maintained a regard for national values:

> During evening conversation got round to Home Rule for Wales. Although I do not agree with severance of connections with England I do believe Wales needs autonomy in connection with internal problems. Dad just said, 'Do you think Wales could pay its way?' – this is a point that needs working out. I said I did not think anything was done in Wales that could not be or had not been paid for by Wales. Of course, if a policy of increasing Wales's industrial strength was pursued, instead of draining away its best workers, Wales would undoubtedly become far richer.[95]

This nicely framed the question that would form the background of Welsh politics after the war. The answer, essentially 'No, Wales could not pay her way', seemed emphatic until the 1960s and after a period of debate was repeated in the negative in 1979. Yet the case for political autonomy would grow in force. That the question persisted would owe most to the slow, grinding work of Gwynfor Evans who brought nationalist politics to the realm of practicability when he became President of Plaid Cymru in 1945.

The Quest for a Political Nation

Gwynfor Evans was a courageous and naïve politician. He drew his strength from what he saw as the invincible integrity of *Welsh* Wales. But he also knew that he could not remain in this redoubt. If less committed or more complicated in his views, it is unlikely that nationalism could have emerged as such a coherent political force in the second half of the 20th Century.

Gwynfor inherited a tiny political estate. Although from 1945 Plaid regularly secured a small measure of electoral support,[96] under Saunders Lewis contesting elections was never a serious consideration and many key figures remained aloof of a political world they thought Plaid could never dominate. Reflecting on Saunders Lewis' famous 1962 lecture,

Tynged yr Iaith, Gwynfor Evans summed up the critical difference in his approach, 'I refused to give priority to a direct action campaign for the language. We were already thought of as being the language party. Many people did not belong to Plaid Cymru because they did not speak Welsh. We would have ceased to be a political party if we had followed his [Saunders Lewis'] advice'.[97]

This was a decisive move because it started to expand Plaid's world view and confront, rather than wish way, the immense changes wrought by industrialisation. Plaid at last accepted the reality and permanence of the Anglo-Welsh and acknowledged the need to meet the demands of an industrial society. Without this development, Welsh nationalism at best would have remained the whimsical political pastime of the more eccentric members of the Welsh-speaking élite; at worst, it would have become but a dim reflection of Scottish experience. It is a mark of Gwynfor Evans' success that for much of the post-war period the intellectual leadership of nationalism in Britain alternated between Plaid Cymru and the SNP, with Plaid often dominating. While there were strands of nationalism in the British parties, they tended to be a ritual practice in the greater British procession. There was nothing urbane or secondary about Gwynfor Evans' nationalism. It was raw and primordial. That is why it changed the face of Wales.

By 1945 Labour was the most unyielding Unionist party in the UK. Opening the debate on the first Welsh White Paper in 1946, Sir Stafford Cripps said 'the Government have considered this suggestion of a separate Minister for Welsh affairs... with the special help, I may say, of the large number of Welsh Members who are in the Government today, we are firmly convinced that, from the point of view of the efficiency of Welsh administration, it would be wrong to institute any such arrangement'.[98] This was cold and distant even by the notoriously bloodless standards of Sir Stafford.

One of the government's big beasts, Aneurin Bevan, was more pungent, 'Is it not rather cruel to give the impression to the 60,000 unemployed men and women in Wales that their plight would be relieved and their distress removed by this constitutional change? It is not Socialism. It is escapism'.[99] A future Prime Minister, James Callaghan, agreed. The Labour government became the 'champion of centralism',[100] and even the National Coal Board did not have a specifically Welsh division.

However, if Labour's state socialism was as centralising as Edward I's regnal practices, like the Plantagenet Labour also recognised the integrity of Wales in a symbolic way. In 1949 the government established the Council for Wales, and although largely toothless, it has been described as 'a landmark in its way'.[101] For those who believed in a unitary British state, this innovation posed the same question that followed the re-establishment of the Scottish Office. If the UK was a seamless constitutional entity, how could such exceptions to uniform administration be justified? Such bells and whistles on the British body politic acknowledged that the UK was not the simple political space it sometimes pretended to be.

Between 1951-64 Conservative governments treated the Welsh question with sympathy but little skill. The Party produced a comprehensive *Policy for Wales and Monmouthshire* in 1949, the first UK party to do so and an event at least equal in significance to the establishment of the Council for Wales. The Party promised to appoint a Cabinet member with responsibility for Welsh affairs when next in government. To some extent, this move recognised the growth of nationalist feeling in Wales, but this potentially imaginative policy was compromised by its dull Unionist application. Churchill gave responsibility for Welsh affairs to the Home Office as if Wales was on a par with the Channel Islands. To make matters worse, the Home Secretary, Sir David Maxwell-Fyfe, was Scottish – the press had much amusement. To be fair to Sir David, he soon won many friends in Wales as he effortlessly combined affability with tact.

Of the five Conservative Cabinet ministers who acquired responsibility for Wales, only one was Welsh. While many senior Tory activists in Wales favoured the creation of a Secretary of State for Wales, Conservative governments refused to yield on this point. Nevertheless, the voluntary side of the Party was often preoccupied with Welsh questions in the 1950s and did not meekly repeat Westminster's mantra. Party members were concerned that Tories were viewed as the English party in Wales. The 'Parliament for Wales' campaign, which attracted a surprising level of popular support in the early to mid 1950s, also caused extensive soul searching within the Party. Yet despite this sincere recognition of Welsh nationhood, senior Conservatives tended to address the national question because it appeared to be a threat to Britishness rather than a way to express it more fully.

Tories were much more comfortable with the ceremonial dimension of nationalism, as demonstrated in early 1953 when Welsh Conservatives urged the inclusion of the Welsh emblem on the Royal Standard. The failure of the Conservative Party to develop its *Policy for Wales* allowed the Labour Party to recover ground on the national question. Labour fought the 1959 General Election with a pledge to create a Secretary of State for Wales, a promise they were able to implement in 1964 when they returned to government. By the 1960s the UK parties were routinely publishing election manifestos for Wales, although they tended to be thin and derivative, a further recognition of the distinctiveness of Welsh politics.

While Plaid did not come close to a parliamentary breakthrough during the immediate post-war period, it demonstrated that it could sometimes attract considerable support in particular contests (usually by-elections). In 1959 Plaid contested more than half of Welsh seats for the first time and achieved a little more than 5 per cent of the vote.[102] Saunders Lewis had never accepted the importance of contesting Westminster elections and he criticised the expense involved in Plaid's 1959 election campaign. However, participation in the parliamentary process indicated a deep-seated faith in constitutional politics which inoculated Plaid from some of the reckless tactics of militant nationalists.

Evans still believed that 'It's a grave mistake to measure the success of Plaid Cymru in electoral terms alone. As well as being a political party, it's a national movement that revivifies the nation...'.[103] One historian of Plaid Cymru has astutely observed that Gwynfor's politics was a 'combination of conservative and radical elements. A respect for the past, for what is deemed natural and traditional, is merged with a rebellious desire for change and improvement'.[104] Some have gone further and characterised 'Gwynforism' as a 'Welsh version of English Toryism'.[105] This commitment to parliamentary methods is all the more noteworthy because it was made at the time of the Tryweryn episode. Despite the overwhelming opposition to the plan in Wales, the Liverpool Corporation secured an Act of Parliament to permit the flooding of the Tryweryn valley to form a reservoir. Even when Welsh MPs of different parties united to defend a vital Welsh interest, Whitehall could be cold and obdurate. The lesson seemed clear. Westminster did not always work well for Wales.

Gwynfor Evans' startling victory at the Carmarthen by-election in July

1966 came just a few months after Labour's greatest performance in Wales. At the General Election Labour won 32 of Wales' 36 constituencies with just over 60 per cent of the vote. Labour's hegemony seemed complete but, like the Liberal ascendancy it replaced in the 1920s, it was a dominance generated by wider British political forces rather than an enhancement of the inner Welsh nation. It could consequently lack imagination and prescience. The Labour Party was sometimes reduced to portraying Welsh nationalism as reactionary and authoritarian. Some Labour politicians went a lot further and labelled Plaid anti-working class and fascist. Partisan political debate is rarely edifying, but the bitterness in the Labour-Plaid exchanges indicated a deep proprietorial fury in Labour ranks as the nationalists made further inroads in the late 1960s.

The parliament that Gwynfor Evans entered was far from its former imperial glory. Back in 1945 most British politicians assumed that African 'nations' would move slowly towards independence. Rather unexpectedly the pace quickened, especially after Ghanaian independence in 1957, and the British Empire ended with astonishing rapidity. This was not the only transformation in British political life. The Suez crisis indelibly marked the end of Britain's world power status. Many assumed that Britishness would not long survive the end of the Empire. To Gwynfor Evans, Britishness was always the malign force that diminished Wales. As he wrote in his memoirs, 'I still believe that Great Britain is a dangerous anachronism and that it is high time for the British state, like others of its kind, to be broken up'.[106]

The view that the end of the Empire posed profound problems for a sense of Britishness became intellectually fashionable after the rise of nationalism in Wales and Scotland. More recently some critics have questioned this simple theory. Bernard Porter has argued that it was only the ruling classes that invested in a common imperial Britishness to any great extent. He notes 'the extraordinary lack of domestic resistance to decolonisation from the 1940s on. If the empire had been central to most Britons' feelings of national identity in those years, this would not have happened. It was because it was absent for most of the 19th Century, and then marginal thereafter, that the majority of Britons were able to cope with the loss of their empire far more easily than later mythology maintains'.[107] Certainly the presence of influential and fairly successful nationalist parties in Wales and Scotland should not obscure the wider point that Britain remained a successful multinational state.

Arthur Aughey has nicely captured the ineffability of Britishness, 'St. Augustine once reflected that he knew something when he did not have to speak of it. When he had to speak of it he realised that he did not know it. This may be the case with the UK…'.[108]

It is true that the character of Australia, Canada and New Zealand as British nations was still strongly felt in the 1950s and 1960s but then declined quickly. Yet Britishness in the Home Nations appears more resilient, perhaps reflecting the fact that a shared community of interests continues to exist at a level that can sustain a common state. National identity is a complex phenomenon and simple explanations of its creation are best avoided. To take an analogous case within the British Isles, the Republic of Ireland has suffered little diminution of Irishness since the sudden lapse of the nation's Catholicism.

Plaid's success, and the SNP's advance in Scotland, caused the Labour government considerable anxiety in the late 1960s. The government established a Royal Commission in 1968 to look at ways in which the constitution could be adapted to meet demands for greater national and, in England, regional powers. For the first time since 1919 devolution was back on Westminster's agenda. When the Commission reported in 1973 it delivered a muddled report that had none of the clarity or succinctness of the options presented to the government in 1920 by the Speaker's Conference on devolution. Yet paradoxically, the debate did not fizzle out as it had done in the early 1920s. In fact, both Labour and Tory commitments were made to some measure of devolution.

Another key event occurred in 1973 when Britain entered the European Economic Community. This made the theoretically simple but highly centralised space of the British state a little more crowded, since the authority of EEC institutions had to be recognised on matters of European competence. This event had ramifications that spread like dry rot through the theory of orthodox Unionism. At first the nationalist parties completely failed to grasp the significance of the European development. Plaid campaigned for a 'No' vote in the 1975 referendum on EEC membership, an anti-EEC stance that lasted until the mid 1980s. By 1991 Gwynfor Evans had changed his mind completely, 'The hope of a national future for Wales lies in her becoming an equal member of the European community. The people of Wales must learn to think of themselves not as British but as Welsh Europeans'.[109] Why the Welsh-European dual identity was coherent but not the Welsh-

British one, was not explained. However, in practical terms Plaid's volte face[110] on the EU was a sound strategic judgement. The General Election of February 1974 boosted Plaid's cause with the election of Dafydd Wigley and Dafydd Elis Thomas to Parliament. Plaid was never again without MPs and constitutional nationalism could always count on powerful expression at Westminster.

This is not the place to consider the 1979 devolution campaign in detail[111] but some general remarks are necessary on its significance both to the national question and the development of the British state. Although the referendums were conceded reluctantly by the ailing Labour government, and were justifiably seen as a hurdle that contradicted parliamentary sovereignty, they had the effect of making the Welsh and Scottish people sovereign on the ultimate question of their constitutional future. The English electorate played no part in determining such a fundamental change to the British state, a strange anomaly that was repeated in 1997. A small majority for devolution was secured in Scotland, although well short of the margin necessary to implement the terms of the 1978 Act.

The rejection of devolution was overwhelming in Wales and it cannot be casually explained away in retrospect as an historical aberration. Even in Gwynedd two thirds of the electorate voted 'No'. One problem was the failure of devolutionists to engage the industrial communities of south Wales. Consequently, Labour supporters had little sense of ownership over their government's own policy which, on the contrary, seemed exacted under duress by the Party's nationalist opponents. Less often remarked upon is the standard and nature of the 1970s devolution debate which at times descended to poisonous parody. It became difficult afterwards to understand what question had been settled. Critics had made a grotesque man of straw to characterise the dangers of devolution and the illusion worked wonderfully. But time soon demonstrated the lack of substance in such exaggerated arguments. While the incoming Conservative government made no attempt to reverse administrative devolution to the Welsh Office, indeed quite the opposite, there was no denying the psychological blow landed on nationalists. Of course Plaid had wanted much more than Labour's fairly weak form of devolution, but Gwynfor Evans fully recognised the value of what was on offer in 1979:

It was true that the proposed Assembly would have been weak

and it wouldn't have had the power to legislate except on insignificant matters, but what I believed to be crucial was not that it should have legislative powers, but that the people of Wales should have an elected Assembly which would draw the nation together and give it direction.[112]

Gwynfor Evans fell into deep despair but he soon had the opportunity to expiate the apostasy of his compatriots. In 1980 the recently elected Conservative government announced a major change to its broadcasting policy in Wales. Instead of devoting the proposed fourth channel to Welsh language broadcasting, an increased output in Welsh would continue to be spread across the TV network. This was a perfectly coherent policy but it required the Conservatives to renege on a manifesto commitment to establish a dedicated Welsh channel. No less serious was the government's failure to recognise the symbolic value of a separate channel for Welsh language broadcasting.

TV had quickly changed the manner in which most people acquired information and enjoyed visual entertainment. It was as strong a force as mass literacy and inexpensive publishing had been in the 19th Century. Ironically, in his famous radio lecture in 1962, Saunders Lewis had not referred to broadcasting at all. Nevertheless, Gwynfor Evans realised immediately the importance of this medium to the *idea* of Wales as a nation and so he announced that he would go on a hunger strike unless the government kept its original promise to establish what became S4C. It seemed that to get its own way, the British state would have to let the father of modern nationalism starve to death. As Jan Morris put it, 'Few Welsh people doubted that he meant it. He had long maintained that the survival of the Welsh language, and so in his view of Welshness itself, largely depended upon the influence of television, so immense was its effect upon the minds and aspirations of the young'.[113]

The government gave in, lost face, but recovered some credibility by acting with good grace in funding S4C generously. The moral of the tale was not that the British connection required Wales to be diminished, but rather that Welsh interests had to be fought for and could not be taken for granted. It must have struck quite a number of people who had voted 'No' to a Welsh Assembly that, while having no truck with political separatism, they had held too benign a view of the British state and the efficacy of its institutions to meet legitimate national aspirations.

Jan Morris has eloquently argued that industrialisation was 'the most fateful and ferocious of all man's successive assaults upon the matter of Wales... It transformed south Wales socially, economically, morally'.[114] Even as late as the 1950s western European politicians considered coal and steel the key industries in any large economy and agreed common policies to co-ordinate heavy industry as a means of preventing another European war. Nevertheless, by the 1980s Europe's post-industrial age was well underway.

Britain faced a clear and crucial choice at the 1983 General Election when Labour offered to cut Britain off from the forces of world capitalism that were tearing through the old industrial regions of Europe. This autarkic vision was firmly rejected by the British people and Labour suffered its worst defeat for 50 years. While Labour remained the largest party in Wales, its margin over the Conservatives was slight (37.5 per cent to 31 per cent) and a record number of Welsh Conservative MPs were elected. Managing such elementary industrial change would have challenged any government, and while the technical task was handled with some skill in the steel industry, the same cannot be said about coal. Mrs Thatcher was too much of a laissez-faire rationalist to entertain traditional Tory arguments in favour of amelioration. Worse, the Prime Minister tended to think that Wales and Scotland were holding England back. Once she berated the veteran Welsh Office minister Wyn Roberts with the acid comment that, 'The only Conservatives in Wales are the English who moved in'.[115] The government's lack of tact in industrial regions rarely represented by Conservatives gave the militant miner's leader Arthur Scargill the opportunity to call a strike in 1984-5 for essentially political reasons. He refused to ballot the miners and only 10 out of Wales' 28 pits backed the strike call, but once it started the south Wales coalfield remained steadfastly out. In 1997 it was in the former south Wales coalfield that the biggest swings in favour of devolution occurred, no doubt in part as former miners and their families reflected on this seminal episode.

The Welsh and Scottish Offices became even stranger anomalies in Britain's unitarian state once successive Conservative victories at UK general elections were not remotely replicated in Wales or Scotland. If British institutions could serve the political interests of Wales, Scotland and England why was there any need for national departments of state? And if the Welsh and Scottish Offices were needed to recognise national requirements in the administration of government policy, why not move to a more formal federal system or at least one with a level of democratic accountability?

These theoretical flaws had little salience until Labour seemed incapable of winning a General Election. Even so, a more pragmatic approach by Whitehall could have managed such dissonance to some degree. Mrs Thatcher rarely thought about Wales, but she did consider the lack of Conservative progress in Scotland irksome. As she remarks in her memoirs, 'There was no Tartan Thatcherite revolution'.[116] Her response was not very Tory, in fact it was alarmingly Jacobin – more concentrated revolutionary medicine needed to be applied by force of will. The results were bleakly predictable as among other measures the poll tax was piloted in Scotland.

Wales was largely left out of this zealous crusade, but after the 1987 election an equally crass decision was taken by the Prime Minister when she appointed an Englishman, sitting for an English constituency, as Secretary of State for Wales. The utter bizarreness of the appointment leaves one struggling for a suitable simile. Perhaps it was as if one of the later Holy Roman Emperors had forced the election of a Protestant as pope. Inevitably, this cultural insensitivity caused significant damage both to the Conservative cause in Wales and to the coherence of Unionism. Unfortunately, the same colonial practice continued during John Major's premiership. In 1995 Francis Pym, the Conservative Party's constitutional spokesman between 1976-79, said of devolution 'I knew we could win once but not again after Margaret turned her back on Scotland'.[117] He could have added, 'and Wales'.

In 1990, during a lunch at Chequers, Mrs. Thatcher expressed her surprise to Wyn Roberts that the Labour Party was returning to a devolution policy. As he recalls the conversation, 'I said that Labour feared the nationalists who were actively challenging them at local level. The truth was that the referendum defeat of 1979 was largely due to the unpopularity of the Callaghan government. I did not add that the next referendum might be a protest vote against us!'.[118]

The British unitary state was now in its final phase of existence, although there was a brief revival in 1992 when John Major campaigned to save the Union in what now appear slightly comic terms: 'the United Kingdom is in danger. Wake up, my fellow countrymen. Wake up before it is too late!'[119]

On a tactical level, the state could still prove innovative in responding to national questions. In 1988, four hundred years after the publication of the Welsh Bible, the Education Act recognised Welsh as a core subject in bilingual schools and as a foundation subject in all others. The 1993 Welsh Language Act strengthened earlier legislation, put English and Welsh on a similar legal footing, and established the Welsh Language Board as a statutory body. These measures were a distinct success for traditional Tory administration under the expert and sensitive guidance of Sir Wyn Roberts. However, a reform of local government in 1994 was much less successful because it failed to secure a consensus in Wales. Despite a poor start on Welsh language issues with the S4C debacle in 1980, between 1979-1997 Conservative governments effectively de-politicised the language through a series of constructive reforms. The language no longer generated fierce controversy as it had done in the 1970s when those opposed to devolution often suggested that a Welsh Assembly would be run by a Welsh-speaking élite. Now the language seemed to belong to everyone in Wales, Welsh-speaking or not. Thousands of monoglot English-speaking parents started to send their children to bilingual schools, a phenomenon that did much to reverse the decline in the number of Welsh speakers for the first time in a century.

The influential journalist and commentator, John Osmond wrote an important defence of devolution in 1977 entitled *Creative Conflict*.[120] Only half of this succinct title captured the mood of the times. In 1995 Osmond returned to the fray with his book *Welsh Europeans*.[121] On this occasion he captured the spirit of the times more completely. His argument was exaggerated in claiming that 'since the 1950s history has been driving Welsh people away from Britishness and towards a new duality in which belonging to Wales is felt more and more in conjunction with a sense of belonging to Europe. We are becoming Welsh Europeans'.[122] Europe is more coherently viewed as an *additional* dimension of identity not an alternative one. Nevertheless, in the late 1980s, as the Cold War's ice sheet receded, problems buried since the end of World War II were suddenly exposed. Quite unexpected threats and opportunities faced Europe's states in the 1990s.

The implications for British constitutional thought were profound. Communism collapsed with revolutionary speed in eastern Europe during the autumn of 1989. Few had expected such epoch defining change, fewer still had prepared for it. The boundaries of European politics were no longer fixed, and it was natural for people in Britain to contemplate adaptations to their constitution in more measured terms. Compared to the overthrow of totalitarian Communism, devolution seemed a modest reform indeed. The European Union's transformation straddled the collapse of Communism, starting in 1986 with the Single European Act and ending with the implementation of the Single Market in 1992. It quickly created political ramifications. After all, the British state had started with its own internal single market in 1707. The European sceptics, most but not all Conservatives, were wrong to fear that this was the start of a federal Europe, but Europhiles were disingenuous when denying the reality of the political changes that were taking place. The European Union was indeed becoming a polity, albeit as a relatively weak confederation. Inevitably this development made Britain a more complicated political space where the simple strictures of Unionism could no longer fully apply. Again, compared to constitutional innovations at the European level – quite unimagined by British politicians in 1979 – devolution appeared far less threatening.

Wales and Britain

While the *Matter of Britain* constitutes a shared inheritance, its particular configuration in time is determined by our *ideas*. The deductions that people make from the premise of common experience can vary enormously. Empirical conservatives will, it is true, ask if a certain interpretation of experience appears coherent. However, this can guard against only the more bizarre creations of political thought. Those looking for compelling justifications either for or against a British state in the *Matter of Britain* look in vain. Even an apparently unambiguous figure such as Edward I can appear on both sides of an argument. Was the Conquest of 1282 akin to the Roman destruction of Carthage, or did it help preserve the *idea* of Wales by leaving much of its culture intact while providing some protection from the Norman Marcher barons and their remorseless anglicisation?

It has been argued that in Scotland the realm survived at the expense of the *idea* of Scottishness. One critic has said of this period, 'it is almost as if there are two Englands and one of them is called Scotland'.[123] In his astute assessment of the investiture of the Prince of Wales at Caernarfon Castle in 1911, John Ellis observes that 'commentators alternately presented King Edward as the ruthless conqueror who had built the castle and as the bringer of peace who had reconciled the Welsh chieftains through his presentation of his newborn son at the castle gates'.[124]

It is more coherent to ask whether the Welsh nation and the British state continue to inspire our imagination? We are left with, in essence, a question of will. There is a strange meeting here between a quintessential English conservative philosopher and a much loved radical Welsh historian. First Michael Oakeshott:

> ...the engagement of constructing a state has remained a permanent ingredient of modern European government. It is an undertaking which has been reflected in five centuries of speculative thought remarkable both for the variety of its arguments and for the inconclusiveness of its outcome, and which comprises also the chequered constitutional histories of modern European states. For a 'constitution' is that in which rulers and subjects express their beliefs about the authority of a Government.[125]

And second, Gwyn Alf Williams:

> There is no historical necessity for Wales; there is no historical necessity for a Welsh people or a Welsh nation. Wales will not exist unless the Welsh want it. It is not compulsory to want it. Plenty of people who are biologically Welsh choose not to be Welsh. That act of choice is beyond reason. One thing, however, is clear from our history. If we want Wales, we will have to make Wales.[126]

While Wales has never been a silent partner in the British enterprise, the Welsh influence on the development of the British state has been secondary, even after allowing for the obvious differences in capacity between England and Wales. Welsh Conservatives must recognise this and move on from a mere appreciation of Welsh history to advocacy of a fuller Welsh political life. Unless this nationalist dynamic is enhanced the *Matter of Britain* will be shaped by those inimical to a British state.

What would have happened if the people of Wales had again voted 'No' to devolution again on 18th September 1997? It would not have stopped devolution. Scotland had already voted three to one for a Scottish Parliament and the peace process in Northern Ireland was predicated on the re-establishment of an Assembly. A Welsh 'No' would have created a more unbalanced constitution than the one that took effect in May 1999. The greatest flaw in Labour's devolution policy was not that Wales and Scotland were on the slippery slope to independence, but that England was left out of the reform altogether. The implications of Britain remaining a unitary state for English matters only are yet to be fully understood. However, the more lurid predictions of Unionists that devolution would quickly lead to the abolition of Britain have proved groundless. It would appear that the *Matter of Britain* can cohere in quite different forms to those envisaged in 1536, 1603, 1707, 1801 or 1921, but without losing its substance.

References *1-77*

1. *Henry V*, Act 3, scene 3.
2. A nice, early refutation of the absurd calumny that Monmouthshire is not part of Wales.
3. *Henry V*, Act 4, scene 7.
4. See Glanmor Williams, *Wales and the Reformation* (University of Wales, 1999) particularly Chapter 10.
5. Ibid, p. 372.
6. King James VI and I, *Political Writings*, Johann P. Sommerville (Ed) (Cambridge), p.135.
7. Ibid, p.169.
8. John Davies, *A History of Wales* (Penguin 1990) p.275.
9. J. Gwynfor Jones, *Early Modern Wales* (MacMillan, 1994) p. 194.
10. John Davies, p.275.
11. Ibid, 279.
12. Entry on Henry Vaughan, *The Oxford Companion to the Literature of Wales* (1986) p. 614.
13. J. Gwynfor Jones, p.213.
14. Ibid, p.209.
15. Quoted in Norman Davies, *The Isles*, (MacMillan 1999) p. 527.
16. Linda Colley, *Britons: Forging the Nation 1707-1837*, (Pimlico 2003) p.13
17. Ibid, pp 367-8.
18. Norman Davies, p. 634.
19. John Davies, p.329.
20. Gwyn A. Williams, *The Welsh in Their History* (Croom Helm 1982) p.47.
21. Quoted in Prys Morgan, *Iolo Morganwg* (University of Wales 1975) p. 42.
22. Gwyn Alf Williams, p.41.
23. Ibid, p.58.
24. John Davies, p. 337.
25. Edmund Burke, *Collected Works Vol. V* (London 1801) pp 180-1.
26. John Derry, *English Politics and the American Revolution* (Dent 1976) p.168.
27. *The Blackwell Encyclopaedia of Political Thought* (1987) p. 417.
28. Ibid, p. 418.
29. Prys Morgan, pp 81-2.
30. Ibid, p. 91.
31. Peter Ackroyd, *Albion* (Chatto and Windus, 2002) p. 422.
32. *The Oxford Companion to the Literature of Wales* (1986) p.220.
33. Gwyn Alf Williams, *The Merthyr Rising* (University of Wales 1988) pp 132-3.
34. Ibid, p. 133.
35. See John Davies, pp 377-8.
36. K.O. Morgan, *Wales in British Politics 1868-1922* (University of Wales 1991) p. 179.
37. Thomas Pakenham, *The Scramble for Africa* (Weidenfeld 1991) p. 25.
38. Ibid, p. 59.
39. Lawrence James, *The Rise and Fall of the British Empire* (Abacus 1995) p.210.
40. Gwyn Alf Williams, *The Welsh in Their History*, p.182.
41. Ibid.

42. K.O. Morgan, p.214.
43. Ibid.
44. John Davies, p. 390.
45. Reports of the *Commissioners of Inquiry into the State of Education in Wales*, Part II, pp 56-7.
46. Ibid, p. 66.
47. Michael Hechter, *Internal Colonialism* (Routledge 1975) p.75.
48. Gwynfor Evans, *Land of My Fathers* (Y Lolfa 1992) p. 369.
49. Quoted in the *Oxford Companion to the Literature of Wales*, p.18.
50. Gwyn Alf Williams, p.161.
51. Marcus Tanner, *The Last of the Celts* (Yale 2004) p. 80.
52. Ibid.
53. Of course this was a Welsh language publication, *Tair Miliwn o Gymry Dwy-Ieithawg ymhen Can Mlynedd*, see John Davies p. 456.
54. Gwynfor Evans, p. 395.
55. Dai Smith, *Wales! Wales?* (George Allen 1984) p. 162.
56. K.O. Morgan, p. 309.
57. John Davies, p. 415.
58. Quoted in, Hywel Francis and David Smith, *The Fed* (Lawrence and Wishart 1980) p. 15.
59. Ibid, p.16.
60. Anthony Jones, *Welsh Chapels* (National Museum of Wales 1984).
61. *Eglwys Loegr* – English Church; *Yr Hen Fam* – the old mother.
62. K.O. Morgan, p. 271.
63. Martin Johnes, *A History of Sport in Wales* (University of Wales 2005) p. 32.
64. Nick Groom, *The Union Jack* (Atlantic Books 2006) p. 292.
65. John Grigg, *Lloyd George: From Peace to War* (Methuen 1985) p.488.
66. Ibid p. 175.
67. Ibid pp 416-7.
68. David Jones, *In Parenthesis* (Faber 1937) p. 160.
69. Ibid p. 176.
70. Ibid p. 162.
71. Martin Gilbert, *First World War* (Weidenfeld 1994) p. 513.
72. Ibid.
73. Alan O'Day, *Irish Home Rule 1867-1921* (Manchester 1998) p. 308.
74. D. George Boyce 'A Place Apart? Ulster, Britain and Devolution, 1886-1939' in Duncan Tanner (et al) *Debating Nationhood and Governance in Britain 1885-1945* (Manchester 2006) p. 61.
75. Andrew Edwards and Will Griffith, 'Welsh national identity and governance 1918-45', in Tanner (et al), p.123.
76. Duncan Brack (ed) *Dictionary of Liberal Democracy* (Politico's 1998) p. 223.
77. Alfred Zimmern, *My Impressions of Wales* (Mills and Boon 1921) p. 29. It seems, no doubt, incongruous that such a title could have been published by this publisher. But many such intellectual essays in fact appeared.

78. Alun R. Jones and Gwyn Thomas (eds.) *Presenting Saunders Lewis* (University of Wales 1983) p. 37.
79. Dai Smith, p. 104.
80. Ray Monk, *Ludwig Wittgenstein* (Vintage 1991) p. 459.
81. Jones and Thomas (eds.) pp 115-122.
82. John Davies, p. 543.
83. J. Barry Jones, 'Changes to the Government of Wales 1979-1997', in J. Barry Jones and Denis Balsom (eds.) *The Road to the National Assembly for Wales* (University of Wales 2000) p. 23.
84. Hywel Francis, *Miners Against Fascism* (Lawrence and Wishart 1984) p. 228.
85. Gwynfor Evans, p. 367.
86. David Jones, *Epoch and Artist* (Faber) p.54.
87. Dai Smith, p. 8.
88. Dafydd Johnston, *The Literature of Wales* (University of Wales 1994) p. 91.
89. Peter Lord, *The Visual Culture of Wales: Industrial Society* (University of Wales 1998) p.14.
90. Ernest Barker, *National Character* (Methuen 1927) p. 130.
91. A.V. Dicey, *England's Case Against Home Rule* (Richmond 1973) p. 189. The work was first published in 1886.
92. Barker, p.131.
93. Iain Macleod, 'One Man's D-Day' in Fiona Glass and Philip Marsden-Smedley, *Articles of War* (Paladin 1990) p. 308.
94. Philip Ziegler in his foreword to, Sandra Koa Wing (ed), *Mass- Observation* (Folio 2007) p.vii.
95. Ibid p. 248.
96. The best individual constituency results for Plaid Cymru in General Elections between 1945-1959 were: 1945 – Meirionnydd (10.3%); 1950 – Caernarfon (13.1%); 1951 – Rhondda West (7.7%); 1955 – Meirionnydd (22.1%); 1959 – Meirionnydd (22.9%); The best by-election result in this period was Ogwr in 1946 (29.4%).
97. Gwynfor Evans, *For the Sake of Wales* (Welsh Academic Press, 1996) p. 247.
98. Hansard, Col 316, 28 October 1946.
99. Ibid, Col 405.
100. Kenneth O. Morgan, *Labour in Power* (Oxford 1984) p. 309.
101. Ibid, 311.
102. A percentage that would have guaranteed representation in some European countries.
103. Gwynfor Evans, p. 126.
104. Laura McAllister, *Plaid Cymru* (Seren 2001) p. 68.
105. Emyr Williams, quoted in McAllister, p. 72.
106. Gwynfor Evans, p. 96.
107. Bernard Porter, 'Empire and British National Identity 1815-1914' in Helen Brocklehurst and Robert Phillips (Eds.) *History, Nationhood and the Question of Britain* (Macmillan 2004) p. 271.

108. Arthur Aughey, 'Three Fables of Britishness' in Brocklehurst and Phillips (Eds.) p. 46.

109. Gwynfor Evans, *Fighting for Wales* (1991) p. 210.

110. I do not intend to be hostile here; I made my own volte face on devolution after the 1997 referendum!

111. See the following Chapter, 'Devolution: the Battle Lost and Won'.

112. Gwynfor Evans, *For the Sake of Wales*, p.213.

113. Jan Morris, *The Matter of Wales* (Oxford 1984) p. 448.

114. Ibid, 290.

115. Wyn Roberts, *Right from the Start* (University of Wales 2006) p. 221.

116. Margaret Thatcher, *The Downing Street Years* (Harper Collins 1993) p. 618.

117. Quoted in Roberts, p.312.

118. Ibid, p. 242.

119. John Major, *The Autobiography* (Harper Collins 1999) p. 303.

120. John Osmond, *Creative Conflict* (Gomer 1977).

121. John Osmond, *Welsh Europeans* (Seren 1995).

122. Ibid, p. 144.

123. James Campbell quoted in RR Davies, *The First English Empire* (Oxford 2000) p. 162.

124. John S. Ellis, 'Reconciling the Celt: British National Identity, Empire, and the 1911 Investiture of the Prince of Wales', *Journal of British Studies*, 1998, Vol. 37, p. 401.

125. Michael Oakeshott, *On Human Conduct* (Oxford 1991) p. 189.

126. Gwyn Alf Williams, p. 201.

Chapter 3

Devolution: the Battle Lost and Won

1997 was, I think, their last chance.. If most Welsh people had not voted 'yes' to devolution, nobody alive would ever see true political nationhood in Wales. For generations no passion of patriots, no ecstasy of linguists, no reasoning of history or ideology would persuade the English State that Wales was really a nation at all..

Jan Morris, *Wales: Epic Views of a Small Country*

The 18 years between the devolution referendums held in 1979 and 1997 barely amount to a generation. Yet the climate for reform was transformed as if a political gulf stream had abruptly altered course and drawn the warm winds of constitutional change across Wales.

For those who wanted Wales to declare itself a political nation, 1ˢᵗ March 1979 was darkest midnight. The Labour historian K.O. Morgan has written of that day, 'However powerful their sense of cultural and historical identity, the Welsh were, in political and economic terms, strictly unionist. Welsh devolution was promptly wiped off the political agenda'.[1] John Davies, the first secretary of the Welsh Language Society, commented that the, 'entire strategy of Welsh progressive patriotism since the 1880s, when Home Rule had first been ventilated by the Cymru Fydd movement, had come to nought'.[2] The president of Plaid Cymru, Gwynfor Evans, considered it the worst day in the nation's history, 'Wales was degraded in the sight of the world and humiliated in the eyes of its own people by the hugely negative result'.[3]

However, on the 18ᵗʰ September 1997 a similar proposition to establish an executive form of devolution in Wales was narrowly accepted by the electorate. Devolution supporters celebrated with that most heady mixture, elation and relief. In his memoirs, Nicholas Edwards remarks that 'few of the arguments changed in the two decades that separated these important constitutional campaigns, although the outcomes were very different'.[4]

What did change? Welsh Tories seem compelled to examine the hypothesis that the most critical variable was 18 years of Conservative government and its affect on the national question. Tony Wright MP, a political scientist and Labour politician, states the charge boldly, 'Mrs Thatcher has good claim to be regarded as the real progenitor of Britain's current constitutional revolution… she provoked a movement for constitutional and political reform that she could not have anticipated and with consequences she would certainly loathe'.[5]

The effulgence of Mrs Thatcher's personality continues to dazzle both friend and foe, but it is unlikely that such a simple explanation can account for so decisive a change in voting behaviour. Other factors must also be considered and their impact carefully assessed. These include the organic growth of the Welsh Office; the exaggerated nature of the 1979 referendum result; the acceptance of bilingualism by the people of Wales; the Labour Party's ownership of devolution in the 1990s; the influence of the European Union in reshaping constitutional concepts; and the economic changes that ended the long age of adamantine industry. It was the combination of these factors and their complementary interaction that explains the remarkable growth in popular support for devolution illustrated in the table below:

Table 1: *The devolution referendums in Wales*

	1979	1997
Yes	243,048 (20.3%)	559,419 (50.3%)
No	956,330 (79.7%)	552,698 (49.7%)
Turnout	1,199,378 (58.3%)	1,112,117 (50.3%)

Some disgruntled Tories protested that such a narrow victory was insufficient grounds for major constitutional change. They had a point, but it was undermined by their equally passionate commitment to parliamentary sovereignty which would logically deny the use of referendums in the first place. The comparative statistics cut through the political arguments and spoke unambiguously: the swing to 'Yes' in 1997 was a massive 30 per cent. Paradoxically, had the 1979 result been less exaggerated, the slender 'Yes' majority in 1997 would have indeed appeared meagre. Every county in Wales voted 'No' by at least two thirds in 1979. Only Monmouthshire recorded such an emphatic rejection of devolution in 1997, although the Vale of Glamorgan also came close. Neath Port Talbot recorded the highest 'Yes' percentage and this demonstrated the Labour Party's 'ownership' of devolution in 1997. The Labour heartlands of Glamorgan and Gwent recorded the biggest swings. It was in Labour's traditional redoubts that the battle was won and the electorate persuaded to whisper 'Yes' to devolution.

Table 2: *The devolution referendums in the counties of Glamorgan and Gwent*

	1979	1997
Yes	119,549 (16.3%)	328,949 (50.5%)
No	612,605 (83.7%)	322,924 (49.5%)

If the narrow but affirmative result of the second referendum inclined Labour to modesty and a desire to be inclusive, no such reserve seemed incumbent on the Conservative Party in 1979. The electorate had shouted 'No' very loudly indeed. A received Conservative view soon emerged in which it was assumed that the Union and the British unitary state had been enthusiastically reaffirmed. Many outside the Conservative Party accepted this unitarian interpretation. *The Western Mail* declared in an editorial, 'Those die-hards who have already announced their intention to carry on the fight are allowing resolution to mask the reality of the situation: the Welsh Assembly is not wanted'.[6]

Conservative policy throughout the 1980s was predicated on the belief that the electorate had indeed rejected *any* form of Welsh Assembly. The Party would pay a heavy price for this naïve faith in the constitutional status quo, and it served to desensitise Tories to the precariousness of their position in Wales. During the long devolution debates which dominated much of the 1974-79 Parliament, Conservatives had taken care to attack Labour's particular plans for devolution rather than the principle of reform itself. Perhaps it was the very scale of the Conservative Party's 'victory' in the referendum that explains the feeling of invincibility that gripped Welsh Tories and distorted their memory of the devolution campaign. In her memoirs, Lady Thatcher recalls the episode with a caution that is nearer the mark of contemporary events, 'Although I had not publicly campaigned for a "No" vote in the referenda in Scotland and Wales, that was the result I wanted… in Wales a large majority of those who voted rejected the proposal. For the moment, devolution was dead: I did not mourn it'.[7] At the beginning of 1979 Conservatives feared that a general election victory might leave the Party responsible for the implementation of devolution in Scotland and Wales. Devolution only became a hopeless cause in the opinion of most Conservatives after the referendum result.

Even this conclusion is perhaps too bold. Donald Walters, then Chairman of the Conservative Party in Wales, believed that the constitutional question had not been resolved, 'Because these Labour proposals have been rejected, it does not mean that devolution is a dead duck'.[8] It was not inevitable that the 1980s would mark a return to unbending Unionism in the Conservative Party. Nor was it inevitable that the Labour Party in Wales would return to a devolution policy in the 1990s after its mortifying experience in 1979. This chapter offers a Conservative interpretation of how devolution became the battle lost and won.

The National Question

Devolution is a child of the 1960s but also a curious genetic throwback to the Victorian era. The British establishment possesses a deep and disturbing ancestral memory of the Irish constitutional impasse that prevailed between 1886-1921. Scotland and Wales had not been inclined to join in the Irish demand for Home Rule in that period. Instead, nationalism in Wales and Scotland followed cultural channels or was sublimated in the British Empire and visions of imperial unity.

Political nationalism returned to spook the establishment at a time when hard realities first experienced in the 1950s took grip of a State that was no longer a world power. The spectre of further Celtic secession haunted the Labour and Conservative parties in the late 1960s. The Welsh Nationalist Party had existed since 1925, but it was a marginal political force that saw its principal mission the defence of Welsh cultural values. Although the creative brilliance and eccentricity of Saunders Lewis had been replaced by the dogged determination of Gwynfor Evans in 1945, Plaid Cymru failed to make an electoral breakthrough in the immediate post-war period.

However, Labour's understandable sense of complacency in Wales was shattered shortly after its most comprehensive general election victory. In 1966 Labour won 32 of the 36 Welsh constituencies, far surpassing all earlier performances. It seemed that in Wales Labour spoke effortlessly for the people. Wales *was* Labour. Then the Carmarthen by-election held on 14 July 1966 produced the most significant result in a Welsh constituency since Keir Hardie's victory at Merthyr in 1900. Gwynfor Evans jumped from a poor third place to beat Labour.

Many senior Labour figures feared that their world might be made of glass, and Plaid Cymru would do to Labour what Labour had done to the Liberals in Wales. A string of pyrrhic by-election victories further unsettled the Labour Party. Labour held on at Rhondda West (1967) and Caerphilly (1968) but on both occasions suffered swings of 29 per cent to Plaid Cymru. The Scottish Nationalist Party matched and then exceeded the success of Plaid Cymru during the late 1960s. In England, Labour suffered only one by-election loss in the 1966-70 Parliament. It seemed that Celtic nationalism was again on the march and a Home Rule crisis imminent. The Labour government responded by summoning that steady night-nurse of the British constitution, a Royal Commission.

Meanwhile Edward Heath concluded that, 'Unless some pressure valve for moderate nationalist aspirations could be created, extreme nationalism might take a grip in Scotland and Wales. This would inevitably lead to the break-up of the United Kingdom'.[9] Edward Heath started to explore the expedient of devolution to prevent a more fundamental constitutional crisis. Between 1967 and 1974 the Conservative Party developed constitutional policies designed to meet the nationalist challenge in Scotland. The process was leadership-led, as indicated in Heath's grandiose 'Declaration of Perth' in May 1968. Wales did not figure prominently in the Party's deliberations and Heath remarked tellingly in his memoirs, 'We had arrived at the view that the outbreaks of nationalist sentiment in Wales and Scotland, although concurrent, were quite different from one another in their root causes, and in the direction which they might eventually lead. Welsh nationalism was more of a cultural phenomenon, whereas the SNP-inspired nationalism was all about independence from the United Kingdom'.[10] Heath qualified his assessment somewhat, 'Once Scotland had its own assembly, there would be pressure from the Welsh for their own as well'.[11] However, it is fair to say that from the beginning Conservative policy on devolution was asymmetric and driven by the Party's experiences in Scotland. The Conservative Party in Wales was a marginal force in shaping devolution policy in the UK.

The Conservative Party has had a more varied tradition on devolution than its opponents are prepared to concede or, indeed, many Tories are inclined to accept. An element of pragmatism befits a Party that identifies itself as Unionist. This belief in the British state is logically prior to any particular constitutional structure whether unitary, devolved or federal. For instance, between 1918 and 1921 the Conservative Party seriously considered a policy of Home Rule 'All Round' in an attempt to keep Ireland in the United Kingdom. An air of desperation did cling to calls for such a panacea, and after the secession of southern Ireland the Conservative Party reverted to simple and confident Unionism based on a unitary state.

Edward Heath was the first Conservative leader since Austin Chamberlain to advocate a measure of Home Rule, but even the bloodless policy eventually proposed for Scotland attracted trenchant opposition from sections of the Party. The outcome of the 1968 Scottish Conservative Conference in Perth was the establishment of a constitutional committee under the chairmanship of Sir Alec Douglas

Home. Among the members of the committee were the former prime minister of Australia, Sir Robert Menzies, and Sir Kenneth Wheare who was the author of the classic text *Federal Government*. Despite the latter's membership, the committee's report *Scotland's Government* rejected federalism on the gnostic grounds that, 'having the advantage of an unwritten constitution, it would be revolutionary and unwise to disturb and discard it'.[12]

Even the term 'Assembly' was thought too aspirational and the report recommended that a 'Scottish Convention' be established to sit about 40 days a year as, in effect, a supplementary chamber of Westminster. The Convention would not have had the power to initiate legislation, but Scotland-only Bills could have had their Second Reading, Committee, and Report stages taken by the Convention. The functions of the Scottish Grand Committee and Scottish Standing Committees would also have moved to the Convention. However, the Convention would not have had an executive and Sir Alec stated that controversial Bills would probably stay at Westminster.

Here the policy ran into difficulty. Although a modest form of devolution, and one with a directly elected body, a Conservative government lacking a majority in Scotland could only allow non-contentious Bills to be dealt with by a territorial chamber of Westminster. John Major faced the same dilemma in the 1990s with his variation of Heath's proposals which sought to enhance the status of the Scottish and Welsh Grand Committees. Nevertheless, the Conservative Party's report *Scotland's Government* was the most serious treatment of the national question by a major party-of-state since the Irish crisis of 1918-21.

Other observations can be made. In its perfunctory rejection of federalism as an option for the UK the Conservative Party set a trend which was to be followed by the Kilbrandon Commission and the Labour Party in the 1970s. All schemes for devolution devised in the UK have failed to demonstrate clear first principles, largely because federalism is assumed to be fanciful. Devolution has been unconvincingly viewed as a system to create constitutional dependencies of Westminster rather than a distinct but complementary apparatus to accord the nations of the UK a political identity within the Union. And the Conservative Party recognised that the real threat to parliamentary supremacy was not devolved law-making but the establishment of separate executives (governments) in Edinburgh and Cardiff.

Edward Heath's administration, unexpectedly elected in 1970, did not consider devolution a priority. The need for urgent action seemed to have passed and the government decided to wait until the Royal Commission had reported before considering devolution further. Both Plaid Cymru and the SNP had a disappointing general election and neither party came close to fulfilling the promise intimated in earlier by-election victories. Comparisons to the Irish crisis could only be sustained if the nationalist parties made significant breakthroughs and sent MPs in large numbers to Westminster. Many in the political establishment had thought such an outcome possible, but these fears appeared an over-reaction in 1970 when the people of Wales and Scotland reaffirmed traditional loyalties.

Heath had criticised the Labour government's response to the nationalist threat as, 'slow and cumbersome',[13] but his administration never even managed to produce the often promised Green Paper on Scottish government. Instead it set about reforming local government, despite the fact that there seemed to be a strong case for tackling devolution and local government re-organisation together. Worse, for those who advocated devolution, the government created a two-tier local government structure in Scotland and Wales. It had been generally assumed that a system of unitary authorities would be best combined with devolution, a consensus that re-emerged in the 1990s.

It took the Royal Commission on the Constitution four-and-a-half years to produce its chaotic and prolix report. The report was not unanimous and two commissioners signed a memorandum of dissent. But that was not the half of it. The majority report was subdivided into three widely different options for devolution. More confusion followed with some commissioners favouring one option for Wales but another for Scotland. Legislative devolution, which involved the devolution of legislative and executive powers, was favoured by eight commissioners for Scotland, six for Wales; executive devolution, which would have left the legislative framework and major policy decisions with Westminster and central government, was favoured for both Wales and Scotland by two commissioners; and a mere advisory council was favoured by three commissioners for Wales, one for Scotland.

In a report that was clear and emphatic about very little, federalism was dismissed in the most conceited terms, 'the United Kingdom has for centuries been governed in a spirit of unity and co-operation, and even if this unity is now being questioned it would hardly be satisfactory to adopt a legalistic system intended for a much earlier stage of constitutional development'.[14] The spirit of imperial superiority lived on in the commissioners.

The minority report was theoretically more convincing but impracticable in the eyes of most critics. It recommended a scheme that would have applied to the whole of the UK with, 'Scottish, Welsh and English Governments and Assemblies' all having 'identical powers and broadly similar structures'.[15] While the minority commissioners stressed that, 'legislative sovereignty in all matters must remain with the UK government and Parliament',[16] their solution was federal in character. The inclusion of England, which the minority commissioners thought essential, would also have required its subdivision into five or more units.

The Kilbrandon Report, as the majority report became known, was greeted 'with bafflement and even mirth'[17] according to the constitutional historian Professor Vernon Bogdanor. It is said that the fate of many Royal Commissions is to report on the burning issues of yesterday. So it seemed in October 1973 as Britain was engulfed by the international oil crisis that followed the Yom Kippur war. Heath's government had also started to head for its showdown with the unions which ended in the 'Who Governs?' election of February 1974. It must have struck the Royal Commissioners as deeply ironic that the 'Who Governs?' election had nothing to do with the national question and devolution.

Neither the Conservatives nor Labour made a manifesto commitment to devolution in February 1974. It was not Kilbrandon's maladroit report that revived devolution but the result of the election which produced a hung parliament. Labour's minority government relied on at least a lack of hostility from the nationalists and the Liberals (the latter a party traditionally committed to federalism). The Queen's speech promised that proposals would be brought forward for devolution to Wales and Scotland. Moving with great haste, Labour just managed to publish the White Paper *Democracy and Devolution: Proposals for Scotland and Wales* before the October 1974 general election campaign started. This slapdash document contained the government's conclusion, 'that the Scottish assembly should have a legislative role',[18] but that the Welsh assembly should only assume, 'certain powers of the Secretary of State in respect of delegated legislation'.[19] With astonishing ingenuity Labour had identified a permutation not conceived by any of the Royal Commissioners. Only Scotland would get a legislature, but both Scotland and Wales would get devolved governments.

A Reluctant Reform

The Conservative Party also fought the October 1974 election on a pro-devolution programme. As Edward Heath recalled, 'If we had been re-elected... we would have honoured our manifesto commitment to set up a single-chamber Scottish assembly to work in conjunction with Parliament. The members of this assembly would initially be drawn from elected councillors on the new local authorities, although we did not rule out direct elections in the future'.[20] The Party had weakened its commitment to a Scottish assembly by abandoning the earlier preference for direct elections. Policy on Welsh devolution was stated explicitly for the first time and promised merely to implement the weakest option in the Kilbrandon Report, a nominated advisory council.

By the time that the Labour government outlined its legislative intentions, Heath was no longer leader. Margaret Thatcher has written that the constitutional theorist who influenced her most was the arch-Unionist opponent of Irish Home Rule, A.V. Dicey. It is only in relatively recent times that Dicey's naïve, but powerfully argued, theory of parliamentary sovereignty has been rejected. Unsurprisingly, Thatcher was no friend of devolution, as she recalls in her memoirs, 'Ted had impaled the Party on an extremely painful hook from which it would be my unenviable task to set it free. As an instinctive Unionist, I disliked the devolution commitment'.[21]

However, with characteristic adroitness, Thatcher pursued a pragmatic course and asked Willie Whitelaw to chair a devolution policy group. Whitelaw proposed, and the shadow cabinet accepted, a directly elected Scottish Assembly. This policy was announced at the Scottish Party conference in Dundee in May 1975. During the first phase of Mrs Thatcher's leadership, the Conservative Party remained committed to devolution and strengthened its policy by proposing that a Scottish Assembly be directly elected.

In November 1975 the Labour government published its White Paper *Our Changing Democracy: Devolution to Scotland and Wales*. The government confirmed its intention to establish a legislative Assembly in Scotland but only an executive Assembly in Wales. A cautious approach was required to convince sceptical Labour backbenchers that devolution would strengthen the British state, 'There are few parallels anywhere for dividing between two levels of government the powers and functions long exercised centrally in a unitary state'.[22] The government agreed, 'wholeheartedly with the Kilbrandon Commission in rejecting also federalism within the UK'.[23] Parliamentary sovereignty was affirmed in comforting if archaic terms, 'Political unity means that the Queen in Parliament, representing all the people, must remain sovereign over their affairs'.[24] This defined the government's concept of devolution for, 'Any surrender of this sovereignty would imply federalism, not devolution'.[25]

The dilemma facing the government was how to turn the theoretical supremacy of Westminster over matters devolved into practical reality. In Scotland, where the Assembly would gain legislative powers, the White Paper proposed that, 'In order to be submitted for Assent the Bill must be both intra vires and acceptable on policy grounds'.[26] A range of measures would also ensure that Westminster remained supreme in executive matters. Although the government emphasised that its reserved powers would be used sparingly, the underlying incoherence in devolution was obvious.

In places *Our Changing Democracy* implied little more than an enhanced form of local government with powers to adapt and modify rather than create policy. Elsewhere the White Paper seemed to be quasi-federal, 'Under the government's proposals, the Assemblies will control policies and spending priorities over a very wide field'.[27] The government attempted to clarify matters in August 1976 with the publication of *Devolution to Scotland and Wales: Supplementary Statement*. Two crucial changes were proposed to the government's scheme for devolution. First, the right of the UK government to reject Scottish Assembly Bills on policy grounds was abandoned; and second, the executive autonomy of the proposed Scottish and Welsh administrations was acknowledged in the government's commitment not, 'to take back devolved functions'.[28] The government was unwittingly moving in the direction of a quasi-federal settlement.

Of course, there was no proposal to formally divide sovereignty in a written and federal constitution, but the supremacy of Westminster over devolved Scottish affairs would have entered what Bagehot called the dignified part of the constitution and have had no practical significance. Quite simply, the government faced the conundrum that executive authority cannot be divided in a unitary state, a fact well understood by Conservatives. All that Labour could do now was restrict the number of subjects to be devolved in an effort to dilute the strength of its devolution proposals. This did not placate the critics of devolution who pointed to the history of the Scottish and Welsh Offices which demonstrated that more functions were likely to flow in time to the devolved executives. The Labour government had little grounds for optimism as its devolution proposals entered the parliamentary process.

For many, devolution remained a poorly understood and unsettling concept. How could devolution both create Welsh and Scottish governments and preserve the unitary state? Labour feared that a Wales Bill might not be carried and so presented a joint Scotland and Wales Bill to Parliament. The Bill, which contained two quite different models of devolution, passed its Second Reading with relative ease in December 1976. However, there was a significant amount of cross party voting amongst MPs and this indicated at best brittle support. The Bill was amended during its Committee Stage by the government to allow for referendums in Wales and Scotland to trigger the implementation of devolution.[29] The government might have hoped for a swift and successful outcome in Parliament given the inclusion of this safety valve, but the reverse transpired. By late February 1977 only a handful of the Bill's 115 clauses had been debated and the government felt obliged to curtail discussion with a guillotine motion. To the consternation of the government, it lost the motion and the Scotland and Wales Bill was effectively dead.

It seemed possible that the government would fall as a result of this debacle, but the following month Labour agreed an informal coalition with the Liberal Party and one of its main conditions was that the devolution proposals would be re-introduced. This time round separate Wales and Scotland Bills were presented to Parliament and they received Second Readings on the 14th and 15th November 1977.

The legislation was further encumbered by the need to gain the support of at least 40 per cent of the electorate in the referendums.[30] Such a threshold was an exacting requirement, but justified by the opponents of devolution on the grounds that major constitutional change should attract the support of a large portion of the electorate, and not merely a simple majority of those voting. It was this measure that translated the small 'Yes' majority in Scotland into a rejection of devolution in 1979. Had the same requirement applied in 1997, Wales would have again rejected devolution.

The Conservative Party had voted against the Second Reading of the Scotland and Wales Bill but denied that it rejected devolution in principle. It was Labour's version of devolution that Tories publicly attacked. Mrs Thatcher stressed that, in contrast, the Conservative plans for Scotland locked devolution into the Westminster structure and avoided the constitutional horrors of a Scottish executive, 'There is a great difference between an Assembly geared into the Westminster structure; an Assembly which has powers of primary legislation, which will then have to come to this House merely for final assent; and an Assembly which has a separate executive, which itself can be a great source of conflict'.[31]

Most Conservative MPs accepted the need for some reform, although many English Tory members remained profoundly sceptical even about a constrained form of law-making devolution for Scotland. Julian Amery MP spoke for many when he said, 'If we concede an Assembly and an Executive we concede a cardinal principle, because once we establish a directly elected Assembly, and still more an Executive, we set up an embryonic state'.[32] Other Tory MPs maintained the need for a comprehensive settlement which would address the concerns of all the Home Nations including England. Devolution, even the Tory brand, remained an elusive if not ineffable concept. It took a heterodox Tory to reach first principles and express the Unionist's dilemma. J. Enoch Powell, reflecting on the previous Home Rule schemes to come before the House of Commons, said:

> All the debates… have led to the only possible logical termination, which is that we can have legislative devolution to the parts of the state only where this state is federal, where the supreme legislature has its own demarcated functions and each legislature has its own entrenched functions…The reason why this ultimate device, the only one that will theoretically fit, is not practical now is not so much that parts of a federation of the UK would be disparate in strength – I see no problem in a federal House representing different parts of the Kingdom in different numbers. The reason why federation is… not a practical possibility is that we do not want it.[33]

Unlike the Royal Commission's dissenting members, Powell thought it fanciful to expect the people of England to agree to the federal re-constitution of the UK simply to meet the vague and unverified political aspirations of Wales and Scotland. Francis Pym closed the debate for the Conservatives with a speech that went a lot further than Mrs Thatcher's in accepting the need for devolution, 'Whatever happens tonight, however, the devolution argument is here to stay... Not many Hon. Members have argued for the status quo. Some would like it, and I understand that, but the more rigidly we try to adhere to a system that is the source of continuous criticism and of continuing frustration, the more possible it is that in the end bigger changes may come about than are desirable or necessary'.[34] After repeating the Party's commitment to a directly elected Assembly in Edinburgh, Pym maintained that only more administrative devolution was needed in Wales. He condemned outright the government's proposals for Wales:

> The Welsh Assembly as proposed in the Bill will be responsible for administrating legislation which it has no power to shape. That is nonsense. It is not wise to have a different form of government for Wales with the result that all four constituent parts of the UK will each be governed by a different system.[35]

The same criticism would be made of Labour's devolution measures for Wales in the 1990s. If Conservatives believed that the Welsh proposals in 1976-7 were half-baked and dangerous, the Party had no intention of promoting a stronger form of devolution. Anticipating later developments in the Conservative Party, leading Welsh Tories emphasised that the real alternative to the status quo was a federal state. Nicholas Edwards, the Shadow Secretary of State, made an intelligent and cogent speech in which he identified the real choices facing Wales, 'Fundamentally, I believe that we either have to choose a system based on a single executive or we have to opt for separation or the federal solution'. He added, 'The government in the Bill have chosen for Wales, from somewhere in the middle of the range of choice, the permutation which seems to offer the least possible chance of success. They are seeking to create a situation in which one government have to carry into effect – and to produce – the secondary legislation for a system of law originated by another government which may be of a totally different political complexion. That is a recipe for administrative and political chaos'.[36]

Edwards offered an alternative which would enhance opportunities for the discussion and scrutiny of Welsh affairs at Westminster. He repeated the Conservative Party's commitment to expand the functions of the Welsh Office, extend the opportunities for the scrutiny of Welsh affairs at Westminster, increase the responsibilities and freedom of local authorities, and to see an enlarged role for a 'Welsh Council as a body to co-ordinate on an all-Wales scale the extended role of the local authorities'.[37]

To summarise, then, in December 1976 the Conservative Party reaffirmed its acceptance of devolution in principle but rejected the proposals of the Labour Party. The status quo was not thought sustainable and a measure of law-making devolution would be required in Scotland, but not in Wales. Devolved executives were rejected outright as a dangerous constitutional innovation which would threaten parliamentary sovereignty. It seemed that the Party had reached a cautious but settled position in accepting a measure of political devolution.

However, the underlying position was dynamic and the strong magnet of simple Unionism started to exert considerable force. Conservatives hostile to devolution became more confident as the Labour government ran into intractable difficulties with its own backbenchers. There were clear intimations that the Party line was shifting and some pro-devolution Tories were not persuaded by the leadership's assurances that voting against the Scotland and Wales Bill did not constitute a rejection of reform in principle. As Douglas Hurd recalls, 'I was cross and thought of resigning my front bench job when the Party finally ditched its commitment to Scottish devolution in 1976'.[38]

The St. David's Day Massacre
The referendums held on 1st March 1979 could not have come at a worse time for the Labour government. Deeply divided, the government had endured an exhausting parliamentary battle during which its devolution policies had been examined in forensic detail. Every conceivable objection had been identified and often exaggerated. What spontaneous enthusiasm existed for devolution in the mid 1970s had evaporated under the heat of economic instability and industrial conflict. James Callaghan, a staunch Labour Unionist, had inherited the devolution commitment when he succeeded Harold Wilson as Prime Minister in 1976. According to Callaghan's official biographer, 'he took the traditional

Labour view of endorsing a nationwide approach to social and economic planning and regarding devolution as a dangerous concession to parochial Celtic nationalism'.[39] As the flesh of Callaghan's premiership turned to grass, he faced the prospect of carrying an unwanted and convoluted constitutional measure at a time of growing political unpopularity. It was a task Callaghan did not relish and he remained intellectually detached from the devolution debate and only managed a single appearance each in the Scottish and Welsh 'Yes' campaigns. Intensely irritated by the 'winter of discontent', the people of Wales, and to a lesser extent Scotland, took the referendum at least in part as an opportunity for a protest vote against Callaghan's failing government.

Labour faced the miserable situation of having to fight for its devolution proposals on two fronts in Wales. On one flank the government faced its traditional Tory opponents and the 'No Assembly Campaign', and on the other a renegade 'Labour No Assembly Campaign'. Ominously for the government, the anti-devolution groups complemented each other without any need for a formal alliance. Chris Butler was the research officer of the Conservative Party in Wales in 1979 and he recalls, 'The Conservative Party... was the party which, to all intents and purposes, formed the No campaign and to the greatest extent was responsible for its funding'.[40] This campaign highlighted the dangers posed by Labour's flawed devolution scheme and stated to the electorate, 'By voting "No" you will be stopping the start of the slide down the slippery slope to the break-up of the United Kingdom'.[41] The cover of an all-party 'No' campaign allowed Welsh Tories to advance a stark and uncompromising Unionist message.

Meanwhile the Conservative Party's official policy was still open to political devolution in principle. As Chris Butler emphasised, 'The referendum is often loosely termed the devolution referendum. The vote, however, was not against devolution, it was against the Welsh Assembly as proposed'.[42] This was a strained, indeed contradictory argument, and one required by political exigencies in Scotland where the Party had to keep the option of devolution open. As Mrs Thatcher assured Scots, 'A "No" vote does not mean the devolution question will be buried'.[43]

The Labour Party–Wales TUC campaign did not focus attention on this contradiction but instead made a crude, partisan appeal in its campaign literature, 'Vote Yes: to maintain the Labour Government. Don't let the Tories win a victory in Wales'.[44] Unsurprisingly, Conservatives interpreted the subsequent 'No' vote in partisan terms. Butler argues that the, 'credit for being totally in step with Welsh voters benefited the Conservative Party in the general election that followed'.[45] In the 1980s Welsh Tories revised history and recalled the 'No' campaign as a heroic battle against the very idea of devolution rather than Labour's proposals in particular. It was difficult for Tories not to interpret the 'No' vote in the most expansive terms and as an endorsement of Conservative policy. However, the sense of euphoria which led to wild expectations of a transformed political situation, was always misplaced. Neil Kinnock, one of the leaders of the 'Labour No Assembly Campaign' got it right, 'We've killed this particular brand of devolution stone dead and we've done it in the main with Labour votes'.[46]

The 'gang of six' Labour dissidents rounded up the Party's traditional supporters and corralled them into the 'No' camp. It was an effective operation and brilliantly executed by the gang's two leaders, Neil Kinnock and Leo Abse. The 'Labour No Assembly Campaign' used to great effect the slippery slope argument and maintained that devolution was a concession to gothic nationalism rather than a means to meet the genuine aspirations of the Welsh people.

Even more devastating was the gang's attack on the government's proposals to reform local government. A provision to review the structure of local government was written into the Wales Act 1978. The government was preparing the way for the creation of unitary local authorities to replace the Conservative reforms of 1973 which had introduced a two-tier system. No doubt the government had reasonable grounds to expect that devolution could be presented as a means to reduce bureaucracy and simplify the process of government. Certainly the public had not taken the county and district structure to their hearts.

However, it was a serious misjudgement. The vast Labour Party élite in Wales found that their local government base was under threat. New battles would have to be fought and many senior councillors would face retirement or the loss of leadership positions. Many councillors also feared that a structure of approximately 25 unitary councils (to replace the 8 county councils and 37 districts) would not be able to prevent the Assembly from usurping many of local government's functions. If the government's proposal to review local government was principled in abstract, it was maladroit in practice. Far from being a strong factor in favour of an Assembly, it became for many Labour

Party activists the primary reason for opposing devolution. The 'gang of six' exploited this issue and helped open up a chasm between local Labour Party organisations and the Labour government.

As the Labour and Tory inspired 'No Assembly' campaigns took it in turns to hack away at the corpse of devolution, Callaghan's government found itself handcuffed to the cadaver. The 'gang of six' were not averse to using hyperbole to unnerve the government still further. The Welsh Assembly was portrayed in Labour's heartland as an alien mechanism to allow north and west Wales to dominate the industrial and socialist south (Tories reversed the argument in north and west Wales to great effect). This was a modern variation of the Orange rant 'Home Rule is Rome Rule'. It was left to the flamboyant Leo Abse to make the necessary rococo convolutions:

> The English speaking majority would be condemned to be strangers in their own land. The Nationalists, by insisting on Welsh being spoken in the Assembly, will ensure the creation of a Welsh speaking bureaucratic élite who will attempt to impose a false homogeneity upon Wales. There is no magic superiority of one language over the others though Nazi and German academics practised that dangerous doctrine.[47]

The 'Yes' campaign failed to turn such gaffes to its advantage. Indeed, these hysterical predictions of a Welsh language conquest resonated with the electorate in south Wales. Quite how 80 per cent of the population could be linguistically coerced by the 20 per cent who spoke Welsh was never explained. The government's response was bloodless. Despite the fact that many of the 'No' camp's arguments were highly tendentious, the government seemed incapable of effective propaganda. Simple and direct rebuttal could have put the 'No' campaigners on the defensive. After all, it could easily have been argued that the Assembly would unite north and south Wales; help create a tolerant and bilingual society; reduce bureaucracy and democratise the Welsh Office; and provide a means to keep Britain united while respecting moderate Celtic nationalism.

The government never really fought to win, perhaps because it feared that with such fervour devolution would gain a life of its own and fuel nationalist sentiments in Wales. In many respects the Labour government's devolution policy for Wales was similar to that of the

Conservative Party's for Scotland. Neither party was enthusiastic about devolution, but at the same time each reluctantly accepted that the status quo was no longer adequate to meet national aspirations. Both parties attempted to create contingent forms of devolution. While the Conservatives proposed to control Scottish devolution by granting a weak legislature without an executive, Labour proposed the converse for Wales: a weak executive without a legislature. The latter was a more risky proposition (to those who wanted contingent devolution) as executives are inherently more powerful than legislatures.

Here the debate crystallised into the question of the Assembly's competence in economic matters. An executive Assembly with wide-ranging powers, including economic functions, would represent a strong (but democratically deficient) form of devolution. John Morris, the Secretary of State for Wales, seemed in no doubt that such an outcome would be avoided and argued that the Assembly would, 'relieve the Welsh Office of responsibility for social matters, including health and housing and leave it free to focus attention on the Welsh economy'.[48] However, the 'Wales for the Assembly Campaign' maintained that the Assembly would provide the, 'Welsh Development Agency with the democratic muscle it needs to plan the Welsh economy and promote economic growth'.[49]

One of Labour's most prominent devolution supporters, Lord Crowther-Hunt, concluded that the Wales Act was so messy, 'it must amount to sabotage by the drafters in London'.[50] With the electorate confused about the government's true intentions for the direction of Welsh devolution, it is not surprising that the referendum was lost so badly. Although the reaction of Plaid Cymru's leader, Gwynfor Evans, was a little too sanguine his remarks contained a germ of truth, 'Because the circumstances of this referendum were so heavily loaded against a Yes vote it cannot be said that Wales has rejected the idea of an elected Assembly'.[51]

The Unionist Revival

The narrow but insufficient 'Yes' vote in Scotland and the resounding 'No' in Wales set the Conservative government elected in May 1979 on a firmly Unionist path. All talk of the constitutional status quo not being an option was silenced. According to Ferdinand Mount, head of the Downing Street policy unit in the early 1980s, under the leadership of

Mrs Thatcher, 'the Conservatives began a long about turn which brought them back to the uncompromising Unionism from which they had departed a decade or so earlier'.[52] This simple Unionism comforted Conservative activists in Wales and Scotland and also led seamlessly to Mrs Thatcher's crusade to restore greatness to Britain.

Yet not all of her senior colleagues were convinced that the national question had been so easily resolved. Edward Heath, predictably, and a number of Scottish Tory MPs believed that political devolution was still necessary. Even some English Conservative MPs thought that the Party's minority position in Scotland and Wales might cause problems. Douglas Hurd feared, 'a colonial situation in Scotland',[53] which could be disastrous. He has argued that the difficulties facing Mrs Thatcher in Scotland, 'could have been avoided with much benefit to the Union and to the Conservative Party if we had held to our 1970 pledge and set up an Assembly when we had the chance'.[54] In Wales the Conservative government implemented its 1979 manifesto promises to increase the functions of the Welsh Office and to set up a Welsh Affairs Select Committee (of course, the latter was part of a general policy to improve parliamentary scrutiny by establishing select committees to track each department of state). The commitment to convene a constitutional convention in Scotland was dropped, although the government did hold all-party talks on methods to improve the scrutiny of Scottish business.

Deep down Mrs Thatcher was not a traditional Tory Unionist. Although the policies followed by her government up to 1987 did fit into the classic category, Mrs Thatcher became increasingly frustrated by the compromises traditional Unionism entailed. A conviction politician needs convictions, and Mrs Thatcher's were those of a Conservative rationalist. She believed that once properly formulated, Conservative prescriptions should be applied universally. Her own words describe this proclivity perfectly, 'There was only one answer. If a small state, low taxes, less intervention and more choice were right then we should argue for them and do so without apology. There must also be the same drive to implement this programme north as south of the border'.[55]

This attitude led Mrs Thatcher, the Conservative rationalist, to a policy of assimilation in economic and social affairs. The Conservative Party performed badly in both Scotland and Wales in 1987. While Wales did not figure prominently in Mrs Thatcher's deliberations, the Party's position in Scotland troubled her deeply. The Prime Minister made an excoriating assessment of the Conservative Party's hierarchy in Scotland and the influence of the Scottish Office. In her memoirs Mrs Thatcher recalls the episode with almost contemporaneous frustration as her colleagues in Scotland, 'regularly portrayed themselves as standing up for Scotland against me and the parsimony of Whitehall… in adopting this tactic they increased the underlying Scottish antipathy to the Conservative Party and indeed the Union'.[56] She also attacked the very purpose of the Scottish Office, 'whose very structure added a layer of bureaucracy, standing in the way of reforms which were paying such dividends in England'.[57]

It would have been impossible for a traditional Tory Unionist to think in this way. The Welsh and Scottish Offices were part of the contract made between the UK state and the Welsh and Scottish nations to compensate them for sometimes having to accept governments they did not vote for (invariably Conservative governments). Mrs Thatcher's rationalist prescription would have been recognised by zealots everywhere: more not less strong medicine. Her St. Paul was ready and waiting and he didn't even need a damascene conversion, 'The real powerhouse for Thatcherism at the Scottish Office was Michael Forsyth, whom I appointed as Parliamentary Under-secretary in 1987'.[58] In July 1989, in the face of stiff opposition from the Tory establishment, Mrs Thatcher appointed Forsyth Chairman of the Scottish Party. His 15 month tenure was miserable and a predictable failure. It is much to Forsyth's credit that he recovered and served John Major skilfully as Scottish Secretary between 1995-97.

What transpired in Wales was even more unsettling for traditional Tory Unionists. Nicholas Edwards had decided to retire at the 1987 general election and to the astonishment of most observers, Peter Walker was sent to the Welsh Office as his successor. Walker had no Welsh connections and a rather whimsical jibe circulated that he could at least see Wales from his Worcestershire home. Mrs Thatcher does not refer to this episode in her memoirs but it is unlikely that she took advice from the Conservative Party in Wales. Nicholas Edwards was informed of Walker's appointment on the day it was announced. In a response which clearly indicates that Edwards' Anglo-Welshness was not always in equilibrium, he replied, 'I am sure he will do it excellently, what a brilliant idea'.[59]
However, with this colonial-style appointment, Mrs Thatcher turned Cathays Park into the new Dublin Castle. There was no malicious intent behind this decision, but it is inconceivable that a 'colonial' appointment

would have been attempted in Scotland. Wales had been diminished and the Conservative cause severely damaged. Ironically, Walker pursued policies that kept the more aggressive aspects of Thatcherism at bay, and his successor, David Hunt, did likewise. There were small tactical advantages to be gained from such 'colonial' appointments (they were always strategically disastrous) and it allowed for the appointment of William Hague as Secretary of State in 1995. However, it also sent John Redwood to the Welsh Office, and he had a strictly assimilationist agenda. Redwood's appointment, had it been made before the age of mass literacy, would have generated many ugly fairytales. It certainly brought a multitude of Welsh souls to the altar of devolution. There have been six Conservative Secretaries of State for Wales: only two have been Welsh and only one of them represented a Welsh constituency. Little wonder that the cause of devolution grew steadily.

Of the three Conservative Prime Ministers to have held office since the re-emergence of the national question in the late 1960s, John Major proved to be the most traditional Unionist. He was not tempted to follow Heath's example and dabble with devolution. But neither did he ever try to emulate Mrs Thatcher's assimilationist approach. Although the comparison is limited in terms of magnitude, Major's second administration (1992-97) was similar to those of Salisbury (1886-92, 1895-1902) and Balfour (1902-05) when Conservative governments attempted to kill off Irish Home Rule with kindness. And just like the attempt to prevent Irish Home Rule in late Victorian and Edwardian times, Major's cogent policies were not pre-destined to fail, although failure was the eventual outcome.

To Major, 'Scotland mattered to me. From the moment I became Prime Minister I could see the danger of it sliding away to independence through a halfway house of devolution'.[60] He concluded a famous election speech in 1992 with a hymn to the Union, 'If I could summon up all the authority of this office, I would put it into this single warning – the United Kingdom is in danger. Wake up, my fellow countrymen. Wake up before it is too late!'[61] It was not only the prospect of a Labour victory that Major feared. He observed that even, 'if we won a majority across Britain, I did not know how we could continue to govern Scotland if we did not have sufficient Scottish MPs of good quality to man the Scottish Office. Devolution would have become inevitable, and I would have had to introduce it'.[62] The thought of an English MP becoming Scottish Secretary was unthinkable, in sharp contrast to practice in Wales. Major was right to acknowledge the difficulties caused by electoral decline in Scotland (and he could have added Wales).

Table 3: *Conservative Party's vote and parliamentary representation in Scotland and Wales 1979 – 1992*

	1979	1983	1987	1992
Scotland	31.4%	28.4%	24%	25.7%
	22 MPs	21 MPs	10 MPs	11 MPs
Wales	32.2%	31%	29.5%	28.6%
	11 MPs	14 MPs	8 MPs	6 MPs

The Conservative Party suffered a significant loss of support in Wales and Scotland between 1979-1992, although the position was worse in terms of parliamentary representation than actual votes cast. John Major was astute enough to realise that some imaginative alternatives to devolution would have to be found from within the Westminster system if the constitutional status quo was to endure.

There is little evidence to suggest that Major's traditional Tory Unionism was informed by the Conservative Party's experience in Wales. Major does not mention Wales at all in his memoirs while a whole chapter is devoted to the constitutional situation in Scotland. In this respect Major shared the attitude of his predecessors Heath and Thatcher. The historical explanation – it does not amount to a justification – for this incongruent approach is not difficult to find. Wales was incorporated into the Union in 1536 in a condition of non-statehood. In 1707 Scotland entered the Union as one of two states combining to form a larger entity. The possibility that Scotland might again become a State has always been latent in the British constitution. Major's government stated the position with a clarity that must have shocked many English Conservatives, 'It should be a mark of Scotland's self-confidence in her own status as a nation that she shares her sovereignty with the other parts of the United Kingdom. But the willingness to share that sovereignty must never be taken for granted'.[63]

Although this statement also implied Welsh sovereignty, it was not explicitly stated by Major's government. Major's record in Wales was mixed. A second Welsh Language Act was passed in 1993 and it recognised Welsh as an official language and placed the Welsh Language Board on a statutory basis. This was a classic piece of Tory Unionist legislation. During the 1980s the expansion of Welsh medium education continued. Given the Party's opposition to constitutional reform, Conservatives were keen to demonstrate their rootedness in Welsh society by supporting the language. These policies both reflected and magnified the shift in Anglo-Welsh attitudes which allowed the concept of a bilingual Wales to be embraced rather than barely tolerated. The language issue, which led to such asperity in the 1970s, was absent from the devolution debate in the late 1990s.

Less credible was the reform of local government carried out in the mid 1990s. The Local Government (Wales) Act 1994 established a single tier of 22 unitary authorities in Wales (a similar policy was followed in Scotland). Critics condemned the government for acting in a way that forced unwanted Conservative reforms on Wales. Actually, the 1992 Labour manifesto had promised a very similar reform, but one linked to the establishment of a Welsh Assembly. While favouring devolution in principle Edward Heath had made it much more unlikely in practice by creating a two-tier local government structure. Now John Major, who opposed devolution, made it more likely by establishing unitary authorities. Had the Conservatives left a county and district structure in place, a greater split in Labour's ranks on the question of devolution might have opened up as it had in the 1970s.

Major's biggest blunder was to send John Redwood to the Welsh Office in 1993. Redwood is unfairly depicted as a pantomime villain who failed to mime the Welsh national anthem convincingly. That he did not know that 'Mae hen wlad fy nhadau' is sung at the Conservative Party's Welsh conference is richly symbolic of the failure of assimilationism. Those who accuse Redwood of failing to speak-up for Wales miss the point entirely. Redwood wanted to speak-up for Thatcherism in Wales. In this respect Redwood was not at all like his English colleagues who also held the office of Welsh Secretary. As Nicholas Edwards observes, 'John Redwood's attitude and his approach to the use of the government's resources were significantly different but, by then, so much had been achieved that little harm was done, and it was not long before William Hague reverted to the general policies of Redwood's three predecessors'.[64] Unfortunately, from a Welsh Tory point of view, it was the actions of a miscreant minister that were more likely to enter political folklore. After this strange, principled but alien Savonarola figure there was the relief of a back-to-earth Yorkshireman in the form of William Hague.

Major's review of the Union focused exclusively on Scotland, although it had repercussions in Wales. The government published its White Paper under a mischievously ambiguous title *Scotland in the Union: a Partnership for Good*. In his foreword the Prime Minister said, 'No nation could be held irrevocably in a Union against its will'.[65] A statement of the obvious, perhaps, but one that Arthur Balfour could never have made in relation to Ireland eighty years before. The contract that formed the UK was not considered irrevocable, as it had been in past Unionist thought, but a free agreement between the nations of the UK that required tacit consent on a continual basis. Indeed, the parameters set out in the White Paper were distinct, but open to subtle interpretation. Parliamentary sovereignty – now depleted by the EU – was not emphasised in the usual absolute unitarian terms. As the document stated, 'While within the Union, the ultimate authority of Parliament at Westminster must remain paramount, the government accept that there is scope for further improvements in the way in which Scottish matters are handled'.[66] The government wanted to push the principle of administrative devolution as a means to further compensate for the inherent tendency towards assimilation in unitary institutions:

> The extension of administrative devolution is very much in line with the government's desire that more decision-making about Scotland takes place in Scotland. It also facilitates the identification of Scottish policies and the essential innovation or adaptation of policy to meet Scottish needs. The government's commitment to this objective is founded on a belief that, while the whole of the United Kingdom should share similar policy goals, the different circumstances of each of its constituent parts mean that greater account in policy formation must be taken of the diversity which is the hallmark of these islands.[67]

Mrs Thatcher would never have allowed such a statement to be made. In the White Paper's proposals to reform the parliamentary process that handled Scottish affairs, the confident stamp of traditional Tory Unionism can again be seen. In particular, the role of the Scottish Grand Committee was considerably strengthened: more time and opportunities for the Second Reading of Scottish Bills (a procedure already established but rarely used); regular meetings, and many more in Scotland, to debate political issues of concern; time for questions to Scottish Office ministers; and the introduction of adjournment debates. The Grand Committee's role was further enhanced in 1995 by a reform which allowed other members of the government – including the PM and senior Cabinet members – to participate in proceedings (but not to vote).

For a time this coherent and imaginative package wrong-footed the pro-devolution opposition. Only Edward Heath – who proposed a Scottish chamber attached to Westminster – had suggested stretching the unitary state further, but his policies were never implemented. In Wales, David Hunt announced that he would seek to enhance the Welsh Grand Committee in a similar way. In the end Major's brand of Tory Unionism was overwhelmed by the tidal wave of antipathy that swept away his government in 1997. Had this policy of traditional Tory Unionism been commenced 10 years earlier it is possible, but perhaps not probable, that calls for political devolution would not have gained momentum in the 1990s.

What really undermined traditional Unionism during the 1980s and early 1990s was the repeated success of the Conservative Party at general elections. The unitary state needed a competitive and sometimes successful Labour Party, although Conservative rationalists would have denied this contention outright. Not only had the people of Wales and Scotland seen four successive governments elected without their support, the position of the Conservative Party in the Celtic nations was declining.

By the time Major apprehended the danger, it was probably too late. He could not have done much more and remain within the bounds of traditional Unionism. For all their ingenuity, his constitutional reforms had one intractable impediment. Traditional Unionism could accommodate distinct legislative practices within Westminster for Wales and Scotland, but the unitary state could only survive if Britain had but one government. This meant that however elaborate the special processes became for Welsh and Scottish legislation, fundamental policy differences could not be tolerated. The establishment of devolved governments – which was the only way to placate those who denied the Conservative Party's authority to govern in Wales and Scotland without a direct mandate – had always been seen by Unionists as the greatest danger to the Union. Traditional Unionism began to look like a constitutional dead-end. It had a rigid external skeleton that prevented the necessary evolutionary adaptation for survival.

In conclusion, after 18 years of Conservative government the climate for devolution had become much more favourable. But devolution was not inevitable. The UK was not facing a constitutional crisis in the mid 1990s, whatever the political frustrations of the people of Wales and Scotland. What the UK was facing – and indeed anticipating with some relish – was a Labour government. If traditional Unionism had failed to prevent the demand for political devolution, it remained to be seen whether the Labour Party could successfully supply the reform.

A Political Nation

The 1979 referendum failure and subsequent general election defeat left the Labour Party traumatised.[68] It had no desire to pursue devolution in the 1980s, although the policy remained technically extant in Scotland. The Wales Labour Party made no manifesto commitment to devolution in 1983 or 1987. Michael Foot had been scarred by the devolution debacle even though he had eventually steered the legislation through Parliament. Now leader of the Labour Party, he turned to a policy of assimilation in the early 1980s that put Mrs Thatcher's caution to shame. Labour's alternative economic strategy needed a strong centralised state and a confident working class consciousness undisturbed by nationalist distractions. Wales was in the vanguard of socialist Unionism and the drive for an autarkic British state independent of Europe and the USA.

Foot's successor as Labour Party leader, Neil Kinnock, had done more than perhaps anyone to help defeat devolution in 1979. Paradoxically it was under Kinnock's leadership that Labour slowly re-engaged with the devolution question in the wake of the Party's third successive election defeat in 1987. Kinnock's views did not change substantially, but bearing the wider responsibilities of leadership he could not assail the pro-devolution wing of the Party as he had done in the 1970s. No doubt he hoped that the renewed calls for devolution would asphyxiate in the depths of the Labour Party's Welsh Executive.

However, the policy did not disappear in the late 1980s but rather received new vigour by being attached to calls for the re-organisation of local government. A hostile force in 1979, the local government sector increasingly believed that it might be worth paying the protection money of a Welsh Assembly to insure itself against future Conservative governments. The poll tax fiasco also pushed many Labour councillors into the devolution camp. Labour's 1992 manifesto promised to establish a Welsh Assembly and introduce unitary authorities. It is difficult to believe that had Labour won the general election, it would not have run into some of the problems experienced by Callaghan in the late 1970s. What is clear is that Labour returned cautiously to devolution. The general secretary of the Wales TUC summed up the mood and said there were, 'no big speeches... no big campaign. It was just there quietly in the Labour manifesto'.[69] One has to seriously doubt that such a cold commitment could have warmed the electorate enough to accept devolution. Under Kinnock, Labour was prepared to be a godparent to Welsh devolution, but it denied paternity.

Between 1976 and 1992 the Labour Party was led successively by three MPs who represented Welsh constituencies. During this time the Party's commitment to Welsh devolution alternated between insipid indifference and active hostility. It took a Scotsman to transform the Wales Labour Party's attitude to devolution. John Smith's short tenure as leader had a profound effect on Welsh politics and encouraged the Wales Labour Party to embrace devolution with enthusiasm. Since the 1970s, when he had responsibility for devolution policy as Minister of State at the Privy Council Office, Smith had never faltered in his belief that devolution would strengthen the British constitution. John Smith found an able ally in Wales when he appointed Ron Davies as Shadow Welsh Secretary in 1992. Ron Davies had voted 'No' in 1979 but over the years he had become a strong supporter of devolution. He recalls the interview he had on appointment:

> 'We'll need a proper Parliament in Wales,' John Smith said. 'Just like we'll legislate for in Scotland'. He railed passionately against those he described as 'silly buggers' – Welsh and, to a lesser degree, Scottish, Labour Party members opposed to devolution.[70]

More than any other Welsh Labour politician, Ron Davies made the Party accept devolution as a priority and a policy it really owned. He skilfully focused on the so called 'democratic deficit' caused by a Conservative-controlled Welsh Office which lacked a popular mandate. Vivid condemnations of the Tory 'quangocracy' followed. Whatever the objective reality, the public came to accept Labour's accusation that Tory placemen were running much of Welsh life through executive agencies. According to Davies, a Tory Welsh Office represented, 'government without ballot and power without scrutiny'.[71] Davies spoke like someone who believed, and the electorate recognised a genuine evangelist. What could the Conservatives do? Just put up a succession of English Secretaries of State for Wales. It was grimly symbolic that after some 16 years of Conservative rule, Tories lacked a Welsh champion.

While Ron Davies wanted to push for a Welsh Parliament, he soon found that the opportunity had passed with the premature death of John Smith. Davies recalls with some frustration that, 'For Tony Blair and New Labour devolution was an unwanted inheritance... The balance of power had shifted and political space had been created for the old divisions to emerge'.[72] This is too sweeping a condemnation. Although the accession of Blair ended any hope of a Welsh Parliament with legislative powers in the first instance, it made devolution more likely as New Labour was prepared to expend political capital on constitutional reform.

Ron Davies was astute enough to realise that devolution could be seen as a 'process rather than an event' and that gaining acceptance of reform in principle was no mean outcome. As he remarked, 'Divided party, devolution down the chute'.[73] Fundamental splits in the Party would have threatened the whole devolution policy as had happened in the 1970s when dissident Labour MPs first forced a commitment to hold a referendum and then campaigned vigorously for a 'No' vote.

The pro-devolution wing of the Wales Labour Party believed that they had won the argument within the Party, but the sceptics were able to apply the brakes and insist on a compromise for the sake of unity. Rhodri Morgan recalls, 'There was a weight of opinion, I would say probably three quarters of the people present who were engaged in debate about devolution, who wanted primary legislative powers'.[74] In its policy document *Preparing for a New Wales* (1995) Labour proposed an executive Assembly with powers over secondary legislation. It was the 1970s all over again with the Labour Party proposing legislative devolution in Scotland but only executive devolution in Wales. This asymmetric approach was no more coherent in 1997 than it had been in 1979.

Some senior Labour politicians have argued that a legislative Assembly would have been rejected by the electorate, but when the Wales Labour Party agreed on the weaker model of executive devolution the Party had no commitment to hold a referendum. Ron Davies suffered a further defeat when the Labour Party's Welsh Executive recommended the retention of the first-past-the-post electoral system, a recommendation endorsed by the Wales Labour Party Conference in May 1995. This was a serious error and it risked alienating many in Wales who feared a Labour-dominated Assembly. Tony Blair became Davies' unlikely rescuer when he insisted that the Party in Wales accept the principle of some proportionality in Assembly elections. In the remarkably close referendum result that followed, this intervention by Tony Blair has the best claim to be the single most critical factor in securing a 'Yes' vote. The decision to hold the referendum was, of course, forced on the Wales Labour Party by Blair in the first place.

On the 18th September 1997 the Welsh electorate endorsed the model of devolution it had so decisively rejected in 1979. Wales became a political nation. A range of factors improved the climate for devolution. In 1979 a moribund Labour government had impaled itself on the spike of devolution. In 1997 devolution was New Labour's key pledge to ensure that Wales would participate fully in a regenerated Britain. The Conservative Party was riding high in 1979 and confident of sweeping gains at the impending general election; not so in the autumn of 1997 as the Party reflected on its most shattering defeat since 1906. Traditional Unionist policies had been tested but found incapable of preventing Conservative parliamentary wipe-outs in Wales and Scotland.

The Welsh economy had been transformed – critics would say reduced – and the reliance on heavy industry ended. Wales was no longer dependent on the industrial largesse of a strong centralised state running nationalised industries. The emergence of a European polity after 1986 (when Mrs Thatcher's government pushed hard for a Single European Market) started to undermine the simple faith some had in an immutable British state based on the absolute sovereignty of Westminster. Devolution was no longer viewed as a nationalist obsession but as a rather common characteristic of modern European government.

Since 1979 the organic growth of the Welsh Office added health, social services, and higher education to the already long list of its responsibilities. Dependence on powerful 'quangos' had also increased. These developments seemed to highlight a flaw in Britain's unitary state. Why have separate Departments of State for Wales and Scotland if Britain's institutions fully express the political aspirations of the constituent nations? And if powerful Departments are necessary in Wales and Scotland, why not make administrative devolution democratic? The Conservative reform of local government which created unitary authorities made room, many argued, for an extra tier of government in the form of an Assembly.

Finally, the 1979 referendum delivered an exaggerated result and in retrospect the 30 per cent swing required to overturn it was achievable. These factors, and no doubt many others, made devolution a plausible policy. Something more, however, was needed to secure a 'Yes' vote second time around. First, the Wales Labour Party had to believe in devolution and fight for it enthusiastically. Secondly, the Assembly had to promise to be more, much more, than a Labour dominated citadel. The use of proportional representation reassured many sceptics that the Assembly could be inclusive. And thirdly, the Labour Party needed skilful tactics to sell a complicated constitutional reform. New Labour did not fail. The devolution referendums were held in advance of legislation and so avoided protracted scrutiny; the polls were held at the earliest opportunity, autumn 1997; and the referendums staggered, the Scottish formality held one week before the less certain poll in Wales.

It was the turn of Tory Unionists to face their midnight hour. Two of the three nations of Britain had declared that they wanted direct control over their domestic affairs. The life of a Union based on one executive and a single legislature abruptly ended. Never again would the Conservative Party win in Wales and Scotland by winning in England. Opposition to what the Victorians called Home Rule could no longer define Unionism.

References

1. Kenneth O. Morgan, *Wales: Rebirth of a Nation 1880-1980*, Clarenden Press, Oxford (1981) p.405.
2. John Davies, 'Plaid Cymru in Transition' in John Osmond (ed) *The National Question Again*, Gomer Press (1985) p.144.
3. Gwynfor Evans, *For the Sake of Wales*, Welsh Academic Press (1996) paperback edition (2001) p.218.
4. Nicholas Crickhowell, *Westminster, Wales and Water*, University of Wales Press (1999) p.128.
5. Tony Wright, 'How Mrs Thatcher Saved the Labour Party (and Destroyed the Conservative Party)' in Stanislao Pugliese (Ed.) *The Political Legacy of Margaret Thatcher*, Politico's (2003) p.365.
6. *Western Mail*, 5 March 1979.
7. Margaret Thatcher, *The Path to Power*, Harper Collins (1995) p.430.
8. *Western Mail*, 3 March 1979.
9. Edward Heath, *The Course of My Life*, Hodder and Stoughton (1998) p. 294.
10. Ibid, p.295.
11. Ibid, p.564.
12. James Mitchell, *Conservatives and the Union: A Study of Conservative Party Attitudes to Scotland*, Edinburgh University Press (1995) p.59.
13. Ibid, p.56.
14. The Report of the Royal Commission on the Constitution (Cmnd. 5460) para. 526.
15. Memorandum of Dissent by Lord Crowther-Hunt and Professor A.T. Peacock (Cmnd. 5460-1) para. 216.
16. Ibid para. 351.
17. Vernon Bogdanor, *Devolution in the United Kingdom*, Oxford University Press (1999) p. 175.
18. Devolution and Democracy: Proposals for Scotland and Wales para. 29.
19. Ibid, para. 30.
20. Heath, p 564.
21. Thatcher, *Path to Power*, p 322.
22. *Our Changing Democracy: Devolution to Scotland and Wales* (Cmnd. 6348) para. 2.
23. Ibid, para. 10.
24. Ibid, para. 19.
25. Ibid, para. 61.
26. Ibid, para. 58.
27. Ibid, para. 16.
28. *Devolution to Scotland and Wales: Supplementary Statement* paras. 15 and 33.
29. Leo Abse, the Labour MP for Pontypool, first proposed the amendment.
30. Proposed by the Labour backbencher, George Cunningham.
31. Hansard, col 1005, 13 December 1976.
32. Ibid, col 1073.
33. Ibid, cols 1816-17, 16 December 1976.
34. Ibid, cols 1856 and 1858.
35. Ibid, col 1863.
36. Ibid, cols 1579-80, 15 December 1976.
37. Ibid, col 1580.

38. Douglas Hurd, *Memoirs*, London (2003) p.247.
39. Kenneth O. Morgan, *Callaghan: A Life*, Oxford (1997) p.629.
40. Chris Butler, 'The Conservative Party in Wales: Remoulding a Radical Tradition' in *The National Question Again*, p.161.
41. All Party No Assembly Campaign document (point one of ten) quoted in Foulkes, Jones and Wilford (Eds.), *The Welsh Veto: The Wales Act 1978 and the Referendum*, University of Wales (1983) p.146.
42. Butler, p.162.
43. Bogdanor, p.193.
44. Foulkes (et al) p.133.
45. Butler, p.161.
46. *Western Mail*, 3 March 1979.
47. *South Wales Echo*, 21 February 1979. Quoted in Foulkes (et al) p.126.
48. Foulkes (et al) p.119.
49. Ibid.
50. Ibid, p.134.
51. *Western Mail*, 3 March 1979.
52. Ferdinand Mount, *The British Constitution Now*, London (1992) p. 253.
53. Hurd, p.233.
54. Ibid.
55. Margaret Thatcher, *The Downing Street Years*, London (1993) p.620.
56. Ibid, p.619.
57. Ibid.
58. Ibid, p.620.
59. Crickhowell, p.52.
60. John Major, *The Autobiography*, London (1999) p.415.
61. Ibid, p.303.
62. Ibid, p. 417.
63. *Scotland in the Union: a Partnership for Good*, (Cmnd. 2225), para. 10.3.
64. Crickhowell, p.35.
65. *Scotland in the Union*, p.5.
66. Ibid, para. 6.7.
67. Ibid, para. 7.2.
68. Here I owe much to the research of Mr Lee Waters. I am grateful to him for sight of his undergraduate manuscript, 'The Dog that Wouldn't Die: The Fall and Rise of Devolution in the Wales Labour Party 1979-1995', Aberystwyth, May 1998.
69. Interview between Bethan Lewis and David Jenkins, 23 March 1998.
70. Ron Davies, Lecture to the Welsh Political Archive, Aberystwyth 2003.
71. Waters, p.39.
72. Davies.
73. Ibid.
74. Waters, p.44.

Chapter 4

Have We Been Anti-Welsh?

South Wales to Toryism is terra incognita, conquerable, if at all, only by force of an economic policy at once radical and fresh

Enoch Powell, *Conservative Party Memorandum, 1948*

If in affectionate memory of Gwyn Alf Williams we ask 'When was Tory Wales?' the answer is between the two great Reform Acts of the 19th Century. In the nine general elections held in that period (1832-1867) the Tories won a majority of seats on seven occasions. With the exception of 1865, Welsh Tories out-performed their English colleagues at every general election. The Anglo-Welsh squirearchy was very much partial to the Tory cause but these pre-democratic 'victories' have come to symbolise the essentially alien nature of Conservatism to the Welsh electorate.

The closest the Conservative Party has come to a majority of parliamentary seats in the democratic era is in 1983 when 14 Tory MPs were returned out of a possible 38. In three general elections – 1906, 1997 and 2001 – the Party failed to win a single seat. It would appear that democracy is incompatible with Tory success in Wales. Many historians publicly and most Tories privately have come to believe that Wales is irreducibly radical and intractably anti-Conservative.

This interpretation overlooks a cardinal fact: Conservatism in England was no better prepared for the arrival of democratic politics. E.H.H. Green has written that Lord Salisbury 'thought there was no possibility of converting "the democracy" to Conservatism: all that could be done was to discipline the masses on their inexorable march to political ascendancy'.[1] The emergence of popular Toryism in England during the 1880s and 1890s was a wonder and a surprise to many in the Party, but few thought it would be a permanent development. Its craft lay in convincing a mass electorate not to be bribed by short-term material gains but to support what the Conservative leadership considered to be the long-term interests of the state. Patriotism, the pint, Protestantism, defence of the Union with Ireland, promotion of Empire, and deference to humane and competent authority as the basis of class co-operation, became the vital elements of popular Toryism.

While the Welsh, or at least the more self-consciously upright, tended to put the Bible before beer, and confessed Nonconformist fragments of Protestantism, little in the Tory mixture strikes one as inevitably vile to the Welsh political palate. Yet the Tory tonic became the quintessentially English tipple, to most Welshmen naughty and not very nice.

Felix Aubel has argued that one 'can largely account for the Tory electoral failure during the period 1880-1914 by the fact that the party was uncompromisingly opposed to church disestablishment, a movement supported by a clear majority of Welsh people, who were overwhelmingly non-conformist'.[2] Anglicanism in the minds of most Welsh believers was Catholicism without the pope. This prejudice was powerfully reinforced by the activities of the Anglo-Catholic Oxford Movement and the conversion to Catholicism of key Anglican churchmen such as Newman and Manning.

Democracy had arrived at a time when formal religion still played a central part in community life. Even in the spiritually becalmed 1880s, midpoint between the great Nonconformist revivals of 1859 and 1904, religion was capable of creating deep political cleavages. The Conservative leadership failed to apprehend this vital element of the Welsh imagination and did not modify the Party's formula for Welsh consumption. It might strike us as curious that the Tories failed to emphasise Protestantism rather than Anglicanism in Wales, but this would have required an acceptance of disestablishment. To the likes of Salisbury, the established Church represented much more than a denominational preference and he was not about to defile the Church of England on the altar of democracy. His sentiments were every bit as intense as those of Welsh Nonconformists. In each *Campaign Guide* published by the Conservative Party between 1892 and 1914 the following section appeared:

> The laws, institutions, and customs of Wales are the laws, institutions and customs of England. The Crown of England is the Crown of Wales, the flag of Wales is the flag of England. To deal with a corner of the country separately in relation to large constitutional questions, such as that of church and state, would be to introduce a system of particularism and parochialism into national affairs which would soon lead to most remarkable anomalies and undermine the whole fabric of uniform and orderly government throughout the country.[3]

To access popular Toryism, the electorate had to accept both that the Irish could not assert Home Rule nor the Welsh defrock the established Church. In 1914 the *Campaign Guide* devoted no fewer than 61 pages to disestablishment – by far the largest ever entry on a Welsh subject. The offence caused to the bulk of the Welsh electorate was exacerbated by the tendency of the Party to emphasise its defence of the established Church. While such sincere missionary zeal was open and honest, a pragmatic reticence might have better served Party interests in Wales. The following leaflet, published by Central Office in July 1895, illustrates the point:

> **Why We Oppose Welsh Disestablishment**
> Because the Church in Wales is absolutely the same as in England, and it is cowardly for those who dare not attack the whole body to try to ruin a small and poor part of it.
>
> Because the Church in Wales, far from being 'alien' is the only really national institution that Wales possesses.
>
> Vote for the Unionist Candidate who opposes Welsh Disestablishment.[4]

Such mock-gothic arguments may have reflected the style of ecclesiastical architecture so favoured by Victorian church-builders, but given Welsh customs they seemed contrived and exotic. Most of the Welsh electorate came to habitually reject the Tory message. The Party became the music hall villain of Welsh politics, always destined to have its base amorous advances spurned by the virtuous heroine to the thrill and delight of the audience. During these seminal times the constructive aspects of popular Toryism were overwhelmed by insensitivity to national questions. Maintaining that 'the customs of Wales… are the customs of England' created an insuperable barrier which ensured that popular Toryism never had a chance of succeeding in Wales.

Meanwhile, as John Davies observes, Gladstone won 'exceptional allegiance' among the Welsh. He lived in Wales, was married to a distinguished Welsh heiress, and regularly spoke in favour of Welsh causes. Unsurprisingly, 'such recognition was greatly appreciated by the Welsh, and the admiration of many of them for the "grand old man" approached idolatry'.[5] The result of the 1900 general election demonstrated a pattern that is recognisable today. A mere 18 per cent of Welsh constituencies returned a Conservative MP compared with a success rate of 73 per cent in England. The six Tory victories came in anglicised boroughs and the rural seats of Glamorgan and Monmouthshire. Even these areas did not constitute a Tory redoubt, the majorities were far too thin for that.

More material factors had reinforced the cultural chasm that opened up between the Welsh electorate and the Conservative Party. Tariff reform was never popular in Wales as it threatened the coal industry by moving the trading world towards protectionism. And throughout this period the Liberal Party's insistence that the individual claims of property could be limited to meet the general demands of welfare, found a ready response in Wales. Nevertheless, it is little exaggeration to say that in defending the established Church, the Conservative Party disestablished itself as an indigenous force in Welsh politics. Meanwhile, in England and Scotland, the Tory cause won popular support in London, Liverpool, Glasgow and Birmingham, and in working class areas such as industrial Lancashire.

When the National Union of Conservative and Unionist Associations held its annual conference in Cardiff in 1893, the Party's head agent, Captain Richard Middleton, acknowledged that the Party's weak organisation in Wales limited its chances of success. Professional agents were few and far between, and the National Union lacked an all-Wales structure in sharp contrast to Scotland. Instead, the National Union was divided into three provinces in Wales and it was not until 1921 that the Wales and Monmouthshire Conservative and Unionist Council (WMCUC) was formed. A general improvement in the Party's organisation occurred in the 1920s, and thereafter most constituency associations had access to a professional agent, although agents often served more than one constituency. It was not until the 1960s that this structure broke down, after which agents were rarely found outside winnable seats.

However, despite the local services of a dedicated band of professional agents, the ability of the Party to organise on an all-Wales basis remained very weak until the 1950s. Little strategy and less policy emanated from the Party in Wales. Next to no Party literature was produced for specific use in Wales, and leaflets in Welsh were rare. The Party's archive contains three Welsh language leaflets published in 1909 and another published in 1927.[6] With disestablishment out of the way (and in truth soon forgotten), the *Campaign Guides* of 1922, 1929, 1931, 1935 and 1945 contained no references to Wales (and few to Scotland).

The lack of local candidates was another sure sign of the Party's failure to spark in Wales. The National Union was told in 1908, when again holding its conference in Cardiff, that Conservative fortunes were hampered by the selection of candidates 'unfamiliar with Welsh conditions'.[7] Thirty years later the same lament was heard and the Finance and General Purposes Committee of the WMCUC was informed that 'every effort should be made to find local people to contest Welsh seats'.[8]

While the 'English' label had firmly attached itself to the Conservative Party by 1914, little happened in the inter-war period to challenge and far less overturn this harmful characterisation. Despite being the most fluid decade in 20th Century British politics, the 1920s did not see the Tory advance in Wales that many hopefully predicted. Although national issues became less salient in a political climate dominated by the growth of socialism and the struggle for European collective security, the collapse of the Liberal Party created few opportunities for the Conservative Party in Wales. Rather it was the Labour Party – which had as many difficulties on cultural and Welsh national issues as the Conservatives – that became the party for Wales.

A Policy for Wales
According to the historian John Ramsden, the Conservative Party emerged from the Second World War 'without a coherent front bench, without an organisation in the country ready and able to fight an election, and without a policy on which to fight one either'.[9] Nonetheless, 'Labour MPs and most independent commentators "still" expected a Churchill sweep to victory in 1945'.[10]

The Conservative Party's landslide defeat was unexpected but it allowed the Party to rejuvenate its organisational and policy-making machinery under the direction of R.A. Butler (Chairman of the Conservative Research Department, 1945-64) and Lord Woolton (Conservative Party Chairman, 1946-55). In Wales the Party's organisation was substantially improved, and an intense and formidably intelligent ex-Brigadier was given the task of drafting a Welsh policy. J. Enoch Powell did not disappoint and he produced the first comprehensive statement of Welsh policy made by a major political party.

Powell made tours of the industrial and rural areas of Wales. In his report on industrial Wales he concluded that the 'Conservative Party, as the national Party, cannot presumably abandon any part of the country as hopeless... But it would be idle to pretend that without sustained and generous financial support, to start or keep up agents and offices and to fight elections, the grip of Socialism on South Wales can be loosened or the foothold of Conservatism in the Valleys extended'.[11] Powell put a series of questions to Conservative associations including how best to turn people away from the Welsh Nationalists. He also asked the disconcerting, but rather Powellite, question that perhaps mass migration out of the valleys might be better 'than attempting to attract new industry to obsolete accommodation and surroundings'.[12] Presumably few Welsh Tories favoured such an approach as such free market libertarianism does not feature in *The Conservative Policy for Wales and Monmouthshire* published in February 1949. The policy marked a major shift in the Conservative Party's attitude towards the Welsh nation, not least by appearing in a bilingual format, and stated that,

> A great part of those living in Wales have kept alive the consciousness that they are a separate and distinct nation. The national individuality expresses itself in the religious and cultural life and the habits of thought and action of the people. There is no economic separateness of Wales to correspond with its national separateness. We believe therefore that the identity of Wales with England as an economic unit and its separateness as a national entity must alike be recognised.

> The traditional policy of Conservatism has always been to acknowledge and indeed to foster, variety wherever found, in individuals or in nationalities. Diversity in unity is our conception of society and of the nation, to which the levelling, standardising and bureaucratic spirit of Socialism is utterly opposed.[13]

This distinction between the cultural separateness of Wales and its economic unity with England became the orthodox Conservative position. The Party would prove both imaginative and responsive to the demands of cultural nationalism, but obdurate and unyielding on questions of political devolution because it believed that such constitutional innovation might threaten the economic unity of England and Wales.

Powell was well placed to understand the cultural aspects of nationalism for he was himself of Welsh ancestry (indeed he learned Welsh and wrote a book on medieval Welsh law). He was also under pressure from the Party in Wales to make a clear statement in recognition of Welsh national identity. In July 1948 the WMCUC called on the Conservative

Party to 'recognise that Wales is a country whose people, climate, terrain and other features often differ considerably from those of England, and that this will be kept in mind when consideration is being given to legislation that will have effect over the whole of the UK'.[14] The WMCUC also stressed that future Welsh policy must reiterate R.A. Butler's promise to appoint a minister for Welsh affairs. Powell recognised the strong support within the Party in Wales for such an appointment. In his report on rural Wales he wrote, 'In most parts of the area visited, the view was strongly held by Conservatives of all shades that separate Ministerial representation for Wales is a sine qua non'.[15] The *Policy for Wales* went further, 'We suggest that one member of the Cabinet should be given special responsibility for Wales'. On the industrial front, the policy committed the Party to diversifying the economy and improving the trunk roads connecting Wales to England.

The *Policy for Wales* was endorsed at the AGM of the WMCUC held in Chester on 28th May 1949[16] as one 'of the most practical statements which the Party has issued'.[17] Although the impetus to develop this policy came from Welsh members, and the constituency associations were consulted by Powell via meetings and a questionnaire, Central Office in London was always in control of the process.

This did not stop a small minority of Conservatives in Wales from ventilating their anger in the press at the Party's 'surrender' to nationalist demands. Lord Merthyr, a particularly active Welsh peer, thundered in the Western Mail's letters page, 'This document is simply a further instalment of Welsh nationalism… How many more wars must we fight before we see that the right way is to draw peoples together; and not as this policy… would do, to keep them apart?'[18] Merthyr received mysterious support from 'Kelticus' of Neath, 'The Conservative Policy has not so far advocated out-and-out separation, but its advocacy of a Minister "responsible" for the Principality and one English county (Monmouthshire) is a dangerous and, happily, an unpopular step thereto'.[19]

Less irritating, no doubt, was the dismissive response of the Labour Party, although the Conservative initiative of developing a specifically Welsh policy was weakly emulated when the Welsh Regional Council of Labour called for a 'Labour Policy for Wales' in 1952.[20] In the post-war era, it was the Conservative Party that established a clear Welsh dimension to British politics.

One consequence of the Conservative Party's bold policy initiative in Wales was that Party leaders made clear and approving references to the status of Wales as a nation. Speaking at an election rally in Cardiff during the 1951 campaign, Anthony Eden said:

> Unity is not uniformity. Wales is a nation. She has her own way of life and her own language. She has preserved and nourished over the centuries her own valuable and distinctive culture. She has her own special needs and conditions and these must be fully recognised and met.[21]

In his message to the electors of Wales, Winston Churchill promised that, 'We shall be very mindful of the national aspirations and special problems of Wales. Unlike the Socialists, we do not believe in putting the United Kingdom in a Whitehall straightjacket'.[22] Although the Conservative Party appeared well placed to make significant advances in Wales, the 1950s turned into a decade of disappointment. A series of blunders blighted the Party's prospects. As Alun Butt Philip put it, 'Each attempt to show that the Conservatives wanted to help Wales was countered by errors of policy. The Conservatives were remembered not for the issue of circular 15 in 1953 which urged full bilingualism in the schools or for the introduction of a Welsh books grant, but by the Tryweryn episode and the decision in 1960 to appoint Mrs Rachel Jones, a non Welsh-speaker, as Chairman of the Welsh Broadcasting Council'.[23] This is perhaps too sweeping a conclusion, but more adroit footwork could have placed the Party on a stronger footing given the divisions within the Labour Party on the direction of its Welsh policy. Perceived, however unfairly, as strangers in the land, the Conservative Party suffered the fate of having its failures remembered, but its successes forgotten.

The first blunder came with the fulfilment of the very promise to appoint a Cabinet Member with responsibility for Welsh affairs. At the launch of the Party's *Policy for Wales*, the press had been briefed by Nigel Birch (MP for Flint) to expect a Welshman to fill the post of Minister for Welsh Affairs, probably in combination with a sinecure office such as Chancellor of the Duchy of Lancaster. The most obvious candidate, the press speculated, was Gwilym Lloyd George.[24] Churchill's decision to appoint the Scotsman, Sir David Maxwell-Fyfe, as Home Secretary and Minister for Welsh Affairs attracted derision from the Conservative Party's opponents, and caused bemusement among its supporters. A confidential Central Office memo was sent to the Party Chairman, Lord Woolton a few days after the general election:

> From all sides I have heard the most alarming reaction to the appointment of Sir David Maxwell-Fyfe as Minister of Welsh Affairs. These private Fleet Street reports have today been confirmed by Mr Garmonsway, the Central Office Agent for Wales. I really do think that we cannot afford to pay a hostage to fortune of this nature. I am sure it will have been considered already, but I believe that the position would be entirely rectified if a Welsh member were appointed as the Under Secretary of State for Wales, with possibly the opening up of an office in Cardiff. This, I would add, is not my personal view, but I have had it from the editor of the News of the World who told me that already they were receiving more letters about this matter than any other subject since the General Election.[25]

The Party's panache in conceiving of such an imaginative office turned to dust in the flames of this fierce criticism. Churchill was forced to allocate the only Parliamentary Under-Secretaryship then at the Home Office to David Llewellyn (MP for Cardiff North) to assist Sir David with Welsh affairs. Unfortunately, the Party learned little from this crass episode. Indeed, future Conservative Prime Ministers took it as a precedent to appoint non-Welshmen to the most senior ministerial post dealing with Welsh affairs.

In the thirteen years of its existence (1951-64) the office of Minister for Welsh Affairs was only once filled by a Welshman (Gwilym Lloyd George). One wonders what Henry Brooke (a quintessential Englishman), Charles Hill (the 'radio-doctor') and Sir Keith Joseph (an English-Jewish intellectual) thought when told that their principal office carried the curious incubus of Minister for Welsh Affairs. We have a pretty good idea what Enoch Powell thought, for in November 1952 he turned down the Under-Secretaryship with responsibility for Welsh affairs when offered to him as what would have been his first ministerial appointment. This refusal surprised and irritated his seniors but, according to Patrick Cosgrave, Powell 'considered a Welsh post difficult for an English MP to handle'.[26] Powell's judgement was tragically erratic, but on this occasion his reaction was clear-sighted. But there again, he knew a bit about Wales.

The 1950s: A Journey Halted

In the 1950s considerable tension existed at times between Central Office and the voluntary party in Wales. With a Conservative government in office from late 1951 there was an inevitable tendency to loyally defend its record, but expectations were also raised when it came to Welsh interests and the prospect of a Tory electoral dividend through the development of imaginative policies to meet them. However, many senior members felt frustrated because the Party seemed unable to project a coherent image of 'Welshness' and sound policies were often implemented in a tardy fashion. In the dying days of Attlee's government a warning was sounded by Brigadier Skaife that that Party needed to work hard to shake off its anti-Welsh label:

> The most damaging anti-Conservative propaganda... is to the effect that the Conservative Party has never taken, does not take, and is never likely to take the slightest interest in Wales and the special interest of the Welsh nation. It is the more damaging because as far as the past is concerned there is too great an element of truth in it.[27]

The Brigadier was Chairman of the Merioneth Conservative association which submitted the following resolution to the 1951 Party conference: 'This conference recognises that the Welsh nation is profoundly disturbed by the increasing degree to which questions affecting their land and national life are being decided by Ministerial decrees drafted by persons without either knowledge of, or sympathy with Wales'.[28] This desire to present the Conservative Party as the champion of regional and national causes against a centralising socialist government was shared by many rank and file members.

A bitter row erupted in 1950 on the future direction of Central Office's secretariat in Wales and the need to develop a stronger Welsh image for the Party through the production of Welsh focused publications. The WMCUC, and particularly its Chairman Colonel Godfrey Llewellyn, favoured the local Party agent of twenty years experience, Miss Winifred James, to head the proposed expanded office. However, Central Office believed that a more professional operation in Wales required a new approach. The Party's Vice-Chairman with responsibility for Wales, J.P.L. Thomas (MP for Hereford) endured an angry meeting of the WMCUC in June. He was mightily annoyed and sent an excoriating memo to the Party Chairman:

The Chairman of the Area Col. Godfrey Llewellin [sic] is a silly little man. He made a long speech about the glories of Miss James. He added that Garmonsway had a good reputation for efficiency, but it was a pity that he was not a Welshman. He made it very clear that... appointments came under Central Office and not the Welsh Area officers.[29]

Garmonsway soon won the confidence of the WMCUC, but at the expense of some support at Central Office. In December 1950 a frustrated J.P.L. Thomas noted in a memo to a senior official, 'Here is Garmonsway, our new Area Agent for Wales, calling for a Secretary of State for Wales'.[30]

The voluntary party organisation, and to some extent Central Office's secretariat in Wales, pushed for a stronger Welsh policy in the 1950s. Although the *Policy for Wales* had been well received, there was a feeling that more attention needed to be paid to developing policy within Wales. In September 1951 a delegation from the WMCUC met with Lord Woolton to urge the establishment of a policy advisory committee to be attached to the Research Department. The WMCUC believed that the Party's policy-making machinery needed to be kept 'in touch with Welsh feeling'.[31] Reporting back on the meeting the delegation emphasised that Lord Woolton 'would be glad if an advisory committee could be formed, but he pointed out the limitations which were imposed upon them by the constitution of the Party in that it was the business of the Leader to make the policy'.[32]

The WMCUC was not put off by this tepid response, and no one was fooled by the argument that all policy emanated unprompted from the Leader. After the general election a further delegation was sent to press the point on Sir David Maxwell-Fyfe. He readily agreed to the formation of such a body, but curiously the Area Advisory Committee did not have a long life and was wound up in 1956. Thereafter more ad hoc arrangements were used, usually in the approach to a general election. The Advisory Committee did make an impact nevertheless. In 1952 it made suggestions on how to strengthen the Council for Wales. The Coronation received the Committee's attention in 1953 when it hoped 'it might be found possible to incorporate the Welsh emblem' on the Royal standard; recommended that a regiment of Welsh-speaking soldiers be formed; and called for 'a Royal Harpist for Wales'.[33] Its most controversial intervention came in 1954 when it recommended:

That in the event of a change in the office of Minister for Welsh Affairs, the new appointment should be:-

    (a) A whole time Minister with Cabinet rank.

    (b) The office should be designated 'Minister for Wales'

    (c) The Minister should be assisted by at least one full-time Parliamentary Under-Secretary.

It is appreciated that the new appointment would necessitate the appointment of extra staff for a Welsh office.[34]

The government's response was to enquire of the Party in Wales what a full-time Minister would actually do? While this demonstrated a lack of imagination, it at least avoided a total rejection. One member of the Advisory Committee, D.V.P. Lewis, who unknown to him and the world was soon to play a central role in Welsh affairs, urged a more expansive vision because 'the time had arrived when we must reckon with the Nationalist movement in Wales as a political party'.[35] Many senior Party members continued to believe that a Secretary of State for Wales should be appointed. When Macmillan succeeded Eden in early 1957 the new PM decided to break the link between the Home Office and the Minister for Welsh Affairs. Instead Henry Brooke, as Minister for Housing and Local Government, was given the Welsh affairs brief. Technically, this decision made sense. As Alan Butt Philip remarks, the 'arrangement was generally considered more successful because the responsibility for Welsh affairs rested with the Minister already in charge of Welsh planning and local government problems'.[36]

However, no warning had been given to the Party in Wales and there was considerable anger that a major change had occurred without consultation. Many members felt that the quid pro quo for not getting a full-time minister was the combination of the Welsh affairs post with a senior ministry such as the Home Office. The whole controversy about the need for a Secretary of State on the Scottish model was re-opened with Colonel Llewellyn leading the malcontents and successfully moving a WMCUC resolution:

> That this meeting representing the Conservative Party in Wales and Monmouthshire… whilst welcoming Mr. Henry Brooke and wishing him well in his new appointment… points out that the link with the department at the Home Office built up over the last few years is now broken and the appointment of an Under-Secretary for Welsh Affairs left unfilled. It is considered that the

time has now come when further devolution should be given and that Wales and Monmouthshire should be granted the privilege of a Secretary of State on similar lines to Scotland.[37]

Given the usual deference of motions passed by the voluntary Party, this was assertive to the point of mutiny. Note the claim to represent the 'Conservative Party in Wales' and the call for further devolution. Henry Brooke moved quickly to repair the damage and he assured members that the transfer of Welsh affairs to Housing and Local Government was not a whim but designed to better meet the needs of Wales. However, given the strength of feeling, Brooke said that the Prime Minister was considering the case for a Secretary of State.[38] This episode coincided with the recommendation to establish a Secretary of State which came from the Council for Wales in its third memorandum *Government Administration in Wales.*

The Party decided to hold an extensive consultation exercise and constituency associations were asked whether they were 'in favour of the recommendation for a Secretary of State?'[39] Twenty-two constituencies responded and 10 favoured the recommendation while 12 did not. One member of the WMCUC suggested that some of the negative responses should be discounted because their executive committees contained a disproportionate number of English members. Colonel Llewellyn still 'believed that the arrangements for Wales now needed a degree of permanency and the best way to secure this was by creating a Secretary of State'.[40]

Macmillan decided against the appointment, but he offered a compromise and created a Minister of State for Welsh Affairs. The intent here was similar to the earlier practice of a Parliamentary Under-Secretary working full-time on Welsh affairs to assist the Home Secretary. Appointing a Minister of State to help the supervising Cabinet Minister gave the role greater authority as the office holder became a half-colonel rather than a mere ministerial subaltern. Yet a Wodehousean farce followed when it was announced that Cllr. D.V.P. Lewis had been flashed the ermine and made Lord Brecon and Minister of State. Rather weakly, the leadership maintained that a member of the House of Lords was ideally placed to spend most of his time in Wales. The Opposition had much sport with the appointment. As *The Economist* commented:

How an obscure Brecon county councillor, visiting London

(in his tweed suit) for the University Rugger match, was called to Downing Street to be made a Baron and a Minister of State, represents one of the most curious political appointments since Caligula made his horse a consul.[41]

If this was comedy, drama followed. The Council for Wales became moribund in 1958 when its Chairman, Huw T. Edwards, and four senior members resigned in protest at the government's summary dismissal of its recommendation to establish a Secretary of State for Wales. Edwards complained that, 'Whitehallism had not the slightest prospect of ever understanding Welsh aspirations'.[42] The Council staggered on until 1966 when it 'expired, almost forgotten'. A Conservative government, to retain authority in Wales where it was the minority party, needed a representative (if unelected) body to give it advice on how to best promote Welsh interests. With the Council for Wales defunct, pressure inevitably grew for the creation of a Secretary of State.

The Brooke-Brecon combination proceeded to tap-dance on the minefield of Welsh politics, smiling affably all the while. Brooke had inherited the question of whether the Liverpool Corporation should be allowed to flood the Tryweryn Valley in Meirionydd. While he recognised the weaknesses in the government's water policy, and moved to address them by establishing an Advisory Water Committee for Wales, Brooke felt the interests of Liverpool outweighed those of a small, Welsh-speaking rural community. Unfortunately for Brooke, the issue was taken as a proxy for the government's general attitude towards Wales. Nearly every Welsh MP across all political parties voted against the government in Parliament, but it was not enough to save Tryweryn. In the opinion of the nationalist historian John Davies, 'Liverpool's ability to ignore the virtually unanimous opinion of the representatives of the Welsh people confirmed one of the central tenets of Plaid Cymru – that the national community, under the existing order, was wholly powerless'.[43] The waters of Tryweryn did indeed germinate the seeds of political devolution.

Lord Brecon, himself the beneficiary of a curious appointment, was responsible for the bizarre nomination of Mrs Rachel Jones as Chairman of the Welsh Broadcasting Council. Once again the Conservative Party dropped a heavy brick on a revered national icon. Mrs Jones was unqualified for the position but well known to Lord Brecon as the wife of the Dean of Brecon Cathedral. The WMCUC loyally supported the decision by passing a deferential resolution, but it did not pass unanimously.[44]

The Conservative Party's minority position in Wales made it particularly vulnerable to having even substantial achievements discounted. However, the Tryweryn affair, Lord Brecon's appointment and his own decision to choose an unqualified candidate to chair the WBC, ensured that the Party was viewed by too many as essentially anti-Welsh. The enduring strength of the cultural antipathy that afflicted Welsh Conservatives was demonstrated by the failure of its Welsh policy to substantially improve the Party's electoral prospects. It had produced the first comprehensive statement of Welsh policy; created the first government minister for Wales and established an embryonic Welsh Office; set up the Welsh Grand Committee; and recognised Cardiff as the capital city of Wales. These achievements were simply swept aside by the casual claims of the Conservative Party's opponents that they could have done all this and more! It was an assertion that the electorate appeared eager to accept.

Senior Party officers like Colonel Godfrey Llewellyn felt that the government was not taking advantage of the opportunities that existed in Wales for a substantial Tory advance. The Party had won four parliamentary seats in 1950, six in 1951 and 1955, and seven in 1959. It was a steady, but certainly not spectacular performance. It was a constant source of frustration to rank-and-file members that the Party did not work harder to dispel its image as the 'English' Party. Many members and several Welsh Conservative MPs continued to favour the appointment of a Secretary of State on the Scottish model. They reflected on the fact that the Scottish Office was established by Lord Salisbury in 1885 and strengthened by Baldwin in 1926. In contrast to its performance in Wales, the Conservative Party won a majority of seats in Scotland in 1955.

In 1964 the Chairman of the WMCUC, Sir Charles Hallinan, asked for assurances that Wales would not be overlooked in the Conservative manifesto as he claimed it had been in 1959. He urged that if 'the Party cannot accept that Wales should have a Secretary of State… then it should agree that the Welsh Office at Cardiff, which is now attached to [the Ministry of] Housing and Local Government, should be given complete independence and be wholly responsible for redevelopment in Wales and all Welsh affairs'.[45] It was clear to some Conservatives that the Labour Party had developed a stronger Welsh policy by committing to the appointment of a Secretary of State, and a great opportunity had been lost for an expansive Tory initiative.

Anglo-Welsh at Last

In 1959 Tom Hooson and Geoffrey Howe published, under the aegis of the Bow Group, *Work for Wales*. It restated the Party's belief in the indivisibility of the economic links between Wales and England and stressed that, 'Welsh Conservatives are also Unionists. We regard a Welsh Parliament as irrelevant to the health of the Welsh economy'.[46] Hooson and Howe called for a ten year programme to modernise the Welsh economy, but:

> The Conservative Party must seek support for this programme by addressing itself purposefully to a Welsh audience. As a first step in this direction its Welsh Area Council should be renamed: 'The Conservative Party of Wales'.[47]

The need to adopt a more distinctive Welsh identity was accepted but rather slowly acted upon. The Caernarvon association proposed that, 'mindful that the Conservative Party has a considerable opportunity to grow in Wales, recommends that the time has come to rename the Party organisation in Wales "The Conservative Party of Wales", whilst retaining the present intimate association of the Welsh Party organisation with Conservative Central Office'.[48]

Both Tom Hooson and Geoffrey Howe spoke in favour of the proposition and stressed the value of having the word 'Party' in the title which would give added emphasis and effect when translated into Welsh as 'Plaid Ceidwadol Cymru'. It was claimed this would go some way to counter the threat posed by Welsh nationalism. Other members favoured the move as a means to rebut the charge that the Conservatives were the 'English' party. Sir Brandon Rhys Williams even suggested that 'Conservative' be dropped altogether. It was eventually decided, with typical deference, to take advice from London. A compromise was reached with the voluntary organisation retaining the clumsy and long title 'Wales and Monmouthshire Conservative and Unionist Council'[49] but for campaigning purposes the title 'Conservative Party in Wales' was adopted. There is more than a semantic difference between the Conservative Party *of* Wales and the Conservative Party *in* Wales, but

152

the move did represent some progress and was welcomed by rank-and-file members.

The Conservative Party in Wales, as it could now be called, issued the Party's first manifesto for Wales during the 1964 general election campaign. *Wales with the Conservatives* was designed to be read with the UK manifesto – a style followed until 1997 when the Party switched to a Welsh edition of a UK wide manifesto. The 1964 manifesto held firm to the decision not to appoint a Secretary of State for Wales, 'We believe that the interests of Wales are best safeguarded by attachment to a department of state whose minister is in the Cabinet and has a strong influence on national policy'.[50] This integrationist approach was reversed by Sir Alec Douglas-Home in Opposition and he promised to retain the office of Secretary of State for Wales with a seat in the Cabinet in any administration he formed.

It was not until 1972 that the Conservative Party in Wales held its first Welsh conference (the last of the major political parties to do so). This was twenty-one years after being first suggested by the Llanelli Conservative association in 1951.[51] The Executive Committee was assured that, 'agendas would be produced in the English and Welsh language, and Welsh would be permitted in the course of discussion and one of the sessions would be presided over by a Welsh speaking chairman'.[52] The conference platform was adorned with the Party's Welsh logo which had been adopted in December 1969.

It is curious that the Party waited so long to take advantage of such an easy opportunity for publicity and a chance to project 'Welshness'. Less amenable to simple reform was the perennial problem of recruiting suitable Welsh parliamentary candidates. In February 1958 Central Office sent a confidential memo to the Wales Agent, Howard Davies, urging progress on recruitment of local candidates, so that the expedient of running English candidates could be avoided for the Party was 'anxious to have as many Welsh candidates as possible'.[53] In November 1973 the Executive Committee was informed that, 'there were 9 Welsh speaking candidates and 17 others who lived in Wales'[54] a reasonable but not ideal outcome. Even in 2005, only 22 of the Party's candidates were Welsh or living in Wales.

In 1966, following its landslide defeat, a survey was conducted for the Conservative Party on *Special attitudes in Scotland, Wales and the West*

Country. The Party was concerned about the growth of nationalism in Scotland and Wales and its own general unpopularity in not being considered able to stand up for national and regional interests. This was followed in 1968 with a survey on the *Scope for Conservative Advance in Wales*[55] which remained until 2006 the only polling data commissioned by the Party specifically on Wales. The main results appear below:

	Con	Lab	Plaid
Completely the Welsh Party	5	12	30
Fairly much the Welsh Party	21	29	25
Not very much the Welsh Party	28	25	17
Not at all the Welsh Party	40	29	21
Completely the English Party	41	21	-*
Fairly much the English Party	38	39	-
Not very much the English Party	7	21	-
Not at all the English Party	7	13	-
Completely sympathetic to Wales	6	12	50
Fairly sympathetic to Wales	42	43	28
Not very sympathetic to Wales	48	27	8
Not at all sympathetic to Wales	21	15	9

* *These middle questions were not put to Plaid Cymru supporters.*

Despite this depressing data, which clearly indicated that the Conservatives were considered 'English' by three quarters of those polled, the polling company concluded hopefully:

> All the conditions exist, over a five to ten year period, for a major Conservative advance in Wales – given that the right strategy is followed…The Conservative Party has a good chance of gaining no less that 45 per cent of votes in Wales if the right strategy is evolved.

Central Office was not so easily fooled, and an internal Research Department memorandum commented:

Have we been anti-Welsh? There is only one major snag and that is that however competent Welsh people consider us, they do not think we are the right ones for Wales. This is rather vital.[56]

The pollsters also asked whether people thought a Welsh Parliament a good idea. Twice as many people thought it good rather than bad, and a majority of Conservatives also supported the idea. Gwynfor Evans' victory at the Carmarthen by-election, just a few weeks after Labour's triumph in the 1966 general election, had put the question of devolution firmly on the political agenda for the first time since the 1890s.

The Central Office Agent in Wales, Mr Wolstenholme, made a detailed assessment of the result, concluding that 'in the next decade it was likely that there would be a marked increase of support for Plaid Cymru... However, it was unlikely that they would ever have more than one member, although their intrusion into local government would prove more fruitful'.[57] The WMCUC's Chairman responded to this contradictory analysis by urging the selection of more Welsh, especially Welsh-speaking, candidates.

In 1968 the Labour government announced a Royal Commission to look at the constitution. Welsh politics seemed to be entering a critical phase and the Conservative Party in Wales responded by resurrecting the policy advisory committee, now termed blandly the 'Policy Study Group for Wales and Monmouthshire'. It was chaired by the Shadow Secretary of State, David Gibson-Watt MP, and was mostly made up of parliamentarians. Consequently, it carried much greater weight in its dealings with Central Office and the group provided the first draft of the 1970 Welsh manifesto.

Edward Heath was preparing to change the Party's policy on devolution to Scotland. Speaking at the Scottish Party Conference in May 1968, Heath said that he favoured a directly elected single-chamber Scottish Assembly, although he thought the question needed to be examined more fully and announced the establishment of a constitutional committee under the chairmanship of Sir Alec Douglas-Home. Not for the first time, events in Scotland directly influenced the development of Conservative policy in Wales. Just before the Declaration of Perth, the Policy Group sensed that trouble lay ahead and adopted a somewhat contradictory response:

> Considerable concern was expressed at a suggestion that the Party might be on the brink of agreeing some form of regional/national elected authority for Scotland. Lord Aberdare argued strongly that any announcement of an elected authority for Scotland would have to be synchronised with a similar announcement for Wales for otherwise considerable resentment would ensue which no subsequent change of policy could appease. Mr. Raymond Gower agreed completely. The Committee agreed most strongly that it was entirely opposed to the concept of an elected Council.[58]

The Party's steadfast opposition to a Welsh Parliament was clearly under threat. Consequently several of the Group's members felt that if devolution was becoming a political inevitability a mild endorsement might be the most pragmatic approach. However, David Gibson-Watt would not accept such a compromise and the Group became divided on the issue. At the meeting immediately after the Perth Declaration, Gibson-Watt 'made mention of Heath's Perth speech on the question of devolution in Scotland; he reiterated his opinion that Wales needed a Welsh answer to her problems and that the reform of local government was the essential first step'.[59] This line was not accepted by all of the Group's members. Lord Aberdare 'repeated his warning that the Committee should keep in close contact with the Scottish to avoid embarrassment'.[60] And Raymond Gower MP again queried 'whether Wales should attempt to form a Welsh Assembly on the lines suggested by the Party for Scotland'.[61] Gibson-Watt's will prevailed, however, and by March 1969 any suggestion of a Welsh Parliament was 'unanimously opposed' by the Group.[62] The Party returned to its traditional policy of advocating a Welsh Council to advise ministers. *Wales into the 70s*, the Conservative Party's 1970 manifesto, declared:

> We will retain an Advisory Council to the Secretary of State which will include a proportion of elected members of the local authorities. With the added powers of the Welsh Office, and with the proposed larger Local Authorities, we do not favour the addition of an elected Council for Wales with executive powers.[63]

To the surprise of many Heath did not appoint David Gibson-Watt Secretary of State for Wales. It is distinctly possible that his aggressive stance against devolution weighed heavily against him.

Devolution

Apart from Leolin Forestier-Walker's flirtation with federal devolution in 1920, when the Conservative MP for Monmouth was indicative of a general trend in Unionism, the Conservative Party in Wales has shown little sympathy for the cause of political devolution. Speaking at Ninian Park, Cardiff during the 1950 election campaign, Winston Churchill, who 38 years earlier had aggressively advocated Home Rule 'All Round', said, 'If I thought a Welsh parliament at the present time would be in the best interests of the Welsh people, I would not hesitate to recommend it to you'.[64] Instead, he insisted that as Wales and England, though two nations, are a single economic unit, such a Parliament could not deal with major economic issues and was therefore pointless.

This rejection of devolution on the grounds that it simply did not make economic sense remained Party policy until the mid 1970s. Little mention was made of the dangers devolution might pose to the Union. In a leaflet published by the WMCUC in 1953, *Some Questions and Answers on a Parliament for Wales*, there was no reference at all to any threat to the Union, merely a warning that such an institution would be based on the model of Northern Ireland and therefore, 'Welsh representation at Westminster would be reduced from 36 MPs to 18 or 19 MPs'.[65]

In a confidential memo sent by the Welsh secretariat to Central Office in 1950, the Party leadership was warned that like disestablishment the cause of a Welsh Parliament might take off and come to symbolise the politics of an age. Two Party members had incognito attended the 'National Conference on Parliamentary Self-government for Wales' and they reported that it was an 'enthusiastic gathering' of some 600 delegates and the 'whole conference gave the impression that the general appeal was to be made through the heart not the head… The petition which is going to be organised is sure to receive a fair measure of support'. Perhaps for the first time, Gwynfor Evans was brought to the attention of senior Conservatives. 'This gentleman is a well known Welsh Nationalist, an accomplished speaker of high intellectual capabilities'.[66]

The following year the warning was reiterated in a letter to the Party's Vice Chairman, J.P.L. Thomas MP. 'There is a good deal of apprehension in certain parts of Wales on the effect of the Covenant. I ought to point out that the Committee responsible for the Covenant are now extremely active and are organising public meetings and door to door canvassing'.[67] As late as September 1953 the Area Advisory

Committee concluded, 'this subject might dominate the election activities in certain constituencies'.[68]

Instead of simply rejecting all of the provisions of the Covenant, the Conservative Party issued a statement that agreed with its first clause which stated, 'That Wales is a nation which lived for many centuries under its own institutions, and which in the face of many difficulties has maintained itself to the present day as a national community'.[69] It was emphasised that, 'The Conservative and Unionist Party' recognises 'the fact that the Welsh people have through the vicissitudes of many centuries kept alive the consciousness that they are a nation. We agree that this national distinctiveness must be respected and fostered'.[70] However, the Party maintained that the 'identity of Wales with England as an economic unit is a fact which no political machinery can alter'.[71] The implications of this statement were that political devolution was inadvisable on economic grounds, but the Union which is the constitutional bedrock of the UK should recognise the multinational nature of the State. Note the emphasis placed on respecting and fostering national distinctiveness. It can be inferred from these statements that the Party was not principally concerned about the danger of a Welsh Parliament dividing the UK. The petitioners' tactic of calling for a Northern Ireland style of Parliament was astute, as Unionists could hardly maintain that it would inevitably fragment the UK.

Labour's decision to appoint a Secretary of State for Wales following its general election victory in 1964 unsettled the Conservative leadership. While Alec Douglas-Home moved quickly to accept the development, after the arrival of Edward Heath as Leader attempts were made to unpick the Party's commitment to continue the Office. Fears that administrative devolution might lead to a more pungent political outcome were expressed by staff at Central Office. The agitprop sounding 'Wales Area Political Education Committee' discussed the issue fully in 1965 at a meeting in Llandrindod Wells:

> Several speakers urged the Party to be bold and abolish the office, but Miss Joan Roberts (Anglesey) warned the Committee that to abolish the post of Secretary of State for Wales might lead to its becoming a pawn between Socialist and Conservative governments. Several speakers, notably Mr. Tuxford (Denbigh) and Colonel Fothergill (Pembroke) felt, however, that it was too dangerous to abolish the office. This was agreed by 10 votes to

four, with eight abstentions. There was no support for giving further powers to the Secretary of State. Members agreed with Colonel Fothergill that the important thing was to make those powers he already held credible and real, so that the Secretary of State should not merely become a red tape barrier between Wales and final executive action in London.[72]

The Conservative Party's voluntary officers in Wales, Sir Godfrey Llewellyn and Sir Charles Hallinan most prominently, had in the 1950s and early 1960s tended to be ahead of rank-and-file opinion on the need for more administrative devolution. In 1958 Henry Brooke had warned Lord Hailsham that, 'Conservatives in Wales are divided on the question of whether it would be better for Wales to have a Secretary of State'.[73] The discussion quoted above indicates a reactive response that critics would come to term typically Conservative. Major constitutional change was instinctively rejected until it occurred, and then it became reluctantly accepted as the final settlement. There is nothing objectionable, and certainly nothing unconservative, in such a response. However, it represents a poor strategy if the aim is to seize the initiative and create new opportunities for the Conservative Party in Wales.

Forty years on, Colonel Fothergill's view that further powers should not be granted to the Secretary of State but that his existing powers should be made 'credible and real' could with only small alteration be used to summarise the attitude of many Conservatives towards the National Assembly. And more sceptical Tories no doubt pine for the day when 'final executive action' will again rest in London. Nonetheless, it should be noted that in relation to the office of Secretary of State the Conservative Party substantially increased its powers when in government, between 1970-4 and 1979-97.

Central Office's misgivings went much deeper, and the very principle of administrative devolution was questioned, if only then to be reluctantly accepted. In November 1969 James Douglas (soon to be Director of the Conservative Research Department) wrote to Sir Michael Fraser under 'Personal and Secret' cover. He analysed Welsh policy since 1949 and noted that the 'ratchet effect in this evolution of policy is apparent'.[74] The anomalous nature of the Scottish and Welsh Offices in Britain's unitary governmental machinery was brought to Sir Michael's attention. Douglas was candid about the Conservative predicament:

There would certainly be a strong reaction to our 'putting the clock back'. Part of the reason for the reaction, I suspect, is that Wales now has like Scotland its own Secretary of State... I suspect that if in a smaller Cabinet there was neither a Secretary of State for Scotland nor a Secretary of State for Wales the reaction would be much milder. While Wales can argue that it has had a member of the Cabinet responsible for it since 1951, I do not see that one can seriously maintain that a Cabinet minister is needed full-time for this. Indeed, it is not easy to see who could take on the job in a Conservative administration.[75]

The office of Secretary of State for Wales created insuperable difficulties for the Conservative Party, although it would be some time before crisis point was reached. In Scotland, up to and including the 1964 general election, the Conservative Party had won a majority of seats on five occasions since 1900. It had been the largest party in another two elections, and had 'lost' ten others. This record was good enough to establish Tory credentials to govern Scotland.

No such legitimacy could be drawn from the Conservative Party's performance in Wales. It had never 'won' a general election in that period and its best result was a mere ten seats out of 36 in 1935. The only factor that mitigated the position was that this 'democratic deficit' was not considered salient by the electorate until the 1990s. Nevertheless, the Party's position was precarious. In 1968 Professor Ivor Gowan, a Conservative academic, wrote that, 'We should do well to remember the inherent political difficulty in the Welsh situation. A Conservative Secretary of State will have the responsibility of policy while the majority of Welsh MPs will be opposed to him politically. His difficulties would be even more formidable if there were an elected Welsh Council on the scene'.[76]

Crisis was avoided in 1970 by Heath's appointment as Secretary of State for Wales of the emollient Welshman and former Welsh MP, Peter Thomas. He pursued a sensitive strategy which went some way to dampen this corrosive issue. His approach was perhaps best demonstrated by the establishment in 1971 of the Water Development Authority for Wales. The Welsh Office also became responsible for primary and secondary education. Nevertheless, the fact that Peter Thomas sat for Hendon South portrayed most vividly the Conservative Party's difficulties. Moreover, until 1972 he also served as Conservative

Party Chairman which made him a part-time Secretary of State.

Despite Heath's earlier desire to tackle the nationalist question quickly, in office he concentrated on other objectives such as British entry into the EEC. Also, the Royal Commission on the Constitution, which had been convened by the previous Labour government, did not report until 1973.

An interesting cameo had occurred in 1967 which did hint at the possibility of a radical shift in Conservative thinking on Welsh devolution. In a typically courteous but slightly naïve manner, Gwynfor Evans approached Sir Keith Joseph and asked him whether Heath would be prepared to receive two papers on the case for Welsh self-government. Heath agreed to do so and asked Sir Keith to analyse the case presented by Evans. Sir Keith's response was startling: 'We could honourably, it seems to me, support greater devolution for Wales and even consideration of independence. Socialism stands for centralisation and we presumably must aim to encourage vitality away from the centre'.[77] Sir Keith, as a former Minister for Welsh Affairs, no doubt understood the challenge posed by constitutional developments, and he seems to have had in mind some form of Home Rule on the Northern Ireland model. However, he warned Heath that such a policy would not be a popular cause.

In the 1970s Welsh Conservatives adopted a fundamentally different approach to territorial politics than did their Scottish colleagues. The Royal Commission's report on the constitution recommended some form of political devolution for Scotland and Wales. It is not necessary here to draw some sense of coherence out of Kilbrandon's Report, a vain task in any event, for it was the political situation following the October 1974 general election that made devolution a pivotal issue. A weak Labour government reliant on a tiny majority needed allies among the much increased Scottish and Welsh nationalists and the dozen or so Liberals. The Conservative Party pursued a dual strategy in mildly condoning devolution to Scotland but rejecting it for Wales.

Vivian Lewis and Donald Walters published an influential pamphlet, *Wales A Blueprint*, under the imprimatur of the Conservative Political Centre. In it we can clearly see a stronger anti-devolution line being developed publicly for the first time. It poured scorn on those who suggested that the establishment of legislative assemblies or elected executive councils would be good for Britain:

> The Conservative Party has wisely taken an entirely different
> course. As a Unionist Party it has no desire to see the
> fragmentation of Britain. It believes that the evolutionary
> process is a surer guide to successful government than
> wild experimentation.[78]

The Conservative Party in Wales was becoming more hard line in its
Unionism than the UK Party, and implicitly critical of Tory policy in
Scotland. Nicholas Edwards told Margaret Thatcher that, 'we are
against any form of directly elected Assembly'. And for good measure
he added, 'Given a free choice I would be equally opposed to the setting
up of an Assembly in Scotland...'[79] No doubt many Scottish Tories
shared this outlook, but it did not become the basis of the Party's
devolution policy in Scotland. Speaking in May 1976 Mrs Thatcher told
Scottish Tories, 'it remains our policy... that there should be a directly
elected Scottish Assembly... We believe that the Union is more likely to
be harmed by doing nothing than by responding to the wish of the
Scottish people for less government from Westminster'.[80]

Meanwhile, the Party's briefing materials insisted that, 'Conservatives
believe that the proposals for Wales are not wanted by most of the
Welsh people. In addition they are unsound in that they create an
Assembly that will have to administer laws passed by another body over
which it has no influence and which may veto the Assembly's
decisions'.[81] This central flaw in the Labour Party's scheme of executive
devolution for Wales was again pointed out by the Conservative Party
in the 1997 devolution referendum campaign.

When the Scotland and Wales Bill was in effect defeated in early 1977,
the Conservative Party in Wales stated that the 'proposed Assembly
would not have brought democracy, or power, closer to the people, it
merely interposed another layer of bureaucracy'.[82] And a little
emboldened, the Party added that it would 'fight to remain part of the
UK'.[83] The Labour Party soon resurrected its devolution proposals and
Welsh Tories responded by urging the preparation of a 'No' campaign
for the promised referendum. The Party in Wales insisted that, 'changes
in our constitution must be on a UK basis only'.[84]

The view that devolution must potentially be applicable to the whole of the UK in the event of it being granted to Scotland, had become official Conservative Party policy. Of course, this was a repetition of the orthodox Unionist position between 1918-20 when Irish self-government was accepted as inevitable. The Conservative Party's main spokesmen on constitutional affairs, Francis Pym and Leon Brittan, cleverly united the Party by opposing the Labour government's devolution plans and calling instead for an all-party conference to discuss devolution. Thus the Party could recommend a 'No' vote in Scotland while maintaining that the principle of devolution was not thereby rejected.

The Conservative Party prepared a 'Preliminary Draft of a Submission to an All-Party Conference' on devolution. It is the most coherent and logically argued document on constitutional change produced by the Party. *The Conservative Party and Devolution* was strongly federalist in tone, although one should note that it was written on the premise that the need for constitutional change had been accepted. It stressed that:

> If a Scottish Assembly with executive and legislative powers is to be established, it should be based on the principles and practices of federalism so that it could evolve smoothly into such a quasi-federal system if in the fullness of time that was thought to be desirable throughout the UK.[85]

The Conservative Party in Wales did not think that the 'fullness of time' had yet arrived and it campaigned aggressively and effectively for a 'No' vote with few qualifications. In November 1978 Nicholas Edwards warned Welsh Tories not to be complacent because a strong government campaign – assisted by an upsurge of romantic nationalist sentiment – should be expected. The Deputy Central Office Agent in Wales, Victor Simpson, outlined the preparations being made to establish an umbrella non-partisan 'No to the Assembly' campaign which the Conservative Party intended to fund with a grant of £30,000. The Wales Area Council resolved that:

> Whilst help would be welcomed from other parts of the UK it should be restricted to members with a clear Welsh background/identity, [and] The Rt. Hon. Margaret Thatcher MP be not involved with the campaign.[86]

On this most 'Welsh' of issues since disestablishment, the Party wanted to appear as Welsh as possible – an adroit tactic that has often since been assiduously avoided. The overwhelming nature of the 'No' vote in 1979 had an intoxicating effect on the Conservative Party as it interpreted the result as the first sign of a fundamental change in the Party's fortunes in Wales. And, indeed, the Party performed well in 1979 and 1983, without quite threatening the Labour Party's hegemony. However, this advance was to prove limited and fragile. In contrast, in Scotland the more astute in Tory ranks realised that the non-acceptance of devolution was tentative and probably temporary. A vocal minority of Scottish Conservatives, including some senior MPs, remained in favour of devolution and urged the Party to convene the promised all-party conference.

The 'inherent political difficulty in the Welsh situation' identified by Professor Gowan in the 1960s, could not be resolved because the Conservative government elected in 1979 ruled out any change to the unitary constitutional arrangements governing Britain. While the rejection of devolution meant that the Welsh electorate accepted the right of a Conservative administration to govern, despite the absence of a mandate generated in Wales, this tacit consent weakened with each successive general election victory after 1979.

It became increasingly apparent that the Welsh electorate was not inimically opposed to devolution, and consequently it would have been more prudent for Conservatives to have interpreted the 1979 referendum result in less absolutely Unionist terms. The lack of such prescience was completely understandable in the early 1980s when the Labour Party was weak and unpopular, but it became less excusable as the decade progressed.

In the run up to the 1979 referendum campaigns the Conservative Party had been dynamic and flexible in its approach to constitutional reform, particularly in Scotland. In office the Party's rejection of devolution for Wales became fixed and final. Yet no attempt was made to weaken the Welsh Office, far less to move towards administrative integration which logically would have reflected the unitary nature of the British constitution. The Welsh and Scottish Offices became the departmental gargoyles on the cathedral of Whitehall, rudely poking out their tongues at any worshiper who offered praise for the uniform nature of the British state.

S4C: Debacle and Defeat

An immediate consequence of the referendum result was that the leverage of the Welsh Office in Whitehall became much weaker. With devolution stone dead, there was no need to kill it with kindness. It is plausible, as John Davies argues, that the Home Secretary, Willie Whitelaw, was emboldened by the devolution result to renege on the costly commitment to establish a Welsh language TV channel.[87]

And while Wales was set to benefit in the long-term from a disciplined economic policy, the Welsh Office was unable to mitigate the severely traumatic affect monetarism had on many industrial communities. Most of those so suddenly struck by this austerity had voted 'No' in the referendum, often on the grounds that it was in their economic interest to do so. It would be in Labour dominated industrial south Wales that the biggest swings in favour of devolution would occur in 1997.

The traditional Unionist argument, that strong unitary government allowed for regional economic imbalances to be evened-out at times of stress, appeared repudiated. The fraternal twins of industrial Wales fared differently in the 1980s. Steel was rationalised and strengthened, at least in terms of competitive production. Coal did not survive at all as a mass industry. In March 1986 Nicholas Edwards hopefully suggested that there 'are good grounds for believing that we have now reached the end of a period of decline that has lasted for many decades in South Wales'.[88] However, it is difficult to avoid the conclusion that the government's rationalisation of the coal industry was more a run-down, and the speed of the process precluded the development of a long-term strategy for the economic survival of mining communities. The trauma caused by this policy was considerable, and the government's policy stands in sharp contrast to the position taken by the Christian Democrats in West Germany where, for example, the Saarland coalfield was closed over a 25 year period.

With the traditional tactics of avuncular Unionism becoming less feasible in a climate of economic austerity, Tories keen on strengthening the Party's Welsh image saw the opportunity to establish a Welsh TV channel as heaven sent. The Conservative Party's 1979 Welsh manifesto stated that:

> There is a widespread desire in Wales shared by English and Welsh speakers to use the fourth television channel for separate

Welsh language broadcasting and there is a very understandable demand among Welsh speakers for an increase in the amount of Welsh broadcasting starting on the fourth channel as quickly as possible.[89]

The Labour Party had reached a similar conclusion and there appeared to be a strong political consensus in Wales for this imaginative solution to an old, nagging problem. Nicholas Edwards recalls in his autobiography that he was startled when Willie Whitelaw informed him, without prior consultation, that the Home Office favoured a two channel solution with an increased Welsh language output continuing on BBC and ITV instead of all Welsh programmes transferring to the proposed fourth channel. Edwards philosophically observes that, 'Fate always seems to decree that ministers face their most difficult problems immediately on taking office... I was only just beginning to feel my way through the Whitehall labyrinth, when I was confronted with a totally unexpected crisis over the government's policy on Welsh language broadcasting... I have always believed that if this affair had happened even six months later, I would not have allowed myself to be persuaded'.[90] Despite these private reservations, he publicly defended the *volte face* because 'the decisions we took in opposition were wrong and the plan described in our manifesto had grave drawbacks'.[91] If this admission unsettled his audience of loyal Conservatives in Narberth, they were no doubt reassured by a diversionary dose of hyperbole:

> The Member of Parliament for Merioneth [Mr. Dafydd Elis-Thomas] put it with spine chilling clarity when he called for 'a Welsh service managed by Welsh speaking Welshmen with correct political attitudes'. Plaid Cymru, rejected by the Welsh people, are making a desperate bid for political control of broadcasting.[92]

The Home Office's proposal was a perfectly rational option, but it failed to apprehend the imaginative aspects of Welsh broadcasting. It also required the Conservative Party to renege on a manifesto promise and this provoked one of the most idiosyncratic but dangerous protests in the history of Wales.

There is no evidence to substantiate Gwynfor Evans' sinister claim that at 'this dark hour the Tory government decided to take advantage of Welsh Nationalism's weakness by striking a sudden and pitiless blow against our language'.[93] Although the Home Office's scheme was penny-pinching, Willie Whitelaw as a latter-day Edward I does not quite work. Ironically, Welsh language policy would become one of the great successes of Conservative administration in Wales. Nicholas Edwards, expertly guided by his deputy Wyn Roberts, did more to facilitate the practical acceptance of bilingualism than any other Secretary of State for Wales. In April 1980 Edwards set the most expansive tone possible for the development of Welsh language policy when addressing Gwynedd County Council:

> We cannot afford to be divided in Wales. We have to work to save the language and culture that is the heritage of the whole nation. I have given my personal commitment, and that of the Government to support the language; but a Government can only support, it cannot and should not direct and impose. Therefore what I have done today is to issue a challenge to all Welsh people and to all who love Wales and a special challenge to the young to build up support for the language, to use it and to use it well. Let us all be united in this task.[94]

This is not to deny that Edwards' urbane, Anglo-Welsh instincts were crushed between the unlikely but hostile forces of Willie Whitelaw and Gwynfor Evans. Whitelaw and Evans seemed to epitomise the gentler aspects of their respective nations, but neither had much empathy with Welsh Conservatism, and their avuncular natures masked steely determination. Both men behaved somewhat out of character during the battle for what would become known as S4C: Whitelaw by mean-mindedly attempting to dump a manifesto pledge, Evans by single-mindedly threatening to starve himself to death unless the promised Welsh language TV station was established. While Evans often appeared beatifical, his tactics now carried a whiff of sulphur. He announced on 5 May that his hunger strike would start on 5 October. For once, overwhelming force – and the iron will to use it – lay with a Welsh rebel.

Gwynfor Evans' threat contained momentous menace. His death in this manner would have radicalised many young Welsh language activists and perhaps inspired them to use similarly thanatist tactics. Welsh politics left the sphere of the rational and became uncontrolled and potentially violent. To be fair to Evans, he recounts the battle with considerable self-doubt:

> I was self-important enough to believe that it was only action

on my part which would be sufficient to touch the heart of Wales and turn the situation around… Perhaps I was suffering from a swollen head in thinking that I was a kind of symbol and that my dying for Wales – for that's what it really entailed – would have a lot more effect than anything I could do with the rest of my life.[95]

The Conservative Party in Wales was trounced. It had no hope other than to surrender to the demands of a would-be suicide faster. Obduracy in the face of such self-destruction was not an option given the Conservative Party's freely made manifesto commitment. Moral force lay with Evans and the political pressure on the government grew relentlessly. Articles in support of Evans appeared in *The Times* and (in Welsh!) in *The Sunday Times*. Nearly all of the British press covered the story and it reached further afield with articles in the *New York Times*, *Time*, and the *Christian Science Monitor* amongst many others. Moderate opinion, represented by men in purple frocks and grey suits told Nicholas Edwards that the game was up. As he recalls:

> The decisive influence was not the fast but a visit to my office by the Archbishop of Wales, Lord Cledwyn of Penrhos and Sir Goronwy Daniel. After that visit I told Willie Whitelaw that, in my judgement, if we could not carry moderate opinion with us, we should change our minds and again reverse our policy. My advice was immediately accepted and we were on the road that was to lead to the birth of Sianel Pedwar Cymru.[96]

Gwynfor Evans never had to start his fast. He probably put on weight in the endless series of dinners given to support his cause. To Evans' regret, the government surrendered early, on the 17 September. 'My first reaction was one of disappointment that the government had relented at least a month too early. If only we had been given five or six more weeks of excitement and national awakening, Plaid Cymru – on which the nation's future completely depends – would have been established in an unassailable position'.[97] He had the grace to add that the 'Government's behaviour after it had been beaten was entirely honourable and there was no quibbling about the cost'.[98]

And so the imprint left on the Welsh soul was not that the Union could enthusiastically enhance the oldest living literary European language and project it on a designated TV channel, but that it took a recently defeated and aged politician to hold the Conservative Party true to what it had freely promised Wales. Of course, Tory propaganda proclaimed the establishment of S4C as a great achievement and a mark of true commitment to the language. The reality was ash in the mouth and it choked the voice of Welsh Conservatism.

Nicholas Edwards had learned a hard lesson, but it says much about his time in office that the S4C debacle did not vitiate his achievements. When he announced his intention to retire in 1987 there was a genuine respect for his record in government. Where room for discretion and independent action existed, Edwards was decisive and carried the authority in Whitehall to get his own way. The range and diversity of his achievements is impressive. Wales was marketed with great success by the Welsh Development Agency and the Welsh Office as an optimum location for inward investment. Record levels of investment were attracted into Wales at a time when heavy industry was in sharp decline. Edwards had the vision to see a new future for the largely derelict Cardiff docklands. In 1986 he announced the establishment of the Cardiff Bay Development Corporation and gave to it the task of turning Cardiff into one of Europe's most attractive cities.

One recalls with incredulity the fact that during the referendum campaign in 1979 some politicians favouring a 'No' vote were predicting that Welsh speakers would soon be forcing Welsh on everyone and demanding such *unreasonable* practices as speaking Welsh in the National Assembly. After Edwards' term as Secretary of State such crass prejudice became risible. It was a natural development of the Welsh language policy initiated by Edwards in 1980 for Welsh to become a foundation subject in all secondary schools. Areas of social policy also received special attention, most notably the all-Wales Mental Handicap Strategy which aimed to enable people with learning disabilities to lead independent lives in the community. This strategy not only established a benchmark for good practice in the UK, it set a standard that many other European countries sought to emulate.

English Again?

It was necessary, but perhaps not sufficient for constitutional rectitude, that in a Conservative government the Welsh Office should be run by Welsh Tories. Heath's expedient of a Welsh Tory sitting for an English constituency worked at a pinch in the early days of the Welsh Office.

However, by 1987 the significantly expanded Welsh Office demanded a more rigorous approach that carried a semblance of accountability to the people of Wales. Thatcher and then Major saw fit to follow the opposite course. The Conservative Party in Wales became an utterly derivative entity without even the modest autonomy usually given to a branch franchise.

The anglicisation of the Welsh Office between 1987-97 meant that for 10 out of 18 years of Conservative administration the Secretary of State was an Englishman sitting for an English constituency. After 1987 Wales either served as the UK's equivalent of a Siberian power station for those sent into internal exile (Peter Walker) or as the Duchy of Lancaster made flesh for the Cabinet's rookies (Messrs. Hunt, Redwood and Hague). The mistakes of the 1950s were revisited and writ large over the Welsh political landscape. The results were predictable. Two seats were lost in Wales at the 1992 election reducing the Tory complement to six. In the 1997 disaster the Tory vote fell by 31 per cent in Wales compared with 26 per cent in England.

The tacit consent needed for the Conservative Party to govern Wales by winning in Britain would have been strained even without the anglicisation of the Welsh Office. By winning four successive general elections the Conservatives unwittingly stretched Britain's unitary constitution to breaking point in Wales and Scotland. To some extent the Party recognised the problem and moved, for instance, to strengthen the legislative role of the Scottish and Welsh Grand Committees.

Key issues needed to be handled with care and in a consensual manner if the Conservative Party's democratic deficit in Wales was not to be seen as salient. Two controversies hit the Party hard in the early 1990s, the reform of local government and the growth and influence of Quangos. The 1992 Welsh manifesto committed the Conservative Party to re-establishing 'the historic counties and county boroughs of Wales'.[99] There were 13 'historic' counties before the reorganisation of local government in 1974 and four county boroughs. Allowing for some rationalisation and adjustment, the manifesto pledge hinted then at about 14 or 15 'unitary authorities in place of the two tier authorities we have at present'.[100]

While in England the Party proposed to set up, area by area, commissions to look at the feasibility of unitary authorities replacing the two tier structure, in Wales the government decided to publish a

'Local Government Reform White Paper' setting out the Welsh Office's proposals. The move to unitary authorities was fraught with difficulty and the approach adopted by the Welsh Office meant that no distance was placed between it and the eventual proposals for reform. An independent commission might have drawn off some of the hostile criticism that followed the publication of the government's scheme in March 1993. *A Charter for the Future* proposed the creation of 21 unitary authorities which would be 'able successfully to address the challenges of the 21st Century'.[101]

It appeared that the District Councils had won the day at the expense of the County authorities. This was certainly the view of the 'Assembly of Welsh Counties' which immediately called for the appointment of an independent commission. Of the 22 new authorities that were eventually established, 12 were wholly or substantially former Districts, and a further six were wholly or substantially amalgamations of two former Districts. Only four of the new authorities were larger entities. The government realised that it had not created optimum units across Wales and that community interests, often strongly amplified by local Labour constituency parties, had prevailed in many areas. Consequently the reform looked weak and confused. *A Charter for the Future* lamely conceded that, 'In cases where it would be inefficient for every authority to plan, manage, secure and deliver the service on its own, the Government will encourage the development of joint working arrangements... The Government expects that some authorities, and especially the smaller ones, will decide to handle many aspects of service provision in this way'.[102]

As a Wales-only measure, the Local Government (Wales) Reform Bill should have been scrutinised by a committee comprised solely of Wales' MPs. The Bill could not have progressed through such a committee, and the government was forced to suspend standing orders and concoct a different arrangement to ensure a majority. As the political commentator Barry Jones has remarked, 'though this was not unconstitutional, the government's action graphically illustrated the ease with which Welsh interests, as defined and supported by the overwhelming majority of Welsh MPs, could be overridden by a government whose parliamentary majority was based upon its electoral support in south-east England'.[103] Many in Wales agreed with this judgement and believed that the political dimension of national identity could no longer be adequately provided by a Department of State in Whitehall. The sum of Welsh political ambition was now greater than the Welsh Office.

Government via Quango became more pronounced in the 1980s as some significant services were delivered by appointed public bodies rather than elected local authorities. Wales had some of the UK's largest Quangos, including the Welsh Development Agency and Housing for Wales. It was significant, for example, that the government established the Cardiff Bay Development Corporation rather than enter into a partnership with the relevant local authorities. Furthermore the Corporation was chaired by Geoffrey Inkin, a former Conservative parliamentary candidate, who was taken as an illustration of the government's tendency to appoint Welsh Tories to a level of influence unobtainable through the ballot box. Geoffrey Inkin proved to be a success and no mean stooge for the government, but other 'political' appointments were less successful.

In 1992 Ian Grist, after losing his seat in the general election, was appointed Chairman of the South Glamorgan Health Authority. Grist was far from unqualified, and his survival as MP for the highly marginal Cardiff Central for 18 years indicated both popularity and diligence, but it was easy for the Conservative Party's critics to parody such appointments as jobs for unelectable Tory boys. Hywel Williams, who served as John Redwood's special advisor in the mid 1990s, describes his master's attitude to such practices with the force of someone settling old scores:

> In Wales, Redwood saw a decadent Party weaned on, and therefore weakened by, governmental largesse. Conservatives were quango-crazy. Unelected to public office, either at Westminster or on local councils, they sated their political ambition in the hunt for a quango. Desperate to be placed on quango boards, they spent their time ingratiating themselves with a Secretary of State who despised such sycophancy.[104]

Gillray could not have drawn a more savage caricature, and as with all good satire it had a germ of truth. Opposition politicians claimed that the Welsh Office was no more than a vice-regal court dispensing appointments to a despised local élite. The reality was far less exotic. Under Major's government public appointments became more open and accountable. Independent advisors became increasingly common and many appointments were publicly advertised. However, the process was far from robust when the Labour government took office in 1997 and set about a successful and praiseworthy reform.

While local government reform was botched, the 1993 Welsh Language Act stands out as a conspicuous Conservative achievement. The Act was both a landmark and the culmination of a process that de-politicised the language. Welsh was largely placed on the same legal footing as English and the Welsh Language Board became a statutory body. Wales had acquired the means to become a bilingual society with a Welsh TV station and the language taught as a compulsory subject in schools. It is doubtful that a Labour government would have been able to act with such expedition in the 1980s and 1990s given the anti-Welsh language rhetoric of senior party members such as Leo Abse (who became the first chairman of the Welsh Affairs Select Committee). When the National Assembly was established in 1999 no one questioned that it would be bilingual. Yet in the 1970s this would have been highly controversial in monoglot English-speaking Wales. The Conservative Party's sensitive development of Welsh language policy inadvertently gave a helpful push to the devolution bandwagon.

Under Siege and Awaiting Conquest

The Best Future for Wales, the Conservative Party's 1992 manifesto, contained an argument that had changed little since the early 1950s. 'The economic separation of Wales from England is unthinkable; the economies of both countries are closely interwoven and inter-dependent... Conservatives believe that all forms of constitutional and political separation could put Wales onto a dangerous road to economic and social secession from the United Kingdom'.[105] Yet during the campaign this clear Unionist line was pursued somnolently and without the alertness of Major's cry in Scotland: 'Wake up now before it is too late'.[106]

To some extent this merely reflected the political situation in Wales. Labour's commitment to Welsh devolution was merely 'parallel with the establishment of similar regional governments in England'[107], as opposed to its promise to establish a Scottish Parliament 'in our first year of government'.[108] Consequently, an aggressive campaign in Wales to save the Union would have seemed obtuse. By 1997 Labour's devolution proposals for Wales were far stronger and Tony Blair's chances of winning office apparently overwhelming. The Conservative election campaign in Wales became something of a crusade to defend the Union as most Tory candidates believed Labour's plans to establish a Welsh Assembly to be deeply unpopular. *Opportunity and Prosperity for Wales* reiterated the economic advantages of stable constitutional structures and warned that:

> A Welsh Assembly is the greatest threat to that stability and security that we have ever had to face in Wales. Only a Conservative government will stand up for the Union and oppose a Welsh Assembly... These dangerous developments [Labour's plans] would drive away future inward investment and reverse the jobs boom that is taking place in the Welsh economy... A Welsh Assembly would begin the process of unravelling the Union and could lead to the break up of the United Kingdom.[109]

The force of this argument was much reduced by the Labour Party's promise to hold a referendum on the question of devolution. Most voters in Wales did not consider devolution a salient issue, but the Welsh Conservative Party continued to press the point in what was an increasingly hopeless campaign. Martin Perry, the most astute Central Office Agent to serve in Wales, warned Central Office that every seat would be lost with the possible (but unlikely) exception of Brecon and Radnor where the popular Jonathan Evans was in a tough contest with the Liberals rather than Labour.[110] For the first time since 1906 the Conservative Party failed to win a single seat in Wales and its share of the vote dropped below 20 per cent. The highest Tory vote was recorded in Monmouth (39 per cent), the lowest in the Rhondda (4 per cent). As Enoch Powell might have observed, it was not just south Wales that was now 'terra incognita'.

The first-past-the-post electoral system so favoured by most Tories exaggerated the decline of the Conservative Party in Wales. A proportional system, at its purest, would have given the Party substantially more seats in 1987 and 1992, and even in 1997 eight Conservative MPs could have been elected. Instead, the Party faced a future without parliamentary representation, despite attracting the second highest share of the vote in Wales.

William Hague, the new Party leader, appointed Jonathan Evans as the chief spokesman in Wales, and while this arrangement worked to a limited extent, it lacked real authority and Evans himself resigned shortly after the devolution referendum campaign. It was to the Party's credit, and a mark of Jonathan Evans' adroitness, that a complete rout was avoided. Without the remission that allowed for a limited recovery in the late summer of 1997, the Welsh electorate would not have had a viable choice in the devolution referendum. The Conservative Party in Wales, lightly disguised as the 'Just Say "No" Campaign', fulfilled its historical destiny as the Party of orthodox and unbending Unionism.

The devolution campaign had really started in 1995 when the Labour 'government-elect' published *Shaping the Vision* and then in the following year *Preparing for a New Wales*. These presented a much weaker version of devolution than the model proposed for Scotland. The ersatz nature of Welsh devolution provided ample opportunity for a Tory counter-attack and William Hague, as Secretary of State for Wales, led the way. Hague asked of Tony Blair, 'If you really believe that a Scottish parliament would work, why would Wales get a second-class version?'[111] The charge that the Welsh were being treated as constitutional lesser beings became a favourite Tory attack. John Major dismissed Labour's discrimination against Wales as 'intellectually incoherent', and on the eve of the referendum William Hague warned the Welsh electorate that:

> You are not being offered the same sort of deal that the government gave Scotland: the Cardiff Assembly would merely take over the existing responsibilities of the Welsh Office and have neither law-making nor tax-raising powers. Why do they want to give the Edinburgh Parliament the powers to legislate, but not the Cardiff Assembly? Why do they trust Scots to decide whether they want tax-raising powers, but not the Welsh? A Welsh Assembly would represent the worst of both worlds. Wales would be deprived of its influence in the UK without gaining a direct say over its own affairs.[112]

Hague was returning to the attack launched on Labour's devolution proposals in the 1970s. If devolution was indeed necessary to strengthen the British constitution, then the 'only logical answer would be the creation of a federal structure'.[113] Perversely the Welsh Assembly posed more dangers than the Scottish Parliament because it lacked 'the basic means of political control or mechanism of accountability'.[114] During the general election campaign an aggressively anti-devolution line was pursued, as John Major put it: 'New Labour would mean no Britain'.[115]

Such a hyperbolic Unionist message would have again been used in Wales during the referendum campaign had the situation in Scotland appeared in any way marginal. It was not. Of all the Home Rule battles – 1886, 1893, 1912-14 and 1979 – what made 1997 distinctive was the resignation of Unionists to the inevitable failure of their cause in Scotland. A subtle shift occurred in Welsh Conservative circles and the dangers to the Union were played down while secondary issues became more prominent. What would happen to the office of Secretary of State for Wales? Would the Assembly not be wasteful and bureaucratic? Could a north-south split be avoided in a political world dominated by Cardiff? That wily old Welsh Tory, Wyn Roberts, summed up the mood of gentle resignation:

> The idea that a National Assembly is going to break-up the UK has stumbled badly and is out of the race; it is as remote as the possibility that my native and beloved Ynys Môn would declare unilateral independence.[116]

Early in 1998 Jonathan Evans announced that he would seek election to the European Parliament. Wales, like the rest of the UK, was set to elect its MEPs by proportional representation for the first time. At least one of Wales's five MEPs would probably be a Conservative.[117] Had Evans instead focused his political ambitions on the National Assembly, the recent history of the Party in Wales might have been very different. It is unlikely that Jonathan Evans would have faced a serious challenge for the leadership and the Party would have adopted a centrist approach and set itself the challenge of locating the optimum centre-right position on the *Welsh* political spectrum. His decision not to lead the Welsh Conservative Party presented Rod Richards with an opportunity for a striking political comeback.

Although Nick Bourne had meanwhile been anointed by William Hague as chief spokesman in Wales, the democratic reforms sweeping through the Conservative Party meant that the National Assembly campaign leader would be elected by the membership. Highly intelligent, articulate and a Welsh speaker, Richards was in some ways more naturally talented than even Jonathan Evans. However, Richards was always a proselytiser and his methods were controversial, assertive and firmly right wing. Rod Richards had no intention of temporising Welsh Conservatism to meet the exigencies of the Welsh political environment. Party members rather liked Richards' old time religion and it provided them with a sense of certainty in a political world that was changing at alarming speed. Using the skills of a battle-hardened politician, Richards fought an excellent campaign and easily defeated his rival Nick Bourne. Welsh Tories had elected as their first leader the most combative politician of his generation.

The organisational reforms introduced by Hague had at last created a Welsh Conservative Party with a small amount of autonomy via its own Management Board. While this was a step in the right direction, Richards had no desire to accommodate nationalist sentiments and he sought to emphasise the 'Britishness' of Welsh Conservatism. In his foreword to the manifesto for the first Assembly elections in 1999, *Fair Play for All*, he proclaimed 'Wales our nation Britain our country' and insisted that, 'We will work hard to make sure that devolution does not become an instrument that undermines our British identity and leads to a break-up of the United Kingdom'.[118]

Such a negative message indicated some failure to adjust to new political realities, but it cannot be criticised as unconservative and many in the Party agreed with Richards' uncompromisingly Unionist line. The real trouble was caused by the manifesto's failure to present a coherent set of policies that could have constituted a programme for government. Instead, the manifesto was cursory and merely identified groups that might be vulnerable to the policies of a Labour dominated Assembly. With wearisome repetition 'Fair Play' was demanded for groups such as business people, the elderly, nurses and most controversially of all for 'non-Welsh speakers'. The employment practices of Gwynedd County Council were highlighted and the manifesto stated:

> The Welsh have always been a tolerant people and we believe that this policy of 'linguistic apartheid' is counterproductive and threatens the social harmony of Wales. The Nationalists have gone too far and are now applying the 'English Not'.[119]

The desired political explosion occurred, but it ripped through the Welsh Conservative Party rather than its opponents. Tory candidates in South Wales Central had submitted a written warning 'against the use of the phrase linguistic apartheid'[120] when the draft manifesto was circulated for comment. Other candidates, such as Nick Bourne and Glyn Davies, disassociated themselves from the Welsh language policy. William Hague did not appear in the manifesto and Rod Richards had to settle for an endorsement in the shape of a photograph with the then spokesman for constitutional affairs, Dr. Liam Fox.[121]

Despite the occasional warning from some of its more perceptive supporters, the Welsh Conservative Party assumed that it would become the official opposition. Rod Richards started the 1999 National Assembly election campaign with a press conference at the St. Mellons Country Club in which he confidently announced his Shadow Cabinet. However, several members of this putative group failed to get elected to the Assembly. Although the few opinion polls that were published in the run up to the election indicated that the Party would finish in third place, it was complacently assumed that such polls underestimated Conservative support. The Party did not bother to commission its own poll and instead allowed itself to be comforted by the knowledge that in past elections it had always finished second, albeit a long way behind Labour. Actually, the Party had lost second place to Plaid in the 1994 European elections, but this fact was ignored. Here the Party's misjudgement reflected its negative policy platform. The Party did not have the imagination to sense that a more expansive vision was required to succeed in the first ever 'Welsh' election. Curiously, this error was partly repeated in 2003 when the Party again considered its fate predetermined, only this time it assumed that Plaid Cymru would inevitably form the opposition. Again the Party fought 'blind' without any polling. The 1999 result was a disappointment: only nine AMs were elected on 16 per cent of the vote, the Party's worst ever performance in Wales. Yet even this mediocre outcome secured the highest number of national representatives the Party had achieved since the 1983 general election. Devolution came at a price even for its enthusiastic advocates. The Tories were back!

Conclusion
The establishment of the National Assembly has transformed Welsh politics as radically as the arrival of democracy did in the 1880s. In the period of traditional 'British' politics that only ended in 1999, the Conservative Party's record in Wales can be summarised as one of failure flecked with intimations of promise.

The failure is objective and a matter of electoral record. Whether the Conservative Party is a foreign entity is a more subjective question. Certainly the failure of popular Toryism to penetrate Wales in the 1880s and 1890s needs explanation. The success of popular Toryism in England, where it pervaded urban and many industrial areas, was striking. In Wales the Liberal Party seemed charmed and blessed, first with the heavenly Gladstone and then the worldly Lloyd George. The Conservative Party behaved rather like Sir John Markby in Oscar Wilde's *The Ideal Husband*, it could not stop talking about disestablishment. Little wonder that by 1914 the 'English' label had attached itself firmly to the Party. It was the Conservative *Party*, and not *Conservatism*, that was rejected. The challenge that proved insurmountable then is almost unchanged today: to discover the most effective way to transmit Conservatism through the Welsh body politic. Today the consequences of failure are much more severe for the Conservative Party and, one can argue, for the Welsh electorate. Unless the Labour Party is effectively challenged, and the possibility of a Welsh Assembly Government without Labour is routinely accepted, the democratic choice available to the Welsh electorate will be limited.

It was in the 1950s that the Conservative Party came closest to reconstructing itself as an indigenous Welsh political party. Inspired by the *Policy for Wales* the Party's officers and several of its MPs believed that the Labour Party's hegemony could be broken by a popular Tory message that championed the cultural interests of Wales. Although London was not hostile to such a development, the UK party failed to take the necessary measures to facilitate its outcome. Instead of securing Cabinet representation via a Secretary of State for Wales and ensuring that a Welshman occupied the office, the half measure of a Minister for Welsh Affairs was adopted. The Labour Party soon realised the merit of establishing the office of Secretary of State and in so doing strengthened its credentials as a party sensitive to Welsh interests. The Conservative Party was not prepared to go the extra mile in the 1950s and so lost all the ground it had gained in being the first to recognise the Welsh dimension to British politics. In 1968 a private poll found that three quarters of respondents saw the Conservatives as the English party in Wales. The image of anti-Welshness has continued to dog the Party.

The fear that devolution would fragment the UK was not strongly felt by Welsh Conservatives in the 1950s. One explanation that might be offered for this is that Unionist antipathy was limited by the essentially ethereal nature of the Parliament for Wales Campaign. However, the evidence does not support such a conclusion. The Conservative Party's secretariat in Wales warned Central Office that the Parliament for Wales Campaign might take off just like the campaign for disestablishment had done over fifty years earlier - quite a warning.

One is struck by the measured and even courteous tone of the Party's initial rebuttal of the arguments for political devolution. They concentrated exclusively on the indivisibility of the Welsh and English economies. It was the Conservative *Party* that was firmly rejecting devolution; no simple rebuttal could be extracted from *Conservatism*. Sir Keith Joseph realised this when he briefed Edward Heath in 1968 that Conservatives could honourably support devolution. The same conclusion was reached by some prominent Welsh Tories such as Lord Aberdare and Raymond Gower MP.

Fear of fragmentation only became a phobia in the 1970s when unbending Unionism embedded itself in the Conservative Party in Wales. Its rejection of political devolution as a dangerous and wild experiment was an implicit criticism of the Party's policy in Scotland. An interesting aspect of this blanket rejection was the view that executive devolution was potentially more dangerous than a Scottish Parliament with legislative powers. Nicholas Edwards in the 1970s and William Hague in the 1990s made this point forcefully. They also agreed on the best form of attack: advocates of devolution should be challenged to offer federalism if they really thought the constitutional status quo dysfunctional.

A strange ambivalence has shaped the Conservative Party's relationship with the Welsh nation. Remarkable achievements, such as establishing a Welsh dimension to modern British politics, have been overwhelmed by errors like the decision to renege on the promise to establish a Welsh language TV channel. The strongest dynamic in this relationship has been that as a minority party in Wales, Conservative failures have carried exaggerated force.

Tories in Wales inhabit a rather cold world. A consequence of this lack of instinctive response to the Tory message has been a certain indifference to Welsh sensitivities emanating at critical times from London. Disestablishment was opposed with futile zeal as if the Almighty were the arbiter of Welsh politics and not the electorate. Tryweryn was flooded to slake the thirst of distant Liverpool despite the near total opposition of Welsh MPs. The Welsh Office was anglicised in 1987 which made a bonfire of Welsh Tory aspirations.

'Have we been anti-Welsh?' The question could only be asked by an outsider and it betrays both over anxiety and an inability to respond confidently to the national dimension in British politics. Certainly when London has played the most prominent role in determining the Conservative response to Welsh questions, the Party has been vulnerable to serious errors. It has not been *anti-Welshness* that has disabled the Conservative Party in Wales but a lack of self-awareness about the destructive strength of its English image.

Devolution is a great reform that will test the greatest political parties. No outcome is predetermined. Opportunity, chance and threat exist in equal measure. The potential for political re-alignment in Wales is greater now than any time since the early 1980s, perhaps even the 1920s. Should the Conservative Party regenerate itself as an indigenous institution in Wales, we might yet say, 'Now is Tory Wales!'

References *1-60*

1. E.H.H. Green, *The Crisis of Conservatism*, Routledge (1995) p125.
2. Felix Aubel, 'The Conservatives in Wales, 1880-1935' in Martin Francis and Ina Zweiniger-Bargielowska, *The Conservatives and British Society 1880-1990*, University of Wales Press (1996) p. 96.
3. Scottish National Union of Conservative Associations, *Campaign Guide 1892*, p201.
4. Conservative Central Office, No. 310 (July 1895), NLW.
5. John Davies, *A History of Wales*, Penguin Books (1994) p. 451.
6. They are: 'Ty'r Arglwyddi' and 'Tair Blynedd o Radicaliaeth' and 'Diwygiad Tollawl: A Blwydd-Dal yr Hen Bobl' in 1909; and 'Cynlluniau: Mr Lloyd George ynglyn a'r Tir, a Rhyddfrydwyr na fynant mo honynt' in 1927. Given the ephemeral nature of such material, other Welsh language leaflets might have been lost, even so supply was obviously very limited.
7. Aubel, p 106.
8. Conservative Party Wales Records (CPWR), Finance and General Purpose Committee, 4 November 1938, NLW, (C/1998/1).
9. John Ramsden, *An Appetite for Power*, HarperCollins (1998) p 310.
10. Ibid, p 311.
11. Conservative Party, 'Report on Industrial Wales', 26 May 1948, Bodleian Library (CCO4/2/183).
12. Ibid.
13. Conservative and Unionist Central Office, *The Conservative Policy for Wales and Monmouthshire*, February 1949.
14. CPWR, Executive Committee of the WMCUC, 6 July 1948, NLW.
15. Conservative Party, 'Report on Rural Wales', 20 January 1948, p. 9.
16. It was not uncommon for Welsh organisations to meet in England during this period. For instance, Sir David Maxwell-Fyfe's first engagement as Minister for Welsh Affairs was to address representatives of the Welsh Local Authorities at Shrewsbury; see Kilmuir, *Political Adventure*, Weidenfeld and Nicolson (1964) p. 203.
17. CPWR, WMCUC AGM, NLW.
18. *Western Mail*, 5 March 1949.
19. Ibid.,15 March 1949.
20. Alan Butt Philip, *The Welsh Question*, University of Wales Press (1975) p 280.
21. *Western Mail*, 12 October 1951.
22. Ibid, 17 October 1951.
23. Butt Philip, p. 299.
24. *Western Mail*, 1 March 1949.
25. Central Office Memo (CPO) to the Party Chairman, 29 October 1951, NLW Film 744.
26. Patrick Cosgrave, *The Lives of Enoch Powell*, Pan (1990) p. 137.

27. Letter from Brigadier E.O. Skaife to Lord Woolton, 14 March 1951, Bodleian (CCO2/2/17). Skaife, the former Colonel of the Royal Welch Fusiliers, was well regarded by Sir David Maxwell-Fyfe who mentions him in his memoirs.

28. CPWR, Executive Committee of WMCUC, 24 September 1951, NLW.

29. Memo from JPL Thomas MP, 28 June 1950, NLW Film 743. Miss Winifred James was left in post as a Central Office Agent but Garmonsway became head of the office in Wales.

30. Memo from JPL Thomas MP to Mr. Clarke, 18 December 1950, NLW Film 744.

31. CPWR, Executive Committee of WMCUC, 24 September 1951, NLW.

32. Ibid.

33. CPWR, Area Advisory Committee, 3 January 1953, NLW.

34. *Ibid*, 11 June 1954.

35. *Ibid*, 7 April 1956.

36. Butt Philip, p 297.

37. CPWR, Executive Committee of WMCUC, 16 February 1957, NLW.

38. Ibid, 25 May 1957.

39. Ibid, 16 February 1957.

40. Ibid, 25 May 1957.

41. Butt Philip, p 298.

42. Kenneth O. Morgan, *Rebirth of a Nation*, Oxford (1982) p 333.

43. Davies, p 664.

44. CPWR, Executive Committee, 2 July 1960, NLW.

45. Ibid, Finance and General Purposes Committee, 11 January 1964.

46. Tom Hooson and Geoffrey Howe, *Work for Wales*, Bow Group (1959) p 24.

47. Ibid, p 111.

48. CPWR, Executive Committee, 7 November 1959, NLW.

49. The short hand 'Wales Area' was increasingly used from the early 1960s.

50. The Conservative Party, *Wales with the Conservatives*, 1964.

51. CPWR, Executive Committee, 19 May 1951, NLW.

52. Ibid, 22 April 1972.

53. Letter from Mr. Kaberry to Mr. Howard Davies, 13 February 1958, NLW Film 743.

54. CPWR, Executive Committee, 17 November 1973, NLW.

55. Opinion Research Centre, 'Scope for Conservative Advance in Wales', Bodleian (CCO 180/32).

56. Memo from Mr. Block to Mr. Sewill, Conservative Research Department, 13 December 1968, Bodleian (CRD 3/37/1).

57. CPWR, Executive Committee, 30 July 1966, NLW.

58. Policy Study Group, 1 May 1968, Bodleian (CRD 3/37/1).

59. Ibid, 21 June 1968.

60. Ibid.

61. Ibid, 6 November 1968.
62. Ibid, 5 March 1969.
63. Conservative Party, *Wales into the 70s*, 1970.
64. *Western Mail*, 9 February 1950.
65. Wales and Monmouthshire Conservative and Unionist Council 'Some Questions and Answers on a Parliament for Wales, 1953, Bodleian.
66. Memo from Winifred James, Central Office Agent in Wales, 5 July 1950, NLW Film 744.
67. Letter from JV Garmonsway, (senior) Central Office Agent in Wales, to JPL Thomas MP, 17 April 1951, NLW Film 744.
68. CPWR, Area Advisory Committee, 22 September 1953, NLW.
69. Ibid, Statement by the Conservative Party, 'Covenant for Wales', 21 March 1951.
70. Ibid.
71. Ibid.
72. Wales and Monmouthshire Area Political Education Committee, 12 June 1965, NLW.
73. Note prepared by Henry Brooke for Lord Hailsham's visit to Wales, May 1958, NLW Film 744.
74. Letter from Mr. Douglas to Sir Michael Fraser, 7 November 1969, Bodleian (CRD 3/37/1).
75. *Ibid*.
76. Policy Study Group, 1 May 1968, Bodleian (CRD 3/37/1).
77. Letter from Sir Keith Joseph to Edward Heath, 17 February 1967, Bodleian (CRD 3/37/1).
78. Vivian Lewis and Donald Walters, *Wales A Blueprint*, Conservative Political Centre, 1974, p 43.
79. Memo from Nicholas Edwards to Margaret Thatcher, 3 November 1975. Lord Crickhowell's papers, NLW.
80. Conservative Research Department, Briefing Note (no. 44) 'The Conservative Commitment to a Scottish Assembly', 9 December 1976.
81. Ibid.
82. CPWR, WMCUC AGM, Annual Report 1976/77, NLW.
83. Ibid.
84. Ibid, Annual Report 1977/8.
85. The Scottish Conservative Party, 'The Conservative Party and Devolution', December 1978, p. 1.
86. CPWR, WMCUC AGM, 18 November 1978, NLW.
87. Davies, *Wales*, pp 680-1.
88. Conservative Research Department, Campaign Guide, 1987, p 451.
89. Quoted in Nicholas Crickhowell, *Westminster, Wales and Water*, University of Wales, (1999), p. 18.
90. Ibid.

91. Nicholas Edwards, Speech on Welsh language broadcasting, 10 November 1979, NLW.
92. Ibid.
93. Gwynfor Evans, *For the Sake of Wales*, Welsh Academic Press, (1996), p 220.
94. Campaign Guide, 1987, p 466.
95. Evans, pp. 221 and 225.
96. Crickhowell, p. 21.
97. Evans, pp. 227-8
98. Ibid, p 229.
99. The Conservative Manifesto for Wales 1992, *The Best Future for Wales*, p. 8.
100. Ibid.
101. Welsh Office, *A Charter for the Future*, CM2155, p 2.
102. Ibid, p 18.
103. J Barry Jones and Denis Balsom (Eds.), *The Road to the National Assembly for Wales*, University of Wales (2000), p 23.
104. Hywel Williams, *Guilty Men*, Auram Press (1998), p 51.
105. *The Best Future for Wales*, p 8.
106. John Major, *The Autobiography*, HarperCollins (1999), p 424.
107. Conservative Research Department, The Campaign Guide 1991, p 557.
108. Ibid, p 538.
109. The Conservative Manifesto 1997, *Opportunity and Prosperity for Wales*, p 53.
110. Conversation with author.
111. William Hague, letter to Tony Blair, February 1996.
112. *Western Mail*, September 1997.
113. William Hague, 'Labour's Dangerous Plans for Wales', in *The Battle for the Constitution*, Conservative Political Centre (1996), p 32.
114. Ibid, p 26.
115. Ibid, p 4.
116. *Western Mail*, 13 August 1997.
117. Assuming past trends.
118. Welsh Conservative Party Manifesto 1999, *Fair Play for All*, Foreword.
119. Ibid, p 12.
120. Memo to Rod Richards from David Melding, Jonathan Morgan and other candidates, February 1999, author's private papers.
121. Hague did not appear either in the Scottish manifesto. *Scotland First* carried no endorsement of any kind from the UK Party, presumably by design.

Chapter 5

The Strange Death of Unionist Britain

Even the English people, in spite of unique advantages, have never acquired more than an intermittent sense of being a single community, and since 1536 they have never alone composed a state; themselves manifold, they have been bound once to three restless partners and now to two.

Michael Oakeshott, *On Human Conduct*

Unionists believe that the United Kingdom of Great Britain and Northern Ireland is a successful and durable state. Logically, this belief stands prior to any preference for a particular constitutional structure. But in practice Unionism, as an ideology, has rarely disguised its zeal to preserve a unitary and centralised United Kingdom. The powerful and often emotional attachment that most Unionists have felt for a unitary state has resulted in the denial of any political dimension to the national identities of the Home Nations.

Devolution has dealt a mortal blow to this simple world view. Unionists must return to first principles and realise that the core purpose of Unionism is to preserve the constitutional integrity of the United Kingdom. A reformed Unionism would accommodate devolution and even look at developments such as federalism. This chapter concentrates on the Tory interpretation of Unionism. In particular, it considers the failure of Tory Unionists to grasp federalism as a realistic response to demands for a decentralised and more explicitly multinational state.

The United Kingdom faced few difficulties as a unitary state with multinational origins until the 1880s. Wales and Scotland were willing partners in a state which permitted no development of its political institutions unless they were directly responsible to Westminster. Even at the height of the Irish crisis, calls for Home Rule were weak in Wales and Scotland. Ireland, the most recent and restless partner in the Union, never accepted the legitimacy of an incorporating Union, although it was not until the advent of democracy that nationalism received its voice and the powerful fillip of popular endorsement. Most Unionists feared that Irish Home Rule would not merely end in separation, but that it might cause the UK to fragment further and even make the Empire ungovernable. These disproportionate fears led Unionists to deny the right of the Irish to domestic self-government despite the repeated and overwhelming desire of the Irish for such an arrangement.

The Union of Great Britain and Ireland was doomed when such unitarian inflexibility entered the Conservative Party. Lord Salisbury and Arthur Balfour, who between them led the Conservative Party from 1885 to 1911, both believed that the unitary state was the most advanced form of political association. They dismissed federalism as little more than the freak show at the end of Britain's political pier. Federalism might serve adequately as a transitionary constitution for more primitive states as they progressed towards fuller union, but in

Britain it would mark the start of fundamental decay.

However, as the legislative Union was not accepted in Ireland, orthodox Unionism could not avoid the continual use of coercion; though this was tempered with imaginative and, for the times, generous measures in an attempt to kill Home Rule with kindness. Although this unitarian outlook dominated the establishment's thinking, the genius of the British constitution still produced systems of parliamentary federalism for Canada and Australia. Yet, that these emerging states were technically subordinate to Westminster until 1931 is a clear indication of the hold that the theory of parliamentary sovereignty had on British political thought.

While the coherence of parliamentary sovereignty was overwhelmingly accepted until the 1970s, it has since received much critical examination. Many critics now consider the theory, at least in its simple and absolute form, inadequate to accommodate developments in international law and membership of international organisations such as the European Union. It has become less a legal fiction and more a half-truth to disguise the need to repair the dilapidated parts of the British constitution. According to the Conservative commentator Ferdinand Mount, this has prevented Parliament from developing a conceptually more modest but practically more authoritative role in British politics.

To evoke the memory of a now forgotten but once prominent Conservative Unionist, Walter Long, the unitary state is as dead as Queen Anne.[1] But not the Union, at least not if the Union is seen as an adventurous journey rather than a fixed destination. Predictions are precarious things, but as Francis Pym and Leon Britten realised in the 1970s, a reformed Unionism would begin with a serious consideration of the application of federalism within the UK.

The British state is tried and tested, but it is not ancient. Created in 1707, it owed its unitary character as much as anything to the fear of a Stuart restoration.[2] Federalism might seem as foreign to us as the Hanoverians initially did to our ancestors. But like that great German dynasty in the 18th Century, federalism could be the lateral thought needed to revivify the British constitution.

Only in the 1880s, nearly two centuries after the creation of the British state, did the need for a Unionist ideology become apparent. Until then, in essentially pre-democratic times, the real test of the state was whether it succeeded in maintaining order and security. Few British citizens questioned the basic premise that Britain was destined to bring an age of progress to the world, nor that the growth of the British Empire marked the unique legitimacy and worldwide significance of the British state. At first, in Ireland this ideology was considered suspect only in so far as it denied the demand for a modest measure of Home Rule. Unfortunately, ideologies at their purest - that is least pragmatic – tend to be strong but brittle. So it proved for Unionism when put to its great test in Ireland.

Ireland: Home of all Unionist Troubles

The brisk progress towards universal male suffrage transformed British and Irish politics in the 1880s. Gladstone struggled to combine the oil and water ingredients of Whig and Radical and maintain a united Liberal Party. Meanwhile, proselytising Tories eyed the Whigs less as class traitors and more like the misguided children of Burke ripe for conversion. Tory populism, surely the most exotic bird of the age, was about to fly surprisingly well on wings of Union and Empire. Defence of the Union acquired ideological rank with the shiny Orange epaulets of an *ism*. In fact, *Unionism* was an import from America, and the supposed lessons of the Civil War became a dominant theme and 'proof' of the inadequacies of federalism.

However, it was in Ireland where the most significant change occurred as Irish nationalism was fused to a popular mandate, and this sent a jolt through the entire parliamentary system. It was in Ireland that the party system failed to come to terms with the ballot box: the Liberals in Ulster, the Conservatives enormously so in the South. As Acton realised, throughout Europe powerful forces had been released as, 'the theory of nationality is involved in the democratic theory of the sovereignty of the general will'.[3] Many politicians in Britain came to believe that the national demands of Ireland – massively confirmed in every election after 1885 – could not be reconciled with the needs of the Empire. It was T.P. O'Connor, Irish Nationalist MP for Liverpool, who observed the explosive potential of the problem. As he put it, Ireland 'represented the government of one people through the public opinion of another'.[4]

Events could have taken a different course. Gladstone had reasonably assumed that Lord Salisbury was considering some form of constructive Irish policy when the Tory premier sent his friend Lord Carnarvon to Ireland as viceroy in the summer of 1885. Although Carnarvon is often dismissed as an intelligent but naïve idealist, it cannot be claimed that Salisbury was unaware of his views. Earlier Carnarvon had written to Salisbury to say that in Ireland 'our best and almost only hope is to come to some fair and reasonable arrangement for Home Rule'.[5]

Carnarvon soon met with Charles Parnell, leader of the Irish Parliamentary Party, and produced an effusive account of the outcome. He assured Salisbury that enough common ground existed for the construction of an imaginative Conservative policy that would attract the support of Irish Nationalists. Salisbury was aghast because a Tory Home Rule proposal would have prevented Gladstone taking up the Irish cause and thereby splitting the Liberal Party. Yet both Gladstone and Parnell thought a Conservative *volte-face* possible. Of course it would have suited them both: Gladstone favoured an Irish settlement on a non-partisan basis, while Parnell realised that only the Conservatives could get a Home Rule measure through the House of Lords.

Confusion reigned throughout the political establishment. According to Elizabeth Longford a 'situation of the wildest improbability had arisen at home. Political parties seemed to be standing on their heads. Parnell ordered every Irishman to vote against Gladstone'.[6] It seemed that Salisbury's low politics had worked. However, the greater prize of an unequivocal Liberal commitment to Home Rule proved elusive because Gladstone refused to enter an auction to secure Parnell's support.

In the late summer and autumn of 1885 the Conservative Party had three distinct options regarding its Irish policy. Salisbury favoured a simple and firm Unionist stance which promised rich dividends if the Liberals split on Home Rule. Carnarvon, influenced no doubt by his earlier experience, when steering through the House of Lords the British North America Bill that established Canada, was open to constitutional innovation and the serious consideration of Home Rule for Ireland. A middle ground position was being explored by Lord Iddesleigh (Sir Stafford Northcote) who wrote to Carnarvon that 'I am strongly impressed with the dangers of leaving this great and cardinal question to be fiddled with, and treated with Parnell in one way and with the British electors in another way. There is both danger and disgrace in that sort of policy'.[7] Iddesleigh's views were prescient but the former joint leader of the Party carried little authority at this time. On purely logical grounds, Carnarvon's response was the most coherent. If the validity of the democratically expressed demands of the Irish was to be acknowledged, there seemed little choice but to grant a measure of Home Rule.

However, such a response soon proved emotionally unacceptable to mainstream Tory opinion in Britain and loyalist opinion in Ireland. Thirty years later the fear of Irish republicanism drove many Conservatives back to a federal variation of Carnarvon's Home Rule option, but by then it was an idea whose day had long since come and gone. Whatever else may be said about Conservative policy prior to the first Home Rule Bill, one fact stands out: faith in unbending Unionism was not universal. Even the view that Home Rule might be proposed by the Conservatives 'was optimistic, but not ludicrous'[8] according to Roy Jenkins.

Salisbury's view eventually won out and Gladstone was forced to introduce a Home Rule measure at great cost to the internal coherence of the Liberal Party. Despite Gladstone's great statecraft the first Home Rule Bill in 1886 had a conspicuous and ugly flaw: it proposed to end Irish representation at Westminster. This would have made Ireland in effect a self-governing colony without an interest in United Kingdom affairs. In 1893 Gladstone presented the diametrically opposite option of retaining Irish MPs at Westminster, which served only to emphasise the incoherence of both approaches.

From the start, Home Rule within a unitary state proved a highly problematic proposition. Today's difficulties with devolution – including the Gladstonian-sounding West Lothian question – are a reflection of Home Rule's central flaw. As Alan Ward succinctly remarks, 'It was clear that allowing the Irish to be represented at Westminster would give Ireland too much power in British affairs, but denying them representation would give them no power in UK affairs'.[9]

Gladstone paid the price for the failure of his Home Rule policy when the Liberals were swept out of power in 1886. It appeared that the Conservative Party had won new ground in Britain and convinced many working class voters to back Unionism. However, the Party could make no adequate response to the freely expressed and settled will of the Irish to exercise responsible self-government. Salisbury offered no more than icy defiance. 'Rightly or wrongly, I have not the slightest wish to satisfy the national aspirations of Ireland'.[10] His Liberal Unionist ally, Joseph Chamberlain, agreed and had earlier remarked, 'I can never consent to regard Ireland as a separate people with the inherent rights of an absolutely independent community'.[11] It caused the 'blindness of a generation', to use Enoch Powell's evocative phrase when speaking in the House of Commons in the Second Reading debate on devolution in December 1976.

The study of history is the basis of all political wisdom. In the early stages of the Irish crisis we can see that Conservatives were confused and split. In the end Salisbury forced the Party to utterly reject Home Rule. This brought electoral dividends in Britain at the expense of any prospect of a constitutional settlement of the Irish crisis.

Federalism: A Fancy for Foreigners?
Federalism has been seen by most Unionists as a foreign and fanciful concept, not at all rooted in British political experience. Balfour famously described the suggestion that federalism could be used to save the Union as being made to eat dirt. Gladstone found federalism so unpalatable that he swallowed the half-baked notion of Home Rule instead.

A century later, the idea of federalism again failed to inspire those promoting devolution. Nevertheless, the proposition that federalism is foreign to British political experience is impossible to sustain. During the first half of the 18th Century Britain's colonies in North America acquired legislative autonomy over their domestic affairs. It proved a workable arrangement, although sovereignty and certainly executive authority remained the preserve of Westminster. Custom and practice developed so strongly that after the War of Independence the Americans had the materials at hand to construct what appeared to be a new and innovative constitution.

Eighty years before, the option of a federative instead of an incorporating Union was discussed and then rejected by the Scots. Andrew Fletcher of Saltoun, a member of the Scottish Parliament, argued for the retention of separate parliaments in London and Edinburgh. Fletcher's plan might have taken its inspiration from the Netherlands' confederation where he had lived for a time in exile.[12] However, it would have required the Scottish Commissioners to jump beyond their times to grasp a fully federal solution. Had they done so, the central concern of the English, the possibility of a Stuart restoration to the Scottish Crown, could have been placated by simply allowing Westminster to determine the matter of succession. Anyway, the Scots saw their Church, rather than their Parliament, as the heart of national life and that institution they did preserve. While it was hardly infused with the spirit of federalism, the Act of Union created a unitary state with glorious anomalies such as two official religions. Uniform it was not.

What had not quite been imagined by the Scots in 1707 was offered in part to Ireland's Protestant oligarchs in the 1780s. This was an Irish Parliament, with legislative autonomy on domestic matters, that accepted the general superintending authority of Westminster over imperial affairs.[13] However, the federal spirit was weak and in the late 18th Century a satisfactory constitutional framework to govern relations between Britain and Ireland proved elusive. Ireland's Protestant elite did not want to concede much legislative independence, and London remained in sole control of the Irish executive. The fundamental division of legislative *and* executive powers between separate jurisdictions that defines federalism was absent.

Rebellion in Ireland during the 1790s, combined with the constant threat posed by revolutionary France, encouraged the British government to impose a unitarian settlement on Ireland. Even so it took a couple of attempts, and ample financial inducements, to cajole the oligarchs to abolish Catholic Ireland's Protestant Parliament. Perversely, the Irish executive was not abolished in the 1800 Act of Union, and Dublin Castle simultaneously became a symbol of oppression and proof of a separate political entity. Britain's unitary state – for 120 years to be known as the United Kingdom of Great Britain and Ireland – had acquired another shocking anomaly.

While British politicians failed to develop or apply the concept of federalism within the Union, by the second half of the 19th Century its use was considered routine in the white dominions of the Empire. Parliamentary federalism, a bold variation of the Westminster model, defined the Canadian (1867), Australian (1900) and a little more ambiguously the South African (1910) constitutions. After 1945 it also became the panacea of choice when de-colonising the non-white Empire.[14]

While the British did become enthusiastic exporters of federalism, it was viewed as an expedient to treat fragile and underdeveloped bodies politic. A partial but temporary exception to this received view was the idea that the Empire might be organised on a federal basis. The Imperial Federation League was established in 1884 to advance such a programme. Speaking in Toronto in 1887 Joseph Chamberlain, Liberal radical turned Unionist and father of two leaders of the Conservative Party, said, 'It may yet be that the federation of Canada may be the lamp lighting our path to the federation of the British Empire. It is an idea to stimulate the patriotism and statesmanship of every man who loves his country'.[15] But one should note that for most imperialists it would have been a case of the UK whole and dominant within an Empire federation. In the aftermath of the Boer War many Conservative politicians linked the concept of imperial federation to imperial preference as a means to create a single economic entity. In 1910 Leo Amery asked what was meant by Imperial unity and provided the following answer:

> We mean that all its [the Empire's] members should remain citizens of a single world state with a duty and a loyalty towards that state, none the less real and intense because of the co-existence with it of a duty and a loyalty towards the particular nation or community within the Empire to which they belong.[16]

Speaking in 1904, George Wyndham predicted 'the birth of an Organic Empire State'.[17] This vision of a supra-state is one of the more curious products of Conservatism. By the 1980s all memory of this episode had been expunged from a Conservative Party that was becoming increasingly Eurosceptic. Of course, the EU is a puny union compared to the one that had been envisaged by some leading Edwardian Conservatives for the Empire.

It remains the case that federalism is an integral part of British political experience and parliamentary federalism is a British invention. What cannot be claimed, however, is that federalism has been a dominant theme in domestic British politics. John Kendle has stated the case well, 'The root objection was to the division of sovereignty entailed in a true federal state. To those nurtured on the sanctity of parliamentary sovereignty the concept of separate but co-ordinate sovereignties was mystifying; even frightening'.[18] Even those prime ministers who have accepted the need for major constitutional change have, with the partial exception of Lloyd George, shied away from exploring a federal settlement. Most Unionists have gone much further and dismissed federalism as at best fanciful and at worst dangerous. In his intemperate polemic *England's Case Against Home Rule*, A.V. Dicey raged:

> Apply Federalism to Ireland and you immediately provoke demands for autonomy in other parts of the United Kingdom, and for constitutional change in other parts of the British Empire. Federalism, which in other lands has been a step towards Union, would, it is likely enough, be in our case the first stage towards a dissolution of the United Kingdom into separate States...[19]

While Dicey believed that the unitary state is the most complete form of political association, few would accept this assertion today. There are no obvious signs that states as diverse as the USA, Canada, Australia and Germany are *en route* to unitary constitutions. Of course Dicey was mischievously upping the ante when he said that 'Colonial independence is better for Ireland and safer for England than sham federalism'.[20] Yet his argument had some substance. Indeed, it continues to resonate today as the consequences of devolution to the Celtic nations slowly reverberate. There is still a surprising level of Unionist support in England for a unitary constitution, and at its least cautious a belief that Scotland and Wales should be forced to leave the UK or rejoin the Union state. It would be deeply ironic if Unionism ultimately ends in the establishment of an independent English state.

Even if an indigenous demand for Home Rule were to develop in England there is still the question of how a federation of such unequal units could be effectively balanced. This occurred to advocates of Home Rule in the critical period 1912–14. Following the 1911 Parliament Act, which removed the veto of the House of Lords, some change to the constitution became inevitable. One significant kite was flown by a rather unlikely convert to Home Rule, Winston Churchill. While paying his annual visit to his constituency in Dundee, Churchill called for the consideration of a federal system of government in the UK. In his view this would best be achieved by establishing local parliaments in England:

> I am not in the least disturbed by the prospect of seeing erected in this country 10 or 12 separate legislative bodies for discharging the functions entrusted to them by the Imperial Parliament. The United States conducts its business through a great number of Parliaments and Germany has not merely Parliaments and States gathered and grouped together within the German Empire, but

has separate kingdoms and principalities and armies woven together in a strong federation of the whole. In the colonies, Canada, South Africa and Australia have found this federal system the only way in which you can reconcile the general interest of an organised State with the special and particular development of each part and portion of it.[21]

Lord Curzon's witty response to such suggestions was to fancy at all these parliaments in our poor little isles! A similar sense of bemusement greeted Labour's scheme for English regional government in the late 1990s. Stephen Dorrell's response was typical, 'I know of no problem to which my constituents think a directly elected East Midlands Parliament is the solution'.[22] Those enthusiasts who advocate federalism *within* England have to confront a tradition of nearly 1,000 years of unitary English administration.[23] However, the argument that England would have to be so divided to balance a federal UK is not quite as unassailable as it first appears. If England would so dominate a federal state, in what sense has England been less dominant in the UK's unitary constitution?[24]

At a time of mortal peril for the Union of Great Britain and Ireland, federalism received its most sustained consideration, but it was a macabre and phantasmagorical spectacle. As image after desperate image flickered on the screen of British politics, diehard Unionists were distorted out of all recognition to become supporters of federal devolution. Even Sir Edward Carson suddenly professed faith in federalism, and Austen Chamberlain reiterated the ideas of his father.

However, events put paid to these latter day federalists. The 1918 General Election effectively ended the Union as Sinn Fein defeated the Irish party by 73 seats to six. Suddenly, independence via dominion status was the least Ireland could then be expected to accept, and that reluctantly by republican and abstentionist Sinn Fein. Undaunted, Parliament proceeded to prepare a panacea to save the Union, and by a majority of 153 voted to establish a body to consider and report on a 'measure of Federal Devolution applicable to England, Scotland and Ireland' and possibly Wales.[25]

Two schemes emerged from the conference and the inevitable confusion that followed vitiated what little prospect there existed for devolution within Great Britain. The Speaker proposed a scheme that would have created legislative Grand Councils for England, Scotland and Wales located within Westminster. The second scheme was an authentic and strong model of Home Rule on largely federal lines. Although the Speaker's scheme was supported by 18 of the conference's 31 members, five of these preferred the stronger scheme (supported outright by 13 members) in the longer term because that 'in our opinion can only satisfy the national aspirations of both Scotland and Wales'.[26]

Leolin Forestier-Walker, the Conservative MP for Monmouth, supported the stronger Home Rule scheme without qualification. Meanwhile, as dominion status for southern Ireland loomed large, the last breath of Home Rule gave voice in Ulster to a Unionist majority that wanted to remain British and used Stormont not as a means to be distinct but as the best way to guarantee the Province's Union with Great Britain. From the start, the United Kingdom of Great Britain and Northern Ireland was not a legislative Union. Britain's unitary state acquired its most bizarre anomaly.

The Sovereignty of Parliament

Federalism's faint echo in Britain can be attributed above all else to the doctrine of the sovereignty of Parliament. Leaving aside times of extreme stress, such as the Irish crisis or the rise of Celtic nationalism in the 1960s, Unionists have instinctively equated the health of the Union with a unitary state governed by a sovereign Parliament at Westminster. But what once seemed so simple has been hugely convoluted by events at home and abroad since the 1960s. It is time to re-consider the traditional Unionist interpretation of parliamentary sovereignty. Lord Hailsham gets us off to a vigorous start:

> There is no doubt that this legislative omnipotence, usually dressed up in the complimentary phrase 'the sovereignty of parliament', has been extremely useful in the past and has afforded an extremely valuable element of flexibility in time of need. However... no other free country has found it necessary to confer these powers or shown any signs of wishing to do so, and when we have conferred freedom on our former colonies and dominions we have not in the main found it possible to export this peculiar feature of the Westminster model.[27]

The nostrum of parliamentary sovereignty can be traced back to the middle of the 17th Century. Charles I failed to establish the monarchy as the absolute source of sovereignty and, after his crass refusal to compromise with the Parliamentarians in 1646, eventually lost his precious head. A new source of sovereignty was required and the Earl of Shaftesbury declared in 1689, 'The Parliament of England is that supreme and absolute power, which gives life and motion to the English Government'.[28] Absolutism, so foreign to earlier British political experience, had survived but it was now located in an assembly rather than an individual sovereign. The influence of Thomas Hobbes in this development was critical, as he stated in the *Leviathan*:

> If the essential rights of sovereignty... be taken away, the commonwealth is thereby dissolved and every man returns into the condition and calamity of a war with every other man, which is the greatest evil that can happen in this life, it is the office of the sovereign to maintain those rights entire, and consequently against his duty, first, to transfer to another or to lay from himself any of them.[29]

All of orthodox Unionism is here in Hobbes' sublime argument! The state is our protector and its sovereign authority is both total and indivisible. Over 200 years later the far from sublime A.V. Dicey would dimly reflect this concept:

> The sovereignty of Parliament is like the sovereignty of the Czar. It is like all sovereignty at bottom, nothing else but unlimited power; and, unlike some other form of sovereignty, can be at once put in force by the ordinary means of law.[30]

Despite Dicey unhelpfully introducing the Czar, parliamentary sovereignty has not been associated with tyranny. In Hobbes' scheme, abuse of power amounts to irrational political behaviour because the purpose of sovereign power is 'the procuration of the safety of the people'.[31] Furthermore, the 'obligation of subjects to the sovereign is understood to last as long and no longer than the power lasts by which he is able to protect them'.[32] To act outside these natural limits is to abrogate the contract by which sovereign power is established. This apart, the sovereign – whether in a monarchy (Hobbes' preference) or a collective assembly – can lawfully do and undo anything necessary for the safety of the people. It is therefore a Hobbesian principle that no Act of Parliament can fetter the sovereignty of a future Parliament to repeal legislation.

Hobbes also emphasised that in much of human activity the law is silent, in 'cases where the sovereign has prescribed no rule, there the subject has the liberty to do or forbear according to his own discretion'.[33] This concept allowed individual liberty to flourish in Britain alongside a theory of absolute sovereignty. There is nothing necessarily illiberal or unconstitutional, therefore, in the concept of parliamentary sovereignty. The problem lies elsewhere, in the constraints on constitutional development that the concept inevitably exacts as its cost.

Even some of its keenest advocates have conceded the essentially fictional nature of parliamentary sovereignty. The Conservative commentator T.E. Utley wrote:

> For over 250 years, the doctrine that Parliament can do anything it chooses has been unchallenged by English lawyers… If Parliament were to repeal the Act emancipating the American Colonies, no English court would declare this amendment to be contrary to the law of England… It is equally clear that this doctrine has never been more than a legal fiction. What Parliament can do at any time is limited by considerations of practical politics.[34]

The first Empire was lost on the altar of parliamentary sovereignty in 1783. More sense prevailed in Britain's relations with Canada and Australia when these dominions moved towards independence. Yet the *Grand Illusion* had to be maintained and it was not until the Statute of Westminster in 1931 that the sovereignty of the dominions was formally recognised and the Colonial Laws Validity Act of 1865 made null and void.

Human rights illustrates the inflexibility of parliamentary sovereignty from another angle, and one increasingly prominent since 1945. Britain's compliance with human rights conventions has been sincere on a practical level, but with little formal redress for citizens who feel their rights have been violated. In 1974 Lord Scarman stated that it 'is the helplessness of the law in face of the legislative sovereignty of Parliament which makes it difficult for the legal system to accommodate the concept of fundamental and inviolable human rights'.[35]

It was not until 1998 that the Human Rights Act gave British citizens access via domestic courts to the European Convention on Human Rights (1951). The incorporation of the Convention into domestic law was made relatively easy by the doctrine of parliamentary sovereignty, but the inordinate delay in passing the Human Rights Act demonstrates the reluctance of successive governments to acknowledge the primacy of international law. This was the case even when the international law in question was largely drafted by British jurists with the full support of the British government.

The area in which parliamentary sovereignty has least coherence is where the EU has competence. Here parliamentary sovereignty does not exist even as a fiction. As Lord Bridge stated in 1991:

> If the supremacy... of Community law over the national law of member states was not always inherent in the EEC Treaty it was certainly well established in the jurisprudence of the Court of Justice long before the United Kingdom joined the Community. Thus, whatever limitations of its sovereignty Parliament accepted when it enacted the European Communities Act was entirely voluntary.[36]

The doctrine of the sovereignty of Parliament is not entirely without value. However, it does need a fundamental reinterpretation and it should no longer be the dominant principle in our constitutional thought. It comes as a relief to many citizens to live in a state that acknowledges the force of international law and is a member of an international polity (for the EU is such). Yet ultimate sovereignty does reside in the state, represented in Britain by Parliament. We remain a sovereign people because our Parliament could repeal the European Communities Act and withdraw from the EU or repudiate the Conventions that establish international law.

But like the Pope speaking ex cathedra, parliamentary sovereignty can only survive as something other than a fiction if it is used in a sparing way, and on questions of ultimate importance. Behind the *Grand Illusion* of omnipotent parliamentary sovereignty lies the real essence that is the genius of the British constitution. While a reformed Unionism is both possible and desirable, it will require the rejection of the *Grand Illusion* so that the real constitutional challenges that face us can be clearly perceived. Conservatives can no longer idle in the land of absolutes and refuse to acknowledge that the constitution is mutable. Consider Dicey in 1886:

> Home Rule is the half-way house to Separation.[37]

Reiterated some 110 years later by John Major:

> Scotland mattered to me. From the moment I became prime minister I could see the danger of it sliding away to independence through the half-way house of devolution.[38]

Such intractable thoughts are ill-suited to changing times. Until the passing of the Parliament Act 1911 Unionists enthusiastically upheld the concept of absolute parliamentary sovereignty because they held an effective power of veto in the House of Lords. Despite facing a government elected with a massive mandate, Arthur Balfour used the House of Lords to frustrate the Liberals' programme of social and economic reforms. It was a fatal misjudgement which culminated in the House of Lords rejecting Lloyd George's 'Peoples Budget' in 1909. As the dominant social purpose of the state was shifting from the protection of property to the promotion of welfare, Balfour was maladroit. It also allowed the question of the House of Lords veto to be judged not on an unpopular constitutional measure like Home Rule, but on economic and social matters central to the programme of a popularly elected government.

In 1908 Lloyd George had said in a jibe that was at once devastating, popular and accurate, 'The House of Lords is not the watchdog of the constitution, it is Mr. Balfour's poodle'.[39] The result of this uneven contest was the Parliament Act which replaced the House of Lords veto with a mere power of delay. At a stroke, Unionists had inadvertently opened the way for Irish Home Rule. Forced now to abandon the concept of parliamentary sovereignty as a means to save the legislative Union with Ireland, the Conservative Party entered its darkest and most destructive hour.

Unionists had believed in parliamentary sovereignty rather like a proud and powerful man might consider a belief in God to be the tiresome cost necessary to sustain his own sense of immortality. Genuine love of parliamentary sovereignty was absent from Unionist hearts. Unsurprisingly, this psychological turmoil brought with it the threat of violence. The menace of Unionist aggression had lurked around the Irish issue since Randolf Churchill's infamous declaration in 1886 that, 'Ulster will fight, and Ulster will be right'. The shock and bemusement felt by many Unionists was acerbically summed up in George Dangerfield's description of Sir Edward Carson, 'He believed in the Union between England and Ireland, not simply as a man who believes in an effective constitutional system, but as a religious man might believe in the marriage between his parents which, if annulled, would turn him into a bastard'.[40] This is not good Canon Law, but it vividly conveys the feeling of existential angst suffered by Conservatives who feared Home Rule would end the Union.

Most Unionists committed crimes of passion in relation to Ireland, but Andrew Bonar Law came close to cold treachery in 1912 when he said, 'In our opposition [to Home Rule] we shall not be guided by the considerations or bound by the restraints which would influence us in an ordinary Constitutional struggle... I repeat here that there are things stronger than Parliamentary majorities'.[41] Britain was sliding towards civil war. And it was Unionists who were doing most of the pushing by suddenly rejecting the sovereignty of Parliament. Here is the text of a contemporary pamphlet published by the National Unionist Association of Conservative and Liberal Unionist Organisations:

> **Referendum or Civil War?**
> To avert that awful danger the Government must submit the Home Rule Bill... to you, the voters of the United Kingdom, in a Referendum – for they refuse a General Election.[42]

That most unparliamentary device, the referendum, replaced the House of Lords as the Unionists' constitutional watchdog.

Some excuse can perhaps be found in the fact that in the period 1912-14 Bonar Law's principal objective was to remove Ulster from the Home Rule scheme rather than prevent the introduction of self-government for the rest of Ireland. Even so it was a reckless tactic to defend the Union to the point of civil and military disobedience. This is what happens when incoherent thought is not challenged and reformed. The best that can be said about Unionist tactics is that they were uncontrolled and dangerous, as illustrated in the following leaflet:

> **Why Ulster will Fight**
> Will you allow the Forces of the Crown, which are your forces, and not the forces of any Political Caucus to be used to coerce loyal Ulstermen, who have asked for nothing but that they should remain with you? The answer is NO![43]

Little wonder that this period of the Conservative Party's history made Lord Hailsham's flesh creep.

The Decline of Old Time Unionism

In 1996, on the eve of the 'repeal' of the remaining Acts of Union, a report for the Conservative Political Centre expressed the core belief of Unionism most eloquently:

> The Union established one constitutional entity – one constitutional people – which has contained national differences and allowed for their distinctive cultural and religious institutions. To be British is to devote an allegiance to the Crown and constitution rather than a national identity. As such, it does not denote the suppression of other identities but rather the expansion of identity, allowing the individual the opportunity to be part both of a national entity and a wider, liberating constitutional entity.[44]

The report argued that political 'devolution would threaten the Union'.[45] However, such an inference cannot be drawn from the passage quoted above in terms of strict logic. It is perfectly possible to argue that a 'wider, liberating constitutional identity' could accommodate devolution. The central fallacy of rigid Unionism is also strongly evident in the report. Equating Unionism with a single UK parliament that generates all law leaves Unionists nowhere to go, other than some form of coercion, should one of the constituent nations wish to reform the Union.

In a section entitled 'The Nationalist Myth' the report stated:

> What is being asserted is the idea of the 'nationalist' people as the 'sovereign people'. It is the idea of the people conceived apart from all constitutional practice. It is the people invested with a metaphysical principle, the right to self determination.[46]

The same logic was used by Unionists to deny Ireland a measure of Home Rule before the First World War. It succeeded in preserving the Union at the cost of eventually driving southern Ireland entirely out of the State. Perversely Northern Ireland was given Home Rule anyway, thus exposing the futility of such a rigid response.

Somewhat surprisingly, Unionism has never attempted to impose a strict integrationist structure on the state. To this extent, the multinational nature of the UK has been accepted. Yet there is often a sense of disdain when Unionists refer to national questions. In a revealing aside the CPC Report maintained that, 'As the Spanish-American philosopher George

Santayana put it, nationality is too deep to be changed honourably and too accidental to be worth changing'.[47] Ferdinand Mount has criticised the lack of development in Conservative constitutional thought:

It must also be said that the historical context of the classical arguments for maintaining strict unitary constitutions derive from the early-modern period of weak central government. Historical experience there did seem to suggest that federations provided weak government. But Dicey's constant repetition of this assertion was already beginning to look old-fashioned in his day. The position now is very different. It is federations which seem, on the whole, to enjoy a massive, even somnolent tranquillity – while unitary states seem to be blown about. And our greater fear is of the overweening power of the centralised state apparatus.[48]

Mount is right to push Conservatives in the direction of new constitutional thought, but his observations were in fact anticipated in the 1970s. In 1978 the Conservative Party's spokesmen on constitutional issues, Francis Pym and Leon Brittan, published *The Conservative Party and Devolution*. They identified four options for constitutional development, from stronger national Grand Committees within Westminster to 'a quasi-federal UK'. No attempt was made to obdurately defend the status quo. Pym and Brittan were not keen reformers, nothing like it, but they grasped the need to reform the Union should the people of Scotland vote for 'an Assembly with executive and legislative powers'.[49] Although still keen to uphold the concept of parliamentary sovereignty, Pym and Brittan were bold and insightful in recognising that devolution would spell the end of the unitary state:

Once it is decided to transfer actual power from parliament to a subordinate assembly, if the principles of a constitutional settlement are not to be abrogated, then the transfer must eventually be to assemblies covering the whole UK. In the absence of that, Parliament would bear a different relationship to Scotland than to the other partners in the UK and Scottish MPs would be placed in a special, privileged position.
Problems such as these have been overcome in federal systems. There every citizen is related to both the federal and provincial parliament in the same way ... In Britain, federalism itself, with this formal division of sovereignty between the two tiers of government and the limitation on the power of the federal parliament, would

be a revolutionary transformation of the role of Parliament rather than a traditional development of existing institutions.[50]

Nevertheless, Pym and Brittan, reflecting on experience in the British Commonwealth, noted that if 'an institutional arrangement which avoided removing overall sovereignty from Parliament' could be found then, 'the principal constitutional and logical objections to a federal system for the UK would have been overcome. The Government of Ireland Act 1920 went a long way towards that'.[51] These views strongly reflected those of many Unionists between 1911-1921 when some form of Home Rule 'All Round' was favoured.

The UK state never became uniform in its administrative structure. As Michael Keating has observed, 'The multi-national nature of the United Kingdom had always carried federal implications and created some tension with the centralist Westminster regime... The traditional response to territorial discontent had been a limited degree of policy differentiation and an extensive system of administrative devolution'.[52] The appointment of a Scottish Secretary by Lord Salisbury in 1885 marked the start of an innovation that would stretch the unitary state to its limits. While the Scottish and Welsh Offices could be seen as examples of skilful 'exceptionalism', they defied the logic of a unitary system which ideally would have administered government through integrated Departments of State covering the whole of the UK. It is a small step from territorial Departments of State to territorial parliaments. Nevertheless, the consensus held for a long time, as Keating puts it:

> Administrative devolution was as far as governments felt able to go before the 1970s in accommodating territorial distinctiveness on the British mainland. By defusing federalist and Home Rule demands, it helped preserve the unitary regime while covering the politics of territorial bargaining with the blanket of Cabinet secrecy and collective government.[53]

Unionists of right and left – and there were many orthodox Unionists in the Labour Party – had reasonable grounds for optimism that this compromise might endure despite its anomalous character. However, two factors that challenged this consensus emerged in the 1980s.

First, the alternation of power stopped and the Conservatives succeeded in winning four successive general elections. The Conservatives won overwhelmingly in England and very comfortably in the UK as a whole, but the Party never won in Wales or Scotland. (In contrast, Labour won a majority of English constituencies in 1997, 2001 and 2005, although by 2005 it had narrowly lost its majority of English votes.) Something stirred in the Celtic gut and a sense grew that such an outcome was not right and that it even diminished the dignity of Wales and Scotland.

Secondly, the idea that major constitutional reform was risky started to decline. Major economic and political developments turned the EU into a polity and ended any lingering pretence that it was merely an international organisation. The collapse of the Soviet Empire and the emergence of free and some new states in eastern Europe reinforced this sense of mutability in political structures. It is hardly surprising that in such a climate the idea of reforming the Union reverberated with many people in Wales and Scotland.

A Reformed Unionism
A reformed Tory Unionism is long overdue. If it is to emerge it will have to draw on both traditional and contemporary Conservative thought. There is no better place to start than Edmund Burke. From Burke is drawn the traditional Conservative reverence for the organic development of political institutions. Yet Burke was not against change when the intent was to preserve the inner essence of ancient traditions. In any event Conservatives are a little too preoccupied with the organic metaphor when it comes to assessing the need for and value of constitutional change. The happy political outcome we call Britain was hardly the product of slow, organic change. The Reformation, the Civil War, the Glorious Revolution, the Acts of Union, the Great Reform Act, Universal Suffrage, Imperialism, the end of the Empire, entry into the EU – these events did not fall like soft drizzle on our political soil!

When William Gladstone was preparing to embark on the last political crusade of his life, the attempt to secure Home Rule for Ireland, he carefully read one of Burke's greatest speeches. It is possible today to visit the Grand Old Man's library at St. Deiniol and handle his notated copy of *On Conciliation with America*. There is no mark next to Burke's magnificent affirmation, 'I am sure that I shall not be misled, when, in a case of constitutional difficulty, I consult the genius of the English Constitution'.[54] However, the once Tory Gladstone was more Whig than Liberal when asking himself the Burkean question *How best to preserve?*

In 1775 Burke's answer was to accept what was already established in practice, and recognise the authority of the colonial assemblies over their domestic affairs. The only other response that could have given the Americans an interest in the constitution would have been to admit colonial MPs to Parliament. Distance made this impracticable (although it became French practice in the 20th Century).

Burke realised that Britain's relations with her American colonies had become what later theorists would call 'quasi-federal'. He did, it is true, uphold the absolute sovereignty of Parliament, but he questioned the wisdom of acting without tact or reference to established customs and practices. Burke's genius lay in his ability to acknowledge change and development in constitutional practice. His flaw was a belief that the English (we would say British) constitution was somehow guided by the intimations of Providence. The view in modern Conservative thought that Westminster is the centre of the United Kingdom's political universe is anticipated in Burke. It has produced the fallacy that representation in Parliament inevitably renders national political institutions both redundant and unreasonable. Nevertheless, if this is the dark side of Burke's influence, his subtle and flexible disposition threw new light on the genius of the British constitution. Gladstone was not foolish in turning to Burke for a guide.

Providential design had no place in the thought of Michael Oakeshott. History is the perceived outcome of a myriad of human actions and nothing is permanent or inevitable. In his remarkable essay *On the Character of a Modern European State*, a sense of fragility and a Hobbesian fear of anarchy seems to pervade every page. 'The history of modern Europe is the history of Poland only a little more so'.[55] Oakeshott's conception of the United Kingdom as a collection of 'restless partners' is unsettling but an inevitable conclusion given his analysis of European political history:

> All European states began as mixed and miscellaneous collections of human beings precariously held together, disturbed by what they had swallowed and were unable to digest, and distracted by plausible or fancied *irredenta*.[56]

The Union cannot be seen as an enterprise sufficient of itself and above the troublesome questioning of its citizens. It is a contingent entity which will continue to survive only as long as most people view it as a coherent State. Nothing of the numinous sanctifies the British constitution. Unsurprisingly, Conservatives have not embraced Oakeshott as warmly as they have Burke. Not only does Oakeshott reject the notion that an enterprise, such as the Union, can be justified by faith alone, it cannot be justified by faith at all. Mystical reference to the *Union* - like references to a *General Will*, the *Common Good*, *Equality*, or any other abstraction – should be anathema to those of a conservative temperament who value instead:

> ...a disposition to be 'self-employed' in which a man recognises himself and all others in terms of self-determination; that is, in terms of wants rather than slippery satisfactions and of adventures rather than uncertain outcomes. This is a disposition to prefer the road to the inn, ambulatory conversation to deliberation about means for achieving ends, the rules of the road to directions about how to reach a destination...[57]

This is Tory scepticism at its most magnificent. The Union is an adventure not a pre-existing entity that was revealed in stages in 1536, 1707, 1801 and 1921. It survives by being modified and re-affirmed by each succeeding generation. We are not compelled to go on affirming this Union, but its longevity indicates coherence and a far greater strength than the recently dissolved unions of Yugoslavia, the Soviet Union, and Czechoslovakia.

Turning finally to Lord Hailsham, we are confronted by a man who, like Burke, was both a politician and a constitutional theorist. His thought is not abstract but a practical response to the political challenges of his day. Writing in the 1970s, a decade of bitter political division and constitutional uncertainty, Hailsham warned that a hard choice had to be made between two options for the development of democracy, 'the two theories are the theory of centralised democracy, known to me as elective dictatorship, and the theory of limited government, in my language the doctrine of freedom under law'.[58]

Hailsham feared that just as Ireland was lost, so too might Scotland and even Wales, unless a reconstruction of the Union was attempted on federal or regional lines. In 1969 he wrote to the former Director of the Conservative Research Department that, 'I am against a permanent Secretary of State [for Wales] in the Cabinet... As you know, I favour regionalism for the whole UK'.[59] He knew also that the conviction that a decentralised state is the best guarantor of democracy was strongly held by Conservatives in Australia, Canada and the USA. Hailsham was dismissive of those who offered devolution merely as an expedient, 'It seems to me that they fail to cross the necessary logical bridges. Compromise may be a splendidly British virtue, but in constitutional matters issues must be faced. You cannot have a system which is at once federal and unitary'.[60] For the first time since the Irish crisis of 1916-21 a senior Conservative was advocating federalism as an option in the face of demands for constitutional change:

> If I am right in predicting the necessity for an assembly in Edinburgh and another in Belfast (as soon as the present troubles are at an end) there will have to be other and similar bodies in Cardiff, and, say, Liverpool, Manchester, Birmingham, Newcastle, Norwich and Bristol, Exeter or Southampton. If we are to come to terms with federalism, it will, I believe, be necessary to do so thoroughly. Why not?[61]

In connecting a call for federalism to a wider programme of constitutional reform, Hailsham added to the canon of British conservatism. Federalism had been grasped at as a constitutional panacea by many Conservatives between 1912 – 1921, but it seemed then the frenetic activity of desperate and disturbed minds. Hailsham, reflecting on the loss of Ireland with composed regret, adduced more positive reasons for embracing the federal principle. He, alone among senior Conservative politicians of the 20th Century, reminded colleagues that in their instinctive rejection of a decentralised constitution, British Conservatives were somewhat idiosyncratic in the English-speaking world.

The first step towards a reformed Unionism has already been taken by most Conservatives: devolution to Scotland, Wales, and Northern Ireland has been accepted. Now the task becomes more difficult but also more vital. The British constitution needs to be balanced so that the rights and privileges of the Home Nations within the UK receive equal recognition. The old way of doing this, through participation in a single and absolutely sovereign parliament, stands utterly obsolete. As Lord Hailsham said, issues have to be faced if we are to strengthen the British constitution. It is now the task of Unionism to lead Britain to a Union that is strongly federal in character.

References

1. Alun O'Day, *Irish Home Rule 1867-1921*, Manchester (1998) p 292.
2. Technically a Stuart continuation, as Queen Anne was the last of the Protestant Stuarts.
3. John Dalberg-Acton, 'Nationality' in *The History of Freedom and Other Essays*, London (1907) p 287.
4. Quoted in D.G. Boyce, *The Irish Question and British Politics* 1868-1996, London (1996) p v.
5. Quoted in J.L. Hammond, *Gladstone and the Irish Nation*, London (1938; new impression 1964) p 377.
6. Elizabeth Longford, *Victoria R.I.*, London (1964) p 605.
7. Quoted in Richard Shannon, *The Age of Salisbury 1881-1902*, London (1996) p 156.
8. Roy Jenkins, *Gladstone*, London (1995) p 525.
9. Alan J. Ward, *The Irish Constitutional Tradition*, Irish Academic Press (1994) p 74.
10. Andrew Roberts, *Salisbury*, London (1999) p 387.
11. Enoch Powell, *Joseph Chamberlain*, London (1977) pp 61-2.
12. See John Kendle, *Federal Britain*, London (1997) pp 3-12.
13. See Ward, *Irish Constitutional Tradition*, pp 15-29.
14. For example the short lived West Indian and Central African federations.
15. Quoted in Powell, *Chamberlain*, p 78.
16. Quoted in E.H.H. Green, *The Crisis of Conservatism*, London (1995) p 199. Green's chapter on Imperial Organisation is insightful.
17. Ibid, p 200.
18. Kendle, p 62.
19. A.V. Dicey, *England's Case Against Home Rule*, London (1886) p 189.
20. A.V. Dicey, *A Leap in the Dark*, London (1893) p 97.
21. *The Times*, 13 September 1912.
22. David Willets, *Why Vote Conservative?* London (1997) p 66.
23. The Marcher lordships were the most significant aberration in England's unitary character.
24. I have attempted to address this question in the essay *Will Britain Survive Beyond 2020?*
25. Hansard col. 2126, 4 June 1919.
26. Conference on Devolution, Cmnd. 692, 1920, p 12.
27. Lord Hailsham, *The Dilemma of Democracy*, London (1978) p 136.
28. A.W. Bradley, 'The Sovereignty of Parliament – Form or Substance?', in Jeffrey Jowell and Dawn Oliver (eds.), *The Changing Constitution*, Oxford (2000) p 27.

29. Thomas Hobbes, *Leviathan*, Indianapolis (1958) p 262.
30. Dicey, *England's Case Against Home Rule*, p 169.
31. Hobbes, *Leviathan*, p 262.
32. Ibid, p 179.
33. Ibid, p 178.
34. Charles Moore and Simon Heffer (Eds.), *The Selected Journalism of T.E. Utley*, London (1989) pp 98-99.
35. Quoted in Bradley, p 51.
36. Ibid, p 45.
37. Dicey, *England's Case Against Home Rule*, p 287.
38. John Major, *The Autobiography*, London (1999) p 415.
39. See Roy Jenkins, *Mr. Balfour's Poodle*, London (1954).
40. George Dangerfield, *The Strange Death of Liberal England*, New York (1935) reprinted London (1997) p 78.
41. Quoted in Alan O'Day, p 240.
42. National Library of Wales, Conservative Party Papers, Leaflets and Pamphlets, 1902-1914.
43. Ibid.
44. Conservative Political Centre, *Strengthening the United Kingdom*, (1996) pp 13 and 15.
45. Ibid, p 10
46. Ibid, p 16.
47. Ibid, p 17

48. Ferdinand Mount, *The British Constitution Now*, London (1992) pp 91-2.
49. Francis Pym and Leon Brittan, *The Conservative Party and Devolution*, The Scottish Conservative Party (1978) p 1.
50. Ibid, p 16.
51. Ibid, p 17.
52. Michael Keating, 'Regionalism, Devolution and the State 1969-89', in Patricia L. Garside and Michael Hebbert (Eds.), *British Regionalism 1900-2000* (1989), pp 160-1.
53. Ibid, p 161.
54. Edmund Burke, *On Conciliation with America*, in the works of Rt. Hon. Edmund Burke (London 1801) Vol III, p 81.
55. Michael Oakeshott, *On Human Conduct*, Oxford (1975) p 186.
56. Ibid, p 188.
57. Ibid, p 324.
58. Hailsham, *Democracy*, p 9.
59. Letter from Quentin Hogg to Sir Michael Fraser, 17 September 1969, Bodleian Library, CRD 3/37/1.
60. Hailsham, *Democracy*, p 167.
61. Ibid, p 169.

Chapter 6

Will Britain
Survive
Beyond 2020?

*The only true conservative is the man
who resolutely sets his face to the future.*

Theodore Roosevelt

In 2007 Britain celebrated the tercentenary of the Act of Union between England and Scotland with a restraint that suggested to some a profound loss of self-confidence. While the case for the Union is defended robustly by the three major political parties, there is a sense that what was once accepted implicitly is difficult to justify explicitly. Britishness, the life-force of the British state, can seem clumsy and archaic; and Britain certainly endures more comfortably as a state than a nation.

Yet political and cultural life in these islands demands a British construction, a fact recognised even by Welsh and Scottish nationalists who predict some form of confederation between the independent Home Nations once their Valhalla dawns. This would not satisfy my dual nationality, whether in the cultural or political sphere. So I advance here an alternative that will unease nationalists and Unionists alike: the case for a federal Britain. Theory rarely moves the empirical British, so I identify below what seem to me the principal practical arguments *against* a federal Britain and attempt to answer them in turn.

Britain cannot adopt a federal constitution because the constituent units of England, Scotland, Wales and Northern Ireland, would be of such unequal size.

This is sometimes called the 'Prussian' problem and it is indeed formidable and easily the strongest objection to federalism being adopted in the United Kingdom. In terms of population and share of wealth England is over five times as large as Scotland, Wales, and Northern Ireland combined. Opponents of federalism argue that England would completely dominate a UK federation as a result. Strictly speaking, in classic federalist theory, units of unequal size are thought less of a problem than a situation where one or two units overwhelm the other members of a federation. K.C. Wheare, for example, wrote that 'The capacity of states to work a federal union is also greatly influenced by their size. It is undesirable that one or two units should be so powerful that they can overrule the others and bend the will of the federal government to themselves'.[1] The USA, Australia and Germany are examples of federations where the size of units varies considerably but no single unit or small combination can dominate. Canada just about fits this pattern, although between them Quebec and Ontario have a population of 20 million, nearly twice the population of the other provinces combined. Here in any event a national cleavage prevents Quebec and Ontario combining to dominate the rest of Canada. If it were made up of the Home Nations undivided, a United Kingdom federation would be very far removed from the classic model of federalism. We must now consider whether this problem is insuperable or merely cause for a distinct mode of federalism to reflect British political experience.

When Britain's latent multinational character became increasingly visible in the 1960s many Unionist politicians feared that the break up of the United Kingdom was imminent. These fears were exaggerated, but not the realisation that the Celtic reawakening would inevitably have constitutional ramifications. Perhaps surprisingly, it took a generation for these consequences to become apparent. Nevertheless, as Simeon and Conway argue, the basic fact that had to be faced was that a multinational state, if democratic, cannot function stably with a unitary constitution. A unitary United Kingdom was only possible when the Scots and Welsh chose to repress their political identities.

At the same time, and somewhat paradoxically, it is Britain's multinational nature that makes an asymmetrical federation possible. While England, Scotland and Wales are significantly different in size, they are very similar in terms of their national coherence. Nations may be 'imagined' but some are projected more vividly than others. The Home Nations of Britain are almost biblical in their intensity. Such nationalism would provide strong cultural defences in a federal United Kingdom. More formally, a range of constitutional safeguards could also reduce the risk of the domestic jurisdiction of Wales and Scotland being encroached by a United Kingdom government. A constitutional court could act as the guardian of national rights. And a reformed House of Lords could contain a disproportionately large number of Celtic members, a useful federalist device established by the American Senate. The strongest safeguard would be a constitutionally enshrined right to secede which would moderate the behaviour of the most diehard centralists intent on assimilation.

Of course, dividing up England would solve the problem of asymmetry in the classic federalist fashion. In 1912 Winston Churchill suggested just such a scheme, and in 2000 a similar pattern was replicated by John Prescott, although for a weaker scheme of devolution. While theoretically more satisfying, this option would require the express consent of the English people and that is unlikely to be forthcoming in the time available to construct a federal United Kingdom. The people of England might agree to one English parliament but not twelve!

Those who dismiss federalism as fanciful fail to appreciate that the United Kingdom has already reached functional federalism and, in a sense, constitutional theory needs to catch up with political practice. Both the Scottish Parliament and Northern Ireland's Assembly are federal institutions, and the overwhelming likelihood is that the National Assembly for Wales will soon follow suit.

Traditional Unionist theory continues to cite Westminster's sovereignty as proof that devolution is power retained, not divided as in a federal constitution. As the Government's Green Paper *The Governance of Britain* puts it, 'Devolution does not cede ultimate sovereignty'.[2] This is a bizarre argument. Could the Scottish Parliament be abolished at the whim of Westminster? Of course not. The devolved institutions are *de facto*, if not *de jure*, entrenched and could only be dissolved at the cost of a constitutional crisis. The Scottish Government's White Paper *Choosing Scotland's Future* acknowledges the notional sovereignty of Westminster over devolved matters but states that 'under a constitutional convention (known as the Sewel convention), the United Kingdom Government and the United Kingdom Parliament have undertaken not to exercise legislative powers in devolved areas, or to change the legislative competence of the Scottish Parliament or the executive competence of Scottish Ministers, without the agreement of the Scottish Parliament'.[3]

Finally, if we accept that the UK is a multinational state, in what sense would England be more dominant under a federal rather than a partly devolved unitary constitution? It would seem more plausible to argue that a unitary constitution would be a more effective vehicle for English domination. This remains, after all, the central contention of militant Celtic nationalism. It is no accident that the SNP and Plaid Cymru have focused on the establishment of national parliaments and assiduously avoid any endorsement of federalism. Formal federalism would confirm the sovereignty of the devolved institutions as well as that of Westminster. Federalism offers sovereign rights to Scotland and Wales without breaking up the British state. It is therefore a vehicle for a reformed Unionism – something recognised and perhaps feared by Celtic nationalists.

A federal constitution would be the first step towards full statehood for the Home Nations of the United Kingdom.

While the advantage of a federation of nations is that the members need not be of roughly equal size, and could accommodate a disproportionately large member, the potential disadvantage is that nations in such a federation might develop an appetite for full statehood. Put simply, the argument is that a federal Britain would be a halfway house to the disintegration of the UK. Among the great federal states of the English-speaking world – the USA, Canada, and Australia – only Canada contains a strong national cleavage. The most successful federal state in Europe, Germany, is made up of non-national units (perhaps with the partial exception of Bavaria).

A federal Britain would break new ground for federalism because it would be made up entirely of nations, and indeed of Europe's oldest nations. In the past Unionists usually maintained that such is the potential force of nationalism that a strong centralised government was necessary to make a British state possible at all. Therefore, in traditional Unionism, cultural nationalism could be permitted, but only once its political dimension had been abjured. In many ways this was a remarkable bargain. England, after all, could have assimilated Wales and Scotland but chose not to do so. While assimilation might have been difficult before the 18ᵗʰ Century, thereafter the state apparatus could have accomplished this bleak task. But the English-British state was on another, essentially liberal, trajectory.

We should not think that classic federalist theory resents national cleavages. It may be true that the USA has lacked a sense of multiple nationalism since the Civil War, but some commentators regret this and consider it to be one of the causes of the decline in state power. Jacob Levy, for instance, has argued that nations can be strong elements of a federal state. 'Provinces that are large enough, stable enough, and aligned with cleavages of sentiment and loyalty can usefully counterbalance the central state. Localities without these traits cannot'.[4] In the *Federalist Papers*, Hamilton argued that the people would naturally support their local governments in any conflict with the federal authority, and this provided a natural safeguard against the potential tyranny of centralised power.[5] Lord Acton echoed similar sentiments in the 19th Century when he argued that it could be healthy for states to contain several nations as this guarded against the idolization of the state, a concept then in intellectual fashion as Hegel's thought received the rather clumsy refractions of his disciples.[6]

Nationalism has not found much favour amongst political philosophers, at least not if the theory is reduced to the essential contention that nations and states should be co-terminous. Wayne Norman points out that if we accept this contention there would be about 600 states in the world, although some think this an underestimate.[7] Many political philosophers believe that such a primordial criterion for statehood is unlikely to produce many liberal democracies. Until the 1980s, Scottish and Welsh nationalism made little headway against this liberal consensus. Something of a breakthrough occurred when Plaid Cymru and the SNP started to argue for full national status within Europe. This allowed for a more liberal nationalist theory to develop as it accommodated a 'higher' entity that would allow for *inter*national co-operation. Today it is difficult to equate Celtic nationalism with separatism as a result of this development.

Given that, despite dire predictions, Canada has not fractured, a federal Britain would seem in little danger of constitutional secession. On a cold rational basis, a federal Britain could be expected to survive and prosper, just as the old unitary United Kingdom survived for so long because it was a successful state. Uniquely in Europe it managed the manifold crises that tore apart the political and social foundations of the Continent between 1789-1945.

More emotionally, Britishness is a national resource that has generated deep loyalty in the past and could do so again in a federal Britain. While the nation-building of Wales and Scotland has enjoyed a modern renaissance, it should not be assumed that Britishness is consequently being blotted out. It is true that the intensity of Britishness has declined since the 1970s, but this is probably more of an historical re-adjustment after the Second World War and its deeply unifying effects, than a decline in its essential character. It is also the case that instinctive values drawn from religious, family and community ties have weakened under the modern, forensic demand for rational justification.

Federalism is artificial and against the organic traditions of the British constitution.

Put simply, many instinctive Unionists believe that federalism is not quite British. And more reflective Unionists dislike the fact that federalism requires the 'Big Bang' of divided sovereignty and a written constitution which, they argue, would be incompatible with our parliamentary traditions. That such views are strongly and sincerely held is beyond question, but they are surprisingly unempirical.

Parliamentary federalism is a British invention, initially developed for use in the large dominions. Even American federalism is partly derivative from British political experience. Federal models were widely discussed in the late 19th and early 20th Centuries as a means to constitute an empire state. Moreover, federalism was belatedly acknowledged to be the most feasible way to preserve the UK of Great Britain and Ireland before its eventual fragmentation in 1921. Britain's lack of a written constitution is not quite as exceptional as politicians maintain. It would be more accurate to say that the British constitution is spread through a constellation of statutes rather than being unwritten and, therefore, somehow 'statuteless'. Nevertheless, federalism remains something of an f-word in British political discourse. Such fastidiousness does not now serve the Union well.

Part of the problem, probably the greater part, is that federalism has not been seen as a resource for use within the British constitution, although it has often been applied abroad. As John Kendle remarks when examining the Anglo-Irish crisis, even 'the promoters of federalism for the UK had but a mechanistic, utilitarian approach to the federal idea and little true appreciation of its possibilities or its resonance'.[8]

Underlying this feeling that federalism is for others is a sense that a unitary state is the superior political association. Generally speaking constitutional reformers, from Gladstone to Blair, have not wanted to go beyond a form of devolution. Labour's devolution proposals in the 1970s were calculated to be an alternative to federalism, and this was the intent also of New Labour's 1990s reforms. However, it is becoming increasingly clear that what starts in theory as devolution – with an assertion of centrally retained sovereignty – quickly becomes quasi-federalism.

The Scotland Act 1998 devolved all legislative power to the Scottish

Parliament other than those items listed for exemption, and this firmly established the Scottish Parliament as a quasi-federal institution rather than a grand unit of local government to be altered or overridden at will by Westminster. That Britain's quasi-federal devolution is not buttressed by a written federal constitution weakens the British state. It is sheer wishful thinking to call this constitutional muddle pragmatic flexibility. There are too many grey areas where devolved administrations can compete for jurisdiction with Westminster. The SNP's anti-nuclear stance on defence illustrates the danger.

To some extent this jostling is found in all federal states. However, without a clear constitutional settlement, Britain risks losing the benefits of a more formal federalism with an agreed set of rules and clear boundaries, while retaining none of the certainties of the former unitary state.

A formal federal constitution would certainly end the fiction of absolute parliamentary sovereignty. However, Westminster, as the United Kingdom's federal Parliament, would be sovereign over those powers allocated to it in a written constitution. Encroachment, such as that attempted by the SNP government on the question of Trident submarine bases, would be much more difficult. While the sovereignty of the Westminster Parliament would be limited, it would be protected and real over those matters under its jurisdiction. The federal Parliaments of Canada and Australia are powerful and authoritative bodies – and Westminster would be no different if recast as a federal institution.

Of course the notional sovereignty of Westminster over currently devolved matters in Scotland and Wales would be abolished. Hence, the Scottish Parliament and Welsh Assembly would also be sovereign institutions with entrenched powers. Is this a great leap in the dark, to paraphrase Dicey? Or is it merely a more elegant and formal recognition of the reality of the constitutional position today? A written federal constitution begins to look less like a 'Big Bang' and more like a skilful reconfiguration of the existing material found in British political experience. If some commentators have mischievously described the USA as a unitary nation wrapped in a federal constitution, it might be time for us to recognise that the UK has been a federation of nations stifled by a unitary constitution.

Finally, in what sense would federalism be artificial compared to the supposedly organic character of the current British constitution? Here we must put aside sentiment and be coldly empirical. The British state was created comparatively recently, in 1707, only 69 years earlier than the USA. It is not an ancient entity justified by processes and decisions lost in the mists of time. As a metaphor, the organic nature of Britain's constitution just about holds true in that since the 17th Century there has been no fundamental revolution comparable to the cataclysms that hit France and Russia. But this metaphor should not be treated as a literal description of British political experience. How else can the distinctly inorganic turning points of universal suffrage, representative government, the promotion of individual welfare, and the protection of human rights be understood? All of these fundamental constitutional and political principles would have been viewed as harebrained in 1707.

Federalism would undermine British national identity and lead to the break up of the UK.

Federation would be a means to formally recognise the multinational essence of the British state. This would give more visibility to the national identities of the Home Nations that have been partially repressed for generations. As a result many Unionists fear, with some cause, that more exclusive Welsh, Scottish and English identities would overwhelm the once robust sense of Britishness that unified so many people in the United Kingdom. This fear is understandable and the expectation of stronger national identities developing in the Home Nations is realistic.

Yet this is happening today even without federalism. Moreover, it might accelerate under the current messy system of what the Conservative political thinker John Barnes calls 'devolutionary shreds and patches'.[9] While it is fanciful to suggest that we would be having any debate on the merits of federalism in the absence of the national re-awakening within Britain, federalism has to be seen by its advocates as less of a pragmatic fix and rather more as a means to strengthen Britain and its constituent Home Nations.

Federalism would not be a panacea, but it would be the best system to unite the nations of Britain in a stable state. A federal state would allow for the nation-building projects of Wales, Scotland, and England, together with those of Britain. There is nothing Unionists could do, of course, should the nations of Britain want to pursue independence and become states. However, federalism offers national autonomy to the Home Nations, while remaining a settlement short of independence. Should this not prove enough to satisfy Celtic nationalism, then at least the people of Wales and Scotland would be making a decisive choice and not one clothed in the confusion and mishap that attends devolution.

Unfortunately, there is currently little prospect of a fuller constitutional settlement under a Labour government. The Green Paper on the constitution, *The Governance of Britain*, hardly mentions devolution at all. In fact it devotes much more space to the discussion of the Church of England and its senior appointments than it does to devolution.[10] While the Green Paper raises the issue of Britishness and its enhancement, the detail is overwhelmingly civic in its focus. The bloodless assertion that there are 'core democratic values that define what it means to be British'[11] hardly manages to distinguish Britain from any other democratic state. The low point in the Green Paper's ample sloppy thinking comes in the warm endorsement it gives to the Victorian constitutional writer A.V. Dicey, who is commended for his 'works of authority'[12] – presumably the same works that did so much to doom the United Kingdom of Great Britain and Ireland.

It is time for Unionists to realise that Britain cannot be defended merely as a state but must also be regenerated as a nation. Some areas of public policy have powerful nation-building characteristics, most obviously education, culture and broadcasting, defence, and foreign affairs (although this list is not exhaustive; some would, for instance, add health policy given the symbolism of the NHS). Federalism allows for these nation-building 'tools' to be shared between national and federal jurisdictions. In a British federation one would expect the field of education, for instance, to rest at the national level, while defence and foreign affairs would be federal powers. Some policy areas with nation-building implications, such as culture and broadcasting, would be shared.

Federalism, then, can accommodate nation-building projects at different levels within a state. As long as the coherence of dual national identity is accepted, then in a federal system Welsh, Scottish or English nation-building could be undertaken alongside the rejuvenation of British national identity. It is only when a strong British identity is necessarily equated with dominance over all but the most trivial aspects of Welsh, Scottish or English identity that federalism could be construed as a system of government likely to weaken Britishness.

There seems little point in going there, although some strident Unionists have done so in the past.

As to the validity of dual identities, even Plaid Cymru and the SNP emphasise the coherence of feeling Welsh or Scottish *and* European. Now if dual (or even multiple) national identities are not only possible but widely felt, federalism seems both feasible and an adroit constitutional response to the challenge of multinationalism. Because federalism offers both the means to share nation-building tools and a system of clear rules – a written constitution – it is the best defence against bombastic nationalism whether attempted at the national or federal level. This is why some thinkers argue that federalism is the *only* way to preserve liberal multinational states.

While the decline in British identity has been much exaggerated, it no longer sits dominant over a hierarchy of allegiances. Unionists find this development unsettling and it has occasionally led to the assertion of a forced and brittle British patriotism. Few would agree with the arch-critic of Britishness, Tom Nairn, when he claims that current attempts at British nation-building are 'a generalisation of Northern Ireland Protestant attitudes',[13] but it is surely true that the once strong voice of Britishness is a little hoarse. If Unionists attempt to reassert the *dominance* of British national identity, then critics like Nairn, who of course long for the demise of Britishness, will prevail.

There are better options for Unionists. To borrow a metaphor from Michael Oakeshott, we need to avoid national *arguments* and instead promote a *conversation* between the Home Nations and Britain. Whether the senior members of the UK and Scottish governments read much Oakeshott is surely doubtful, but both *The Governance of Britain* and *Choosing Scotland's Future* seek to promote 'a national conversation'.[14] The grammar of federalism could help to keep this conversation going.

However, before the conversation can begin in earnest, Unionists must abandon any belief that Britishness somehow sublimates Welsh, Scottish or English national identity. Similarly, Unionists should not make the opposite mistake of lacking the confidence to speak through fear that a once dominant sense of Britishness is being replaced by equally dominant Welsh, Scottish or English identities.

The growth of Welshness, for example, does not come at the cost of

Britishness, although it certainly alters the environment in which British identity is formed. In the formation of national identities we do not have a system akin to mercantilism, where if one national economy increases it is thought that other economies must diminish. Britishness is changing rather than declining, and the growth of nationalism in Wales and Scotland is one of the many stimulants producing this change.

The modern apostles of Britishness are not yet very eloquent, it is true, and it is likely to be a while before more articulate idioms are available to match those found in Welsh and Scottish nationalism, but Unionists should have the confidence to persevere. These new idioms can only form if Unionists accept the need for a modern language of Britishness, one that describes the national experience of being British now, one that is civic and national and not designed to shout-out the voices of the Home Nations.

Unionists must take seriously the possibility that the British state might fragment within the next 20 years. Only when a risk is acknowledged can it be managed and mitigated. Whatever happens, by acknowledging the fragility of Britain, Unionists can at least prevent its dissolution by stealth or neglect. But why should the secession of one or more of the Home Nations be considered permissible at all? With a referendum on Scottish independence possible in 2010, this is far from an abstract question.

However ethically dubious (and few political philosophers take the dissolution of liberal multinational states lightly) on a practical level it would seem highly problematic to deny, should it form, the settled will of the Scottish people to leave the United Kingdom. One key test illustrates the point. The United Kingdom is a political association that values above all its character as a liberal democracy. Should Scotland, Wales or even England ever secede, would they inevitably become liberal states? In all but the most fantastic scenarios they would (if nothing else, membership of the EU or NATO would require it). Yet if the United Kingdom government wanted to deny the right of one of the Home Nations to secede, could it do so without using illiberal means? Almost certainly not. Consequently, Britain is only an immutable state if it is ultimately prepared to surrender its liberal values.

This does not mean that Britain will fragment, but it could do so under certain circumstances. Here Britain is no different from other European states. As Michael Keating has observed 'The only

European state that has the same boundaries in 2001 as in 1648 is Portugal, and that has lost an empire which profoundly shaped its internal politics'.[15] The UK will survive as a political association only if the people of Britain make an active choice that it should do so. The possibility of fragmentation is merely the dark side (to Unionists) of this existential choice.

A federal Britain would be complicated, bureaucratic, and over governed.

Compared to the simple and elegant constitutional lines of a unitary state, at first sight federalism looks complicated and ungainly. A.V. Dicey thought federalism a transitionary solution for political associations not ready to form unitary states. While the British unitary state fell some way short of the ideal model (after all, it contained two established churches and disestablishment within one kingdom – a curious trinity) it is fair to acknowledge that federalism would make Britain a more complicated political space than it was before 1999.

However, the current hybrid constitution, created to accommodate devolution to Scotland and Wales, seems more convoluted than federalism. John Barnes sees this constitutional jumble as a particular danger to Britain. He warns that 'Lopsided decentralisation within what purports to be a unitary state will lead to the Balkanisation of politics and threaten the disintegration of the United Kingdom'.[16] This view echoes the warning given by Lord Hailsham in the 1970s:

> You cannot have a system which is at once federal and unitary. You cannot have local assemblies with jurisdiction concurrent to that of Parliament. I know that in theory this is what occurred at Stormont, but that is partly because the system was operated by conventions observed on both sides as if it were a federation which in fact it was not, and partly because the permanent majority at Stormont was determined to get on with Westminster and the minority largely opted out altogether.[17]

There is already ample evidence in Scotland that devolution is delivering the dangers anticipated by Barnes and Hailsham. The SNP's skilful programme of nation-building is designed to come at the expense of the Scottish people's British allegiance. It is because devolution is messy and lacking in clear boundaries that the SNP can play so fast and loose, leaving the British government flat-footed.

Why then do Unionists in the Labour and Conservative parties cling so resolutely to what 'purports to be a unitary state'? Conservatives oppose federalism for rather instinctive reasons. The 'Big Bang' of federalism does not seem an organic solution to Britain's constitutional crisis. The Labour Party's opposition has a sharper edge because it is essentially ideological. Labour is deeply committed to the concept of universal and equitable public services. And it should be said that since the introduction of the welfare state, the British people have largely shared this commitment. Variations in public services are viewed as unfair 'post code' lotteries. Few English voters know much about Welsh politics, but many do know that NHS prescriptions are free here and they consider this unfair in a national health service.

However, such policy differences are the life-blood of federalism because they allow for local decisions to be made according to local priorities. Of course some services in federal states remain universal and equitable because they are delivered at the federal level. Nevertheless, under federalism the principle of equal services to all citizens is undoubtedly weakened. Labour Unionists cling to devolution as a means to maintain the notional right of the United Kingdom government to intervene if devolved governments move too far away from a uniform standard. Yet it is highly questionable whether such a power could be exercised in practice.

In one important respect a federal Britain would be more equitable than a devolved Britain, and that is in the application of a uniform system of government. In federal states government operates at the local, national (or provincial) and federal levels. Wales, Scotland and Northern Ireland would no longer retain exceptional rights because England would also have its own parliament.

The importance of a uniform system of government was often emphasised during the Irish crisis, and it produced a scheme called 'Home Rule All Round'. This failed largely because many Unionists felt it unreasonable for the rest of the United Kingdom to accept Home Rule just because the Irish wanted it. The cure was thought worse than the disease, and so southern Ireland eventually seceded. Today the cause for an English parliament is unlikely to succeed merely on the grounds that it would help balance the anomalies of devolution. Federalism offers the opportunity of presenting a more positive justification for an English parliament as part of the rejuvenation of Britain.

As it stands, devolution carries a dangerous but infrequent risk: it is possible that the English will one day be governed by a party they did not elect to office. Technically, in terms of raw votes, this happened in 2005 when the Conservatives narrowly polled more than Labour but won fewer seats. This itself attracted some critical comment at the time, but the scenario of a United Kingdom government having a minority of MPs in England would be daunting. Although this is unlikely to happen, as England has 85 per cent of the United Kingdom's population, it did occur in 1964 and February 1974. A government elected in such circumstances would have the option of forming a coalition to generate majority support in England. Alternatively, a mechanism for 'English votes for English laws' (that is, an English legislative process *within* Westminster), could be established as long as this did not inadvertently create two executives answerable to the same Parliament. Another solution would be the introduction of PR for Westminster elections. Whichever way the 'West Lothian' question is answered, within the bonds of devolution, it is complicated – more complicated than federalism by far.

A federal constitution need not create a vast number of additional politicians and civil servants. The aim of federalism is to divide not multiply governmental functions. However, there are likely to be more politicians and civil servants than in a lean unitary state. The House of Commons is not very lean – it has half as many members again as the US House of Representatives. Should Westminster evolve into the United Kingdom's federal parliament it could be cut back to 300 or so members without inhibiting the execution of its functions. Whether a particular political association suffers from the vices of over government, bureaucracy or needless complication owes as much to cultural as constitutional factors. Britain's unitary state as it existed before 1999 was notoriously complicated and relatively bureaucratic, and not at all transparent.

When thoroughly examined none of the arguments against federalism seem very convincing. If Britain wanted to become a parliamentary federal state it could do so without great risk to its traditional political culture. New dynamics would be created, of course, and they cannot be precisely anticipated. But the simple truth is that a parliamentary system can be either unitary or federal. Some parliamentary democracies are a hybrid, such as South Africa and Britain as presently constituted. However, there is strong evidence to suggest that Britain's hybrid constitution might be ill suited to the management of stronger national identities within the UK.

IS THERE A CASE FOR WELSH INDEPENDENCE?

While I believe that all Unionists in Wales should be patriotic Welsh nationalists, in this section I will examine the practical and moral case for an independent Welsh state. Following the methodology of the preceding section, I will set out what I consider to be the principal arguments against an independent Wales and consider their validity.

Wales is too small to be an economically prosperous and stable state.

This has been the most frequently used practical argument against independence. Economically, Wales is unquestionably deeply integrated with England, so much so that the very concept of a Welsh economy has to be qualified. However, other European states have shared a common economic space. In the 1950s the concept gave birth to the 'Benelux' economy made up of Belgium, the Netherlands, and Luxembourg. In any event, even in large states like Britain and Germany the concept of a national economy is clearly weakening under the demands of globalisation. Furthermore, if a member of the EU as seems safe to assume, an independent Wales would have access to English and European markets. The only scenario in which severe economic dislocation could be anticipated is if an independent England were to leave the European Union. Otherwise, the natural geographic bonds that unite the Welsh and English economies would surely continue to promote trade and commerce.

An independent Wales would certainly face economic costs, although how long these would last is a matter of conjecture. Public expenditure in Wales considerably exceeds taxation receipts and this deficit would be difficult to fund even in the short term by borrowing. In the longer term it is impossible to say whether an independent Wales would be better or worse off economically than if it had remained part of Britain. It would depend on the quality of government policy and the entrepreneurship of the people. Ireland remained one of Europe's poorest economies for 70 years after independence but has witnessed an economic transformation in the last 15 years or so. Even if the economic cost of Welsh independence is considered likely to be substantial and long lasting, this is hardly justification for denying the feasibility of independence. All it does establish is that independence would carry a significant economic cost. Wales would not be the first nation to consider independence worth the price.

Some nationalists have turned this argument on its head and asserted that an independent Wales would quickly become more prosperous. Helen Mary Jones AM has argued that:

> The Unionists say we are too poor to become an independent nation. That's just not the case. Global experience demonstrates that, in today's developed world, neither a country's size nor its location are barriers to success. Take Iceland as an example. It … is the 10th most prosperous country in the world … If Iceland can do it, Wales can. Norway is the third most prosperous country in the world. Ireland is the seventh most prosperous country in the world. The people of Wales could be just as prosperous as those small independent countries.[18]

These remarks were made before the world economic crisis worsened in the autumn of 2008. Leaving this aside, it is clear that the nationalist treatment of the economic costs and benefits of independence is no more robust than the hard Unionist interpretation. In time, Wales may be better or worse off. Either outcome would be possible in an independent Wales that had more control over economic leavers. However, such control might not always compensate for the security of being part of a larger state when economic storms hit. Helen Mary Jones' list is instructive even if we overlook how recent events have torn through its 'small is beautiful' assumptions. Iceland, a micro and niche economy, was already in deep and over-heated economic water. Ireland achieved considerable prosperity at the cost of policies that would probably make Helen Mary faint. Meanwhile, Norway has benefited from massive oil and gas wealth, a windfall rarely available to small economies.

Let us make a more sober prediction. Independence is unlikely to make Wales so poor that the durability of democratic institutions would be threatened. However, any initial and significant economic cost could, certainly if unanticipated, pose a tough challenge to an independent Wales.

In gaining independence Wales would set a bad example to other small nations currently in democratic multinational states and encourage them to secede.

Here we find the strongest ethical argument against Welsh independence – its affect on other nations. Many political philosophers believe that a liberal theory of the state cannot be based on the premise that nations and states should be necessarily co-terminous. The federalist thinker Wayne Norman argues that there are compelling 'reasons for seeking out federal solutions to the problems of multinational states. The world surely has little to gain from being divided into 600 states (with 600 tetchy armies and who knows how many ethnic and religious militias), and still less from going through the 'liberating' process (Yugoslav-style) of fighting to become 600 states'.[19] It might seem a little unfair to stand against Welsh independence on the grounds of what it might incite in the Caucuses, but recent experience of state disintegration surely does counsel caution. Certainly some senior figures in Plaid Cymru have reservations about the liberal credentials of absolute nationalism. For example, in 2004 Lord Dafydd Elis Thomas AM said:

> Plaid Cymru has not adjusted to devolution because you have this improbable allegiance of some people to something called Welsh independence. Not since the 7th Century was this ever a real political project. And yet there are still people who still pursue the goal of Welsh independence and Scottish independence as if this was the real issue. If you look at mainland Europe and North America with people like the Party Québecois the only role for autonomous parties is to transform themselves from opposition to the overall state to one of the parties of government in the areas they represent.[20]

These remarks helped pave the way for Plaid's entry into coalition government in 2007, and they followed a sometimes acrimonious debate on the desirability of independence. Some in Plaid held that independence had never been a goal of Plaid Cymru at all, and even if it had there was little sense in pursuing it further. Rhodri Glyn Thomas AM, a contender at the time for Plaid's leadership, said that 'logistically Wales is and will always be a part of the United Kingdom. But we need a more equal partnership based on free association, which will give us sovereignty without separation'.[21] Unless delivered in a federal constitution, however, it is difficult to see how sovereignty without separation is possible. Plaid have swung back in favour of independence, but there are still influential sceptics who hint that a thoroughgoing federalism would be a more liberal option. The former AM and MP Cynog Dafis has stated that:

> I think independence ought to be regarded as an option for the future, rather than as an aim. The other danger is that by putting the emphasis on independence, we take our eye off the really important ball, which is to achieve things for Wales in the here and now.[22]

An independent Wales could, of course, pursue a foreign policy that promoted international co-operation and emphasised interdependence. A self-denying ordinance could be placed on the discussion of national disputes in other states. Nevertheless, it is difficult to see how Welsh independence would not be part of a wider process of state disintegration. Yet states, like nations, are not fixed and final entities. It is possible that the disintegration of multinational states will be counter-balanced by new models of political association such as the confederal European Union. While this is a reasonable point to make in the case of western and central Europe, it seems a very optimistic expectation for supra-national developments elsewhere.

In my view, international order is unlikely to be promoted by the emergence of hundreds of new states in the next 25 years or so. While it is fanciful to suggest that Welsh independence would be a direct cause of such an outcome, it should be placed in the context of this wider question: what is likely to happen if states and nations become increasingly co-terminous? This creates a strong presumption in favour of preserving democratic multinational states such as Britain. Wales should remain within the United Kingdom and nationalists should only seek independence if their (our!) legitimate nation-building projects are suppressed.

To seek independence for its own sake, as Dafydd Elis Thomas hints, would take Wales close to what Wayne Norman calls 'vanity' secession – and that cannot be justified on liberal grounds. While this ethical objection to independence has moral force, it cannot be considered a total bar to independence nor does it give to Unionists the right to use force to prevent secession should that be the settled will of the Welsh people.

A Welsh state would contain a troubling linguistic division and not be a coherent national community.

Just as few existing states have been formed without a degree of conflict and coercion, and continue to live with the lingering consequences, any new states more aligned to national communities are likely to contain similar seeds of conflict and have their own minorities, embedded populations bearing allegiance to the old state, and cultural and linguistic divisions. Russia, for instance, justified its occupation of Georgia in 2008 on the grounds that it was protecting embedded Russian populations in Abkhazia and South Ossetia. Georgia was said, by the Russians, to lack national coherence (at least in these territories). Perhaps with a tinge of moral pessimism Michael Oakeshott warned those seeking elevated forms of political association against believing they would be miraculously free of profound tension:

> There have always been people who have wished for more, who have wanted a state to be an integrated community set on a common course and pursuing a common purpose... But those who, under the spell of a supremely inappropriate analogy, have expressed their belief that more has already been achieved by speaking of the states of modern Europe as 'nation states', have confused their dreams with the conditions of waking life.[23]

Paradoxically, the various communities in an independent Welsh state – Welsh speakers, Anglo-Welsh, English-born citizens, ethnic minorities and so on – might interact in such a way as to make Wales *less* coherent as a nation. The demands of a state are formidable. Cleavages of relatively little salience when a nation exists within a wider multinational state could become aggravated by independence. Should an independent Wales falter in the economic sphere, would Wales' linguistic divide suddenly become a proxy for more general anxieties? Wales may appear a simpler political space than the United Kingdom as a whole, but the divisions that are unavoidably present in a population of some three million inevitably take on a different character, and carry different possibilities, when contained in a state.

The most pressing existential question that would face an independent Wales is what future would there be for the Welsh language? Within the United Kingdom, the policy of bilingualism in Wales has generated little tension since it started to be applied with increasing rigour in the 1980s. Indeed, it is remarkable how enthusiastically bilingualism has been actively supported by monoglot English speakers. A Welsh state would probably (with cause) want to go further and initiate a programme of rapid Welsh language recovery, perhaps along the lines of the policy pursued by the Israeli state after independence in 1948. This is not a fanciful suggestion. Arguably, Plaid Cymru was dogged by this very issue – how to make Wales once again Welsh-speaking –until the establishment of Cymdeithas yr Iaith Gymraeg in 1962. Saunders Lewis and his disciples maintained that Wales was the language. While Gwynfor Evans pursued a more pragmatic course, he had to cope with the constant pressure for a more aggressive Welsh language policy. While I doubt that the minority of Welsh speakers could, and far less would want to, oppress the majority Anglo-Welsh population, the language question would clearly be framed in a radically different manner in an independent Wales.

These are profound questions indeed. However, they appear to challenge most if not all nations and states. Cultural diversity, which in modern society is inevitable, would not constitute an objection to Welsh independence in particular, but it should stand as a warning to any naïve nationalists who believe that Wales would somehow become spiritually elevated as a state. It would not. Like the British state today, an independent Wales would not be a uniformly coherent entity but an untidy and ambivalent mixture of social, cultural, religious and ethnic groups. Nevertheless, this is the condition of all but the smallest states and it cannot be considered a strong argument against the case for Welsh independence.

Wales, unlike Scotland, has never been a state and therefore secession from the UK cannot be justified.

After a long process of negotiation, the ruling class of Scotland agreed to join with England (and Wales) to establish a British state in 1707. At the time Scotland could claim to be one of Europe's oldest kingdoms, although also one of its weaker states. There is the possibility that Scotland's consent to form a Union may at some point be rescinded because it no longer serves the best interests of the Scottish nation. Once a state, always a potential state – this is the general thrust of the argument. As the Scottish Government recently put the case, 'The Act of Union 1707 is the focus of the debate for further change or indeed repeal'.[24]

Wales never achieved statehood. Indeed, it was only intermittently a unified Principality, and it was incorporated into England by conquest, a commonplace device in state formation (although one with manifest ethical difficulties). However, that Wales contained in the later medieval period the potential for statehood is undeniable. Owain Glyn Dŵr's programme, set out in the Pennal letter to the king of France, was an accomplished sketch of an early modern state. But these dreams evaporated and they provide but scant historical justification for Welsh independence. Even had Glyn Dŵr established a state that endured, it is distinctly possible that Wales would have followed the path of Scotland and voluntarily joined the Union.

Whatever weight we choose to place on these deeply historical judgements, we can perhaps say that Scotland has a stronger precedent for independence than Wales. Yet Wales was recognised as a distinct political entity in medieval Europe. This may form the basis for an argument that, as Wales did not join the Union with England voluntarily, Wales' membership of the UK remains open to question even without the historical precedent of once being a state. While the Welsh gentry acquiesced to the Act of Union in 1536, they can hardly be said to have negotiated with Henry VIII's government.

In his study of *Secession: The Morality of Political Divorce* Allen Buchanan identifies involuntary annexation as grounds for secession. However, he acknowledges that opponents of secession have a strong argument when they maintain that, 'To fail to acknowledge a moral statute of limitations would produce unacceptable disruption of the international order, with endless recriminations about ancient wrongs vying for priority'.[25] There is also a sense, opponents of secession argue, that we 'cannot be held hostage to history' and that 'historic grievances fade with time'.[26] Buchanan suggests that if these arguments are accepted then a statute of limitations might commence after three or four generations have lived peaceably within the coerced state. However, he remains sceptical that these arguments against secession are likely to work in practice. In the case of Wales, many generations have lived peaceably within the British state since 1536. Whatever historical grievances may have existed in Tudor times, they can have little contemporary significance for Welsh citizens now. Indeed, many Welsh citizens today would not have had Welsh ancestors in the 16th Century, others have ancestors who only settled in Wales because of the Tudor annexation.

History is often a reliable guide but we must guard against being enthralled by its so-called (and often highly subjective) lessons. It is doubtful that states require such an historical justification. States are political associations and most philosophers agree that they can be dissolved and reconfigured under certain circumstances. History cannot have an absolute veto on this process. If the British state ever pursued a policy of discrimination and cultural assimilation in Wales, it would simply be illiberal to argue that the Welsh people could not demand to secede because Wales has never been a state. On this reasoning, the USA is not a legitimately constituted state. Wales has enough cultural, geographic and political coherence to give any demand for secession arising out of oppression great moral force.

Welsh independence is impermissible unless it is the sovereign will of the people of the United Kingdom as a whole.

The most fundamentalist objection to Welsh independence comes from Unionists who contend that the United Kingdom is a single constitutional entity. For any change in the composition of the state to be valid, agreement should be secured on a United Kingdom basis.

During the Irish crisis such agreement originally meant a decision by Parliament, but Unionists later argued that it required a specific UK-wide referendum (the shift occurred when Unionists lost their parliamentary majority). There is no acceptance here of the contention that sovereignty ultimately resides with the Home Nations separately. This hard Unionism explains why the overwhelming and democratically expressed wish of Irish voters was denied in the late 19th and early 20th Centuries. The sovereign will of the Irish people was not recognised because Unionists argued there existed only the sovereign power of the

United Kingdom as represented by the Sovereign in Parliament.

The Irish crisis discredited the moral assumptions of such fundamentalist Unionism because in practice it required the frustration of a democratically expressed demand by coercive means – and such a situation cannot be sustained in a liberal state. While few Unionists now hold these absolute views, they still linger in the ideological DNA of some Conservatives and to some extent explain the antipathy they feel to any significant constitutional change. John Major was more realistic in 1993 when he stated the obvious in the foreword to the White Paper *Scotland in the Union*, 'no nation could be held irrevocably in a Union against its will'.[27] The White Paper left no room for ambiguity, 'It should be a mark of Scotland's self-confidence in her own status as a nation that she shares her sovereignty with the other parts of the UK. But the willingness to share that sovereignty must never be taken for granted'.[28] By logical inference, sovereignty rests with the Welsh people in the same way.

In conclusion, we can say that there is no absolute argument against Welsh independence in all circumstances. This is not to say that independence is suddenly the most coherent option available to the people of Wales. Rather, the secession of Wales from the United Kingdom would be permissible on moral grounds in certain circumstances, assuming that this was the settled will of the people.

The strongest ethical argument against Welsh independence is that it might have a deleterious affect on international order by sparking off 'vanity' nationalist programmes elsewhere. However, this would not be a justifiable reason for overriding the sovereign will of the Welsh people to form a liberal state committed to international co-operation and lacking aggressive military and foreign policy objectives. Nevertheless, and even under such benign conditions, an independent Wales is only likely to emerge within a process that would end in many more sovereign states being created in the next 25 years or so. This would not be a constructive development and therefore I believe there exists a strong presumption against Welsh (and Scottish) independence. Celtic nationalists should, it seems to me, explore the possibility of fuller domestic autonomy within a federal British state.

WHY ARE WE BRITISH?

So much of Britishness lies in the elusive realm of sentiment that it cannot be easily encapsulated in a set of precise characteristics or values. In *The Governance of Britain* the whole country is urged to 'come together to develop a British statement of values'.[29] The Government promises 'to work with the British people to achieve a stronger sense of what it means to be British, and to launch an inclusive debate on the future of the country's constitution'.[30] It is instructive that here the Government quickly falls back onto a civic issue – the future of the constitution – and avoids any contemplation of the question what is Britishness?

We are left with the impression that Britishness has to be tightly defined in constitutional terms because it is no longer loosely felt as an instinctive identity by a large and growing part of the population. Yet establishing what are Britain's core national values can quickly become a didactic and unconvincing exercise. One cannot help but wonder that a loose fitting British nationalism, a little worn from instinctive use, is not actually closer to the ideal and much more suited to meet the practical demands of modern life. Critics of Britishness argue that it cannot be convincingly expressed by politicians because it is no longer strongly felt by the public. They believe that Britishness has had its day. Yet definitions of Welshness and Scottishness sound equally shaky and archaic when spelt out. It is noteworthy, for example, that *Choosing Scotland's Future* completely avoids giving a definition of Scottishness and concerns itself entirely with Scotland's constitutional future.[31]

The civic and sentimental aspects of Britishness are, of course, closely interwoven. The development of the British state was greatly helped by the cultural bonds that inevitably grew in such a geographically distinct space. And indeed the concept of Britain had deep roots. As the historian R.R. Davies has written, 'The idea of Britain exercised a powerful hold over the medieval mind. It had a depth, a resonance, a precision, and an incontestability which did not belong to its imprecise, contestable, and Johnny-come-lately competitors – England, Scotland, Wales'.[32]

Nonetheless, the Norman-Angevin kings struggled to extract political outcomes from this rich seam of sentiment. Their vision of a united Britain looked too much like English domination of an insular empire. The Tudors, notionally Welsh, and the Stuarts, actually Scottish, did not make this mistake. They realised that any convincing ideology of Britain could not merely be written with an English pen. Of course, Wales was annexed by England while Scotland joined in a more equal Union, though very much as a junior partner. Nonetheless, the Celtic nations participated in the political institutions of the realm and slowly transformed them into British institutions. Although this has been described by some as 'internal colonisation',[33] the British state worked because it erected few barriers to keep out those Celtic citizens with the requisite social standing or raw talent to participate in political life.

In divorcing Britain from Catholic Christendom, the Tudors perhaps inadvertently turned away from Europe and created the conditions for Britain to project itself as a global state. This started a process that eventually created the English-speaking world and caused cultural ramifications which are still massively pervasive today. Distinctiveness is at the heart of national identity. While geography had made Britain naturally distinct, the Reformation and its aftermath made it culturally distinct also. Sir Thomas More was horrified by the implications of political and religious autarky. At his trial he said:

> This Realm, being but one member and small part of the church, might not make a particular law disagreeable with the general law of Christ's universal Catholic church. No more than the city of London, being but one poor member in respect of the whole realm, might make a law against an act of parliament to bind the whole realm.[34]

How the passing of time has dulled our senses! Thomas More immediately saw the revolutionary nature of the Tudor state-building project. Although piecemeal and not systematically planned, it nevertheless established the realm as an *Imperium*. It was a state self-sufficient as a temporal and spiritual entity and therefore the *only* source of authority. First the Crown and eventually Parliament was acknowledged as the sovereign power.

Many critics of Britishness ignore its long antecedence and focus on the imperial episode of British history. They argue that Britishness is no more than a false-consciousness and an epiphenomenon of the Victorian-Edwardian British Empire. Yet this period barely lasted 50 years. Rather than viewing this short spell in our history as a particular episode in the development of Britishness, it is taken to be its epitome. Without the high-age of Empire and its ideology of imperialism, such critics argue, the Union would have decayed in Wales and Scotland as it did in Ireland in the late 19th Century. Instead, Wales and Scotland were fooled into thinking themselves partners with, rather than colonies of, England. These critics often long for the growth of English nationalism as they predict that this would be the final sign that Britishness is defunct. To be fair to these trenchant critics of Britishness, it is Britain as a state that they find objectionable. As Tom Nairn puts it:

> The best, and possibly the only, way of saving the many worthwhile features of the UK inheritance is for Scotland and Wales to become independent… In the longer run, 'Britain' will only survive as a confederation of independent states … and that survival will indeed represent a 'New Britain'.[35]

Nations exist when people *think* they exist. People generally think nations exist when they *want* them to exist. Consequently, the forensic tools of modern scholarship are of only limited use in examining the substance of national identities. Under any robust analysis, tartan is as risible as the Gorsedd or the state opening of Parliament when presented as some kind of ancient tradition. This is not the point, however. All traditions are invented, but they can only endure if they make visible some deep, inner truth and satisfy a people's need for an historic narrative and purpose.

It is of little wonder that national symbols can be so bizarre, pungent and colourful. To ask whether a particular national symbol is true makes as much sense as asking whether a particular colour is true. The materials of nation-building are rather like colours on a palate – they await the creative power of the artist to produce an authentic depiction of human experience. The most meaningful question we can ask is whether a certain depiction of national identity appears authentic. But what can appear to one generation as authentic may to another seem archaic or even disturbing. The work of nation-building is never complete nor ever entirely convincing. Just like the human character, nations are not fixed or final entities and remain frustratingly elusive.

Unlike the civic architecture of a state, nations cannot be made objective. To our recent ancestors, speaking Welsh as the mother tongue was what most clearly defined Welshness. That definition cannot sustain a general sense of Welshness today. While the British Empire may have seemed an awesome symbol of Britishness just a hundred years ago, it only lingers faintly now in the Commonwealth and the history books. Reinvention is the existential challenge facing all nations.

Britishness has meant something a little different to each Home Nation. The Welsh and the Scots have had the strongest British identity, the Irish the weakest, and the English the most diffident. In Wales and Scotland the injury to national pride caused by the failure of political institutions either to fully develop or to be sustained was assuaged by a partnership in a British state that was not under exclusive English ownership. Only in Ireland did this political assimilation fail entirely (initially because it was not accompanied by Catholic emancipation). Ultimately the possibilities offered by Britishness appeared to the Irish less promising than those contained in Europe's national reawakening in the 19th Century.

For Wales and Scotland, Parliament's somewhat reluctant transformation from an English into a British institution was a key development. The Crown, of course, had long juggled with multiple identities, celebrating its historic Welsh and contemporary Scottish roots. Consequently, the civic projection of Britishness became vivid and powerful. Even today *The Governance of Britain* affirms with little hyperbole that Parliament 'is a major symbol of what it means to be British'.[36] And *Choosing Scotland's Future* concedes a similar point when it reassures Scots that 'the Union of the Crowns of 1603 would continue even after repeal of the 1707 Act'.[37]

The other mischievous alchemist of Britishness, critics argue, was Protestantism. Linda Colley maintains that 'Protestantism was the foundation that made the invention of Great Britain possible'.[38] Predictably, some critics of Britishness have jumped to the conclusion that the decline in religious observance means the end of Britain. Protestantism was in fact a weak unifying force because it was so fractured. Calvin's followers had little in common with the latitudinal Church of England. On the other hand, what Protestantism did symbolise was distinctiveness. Britain was much more than Protestant, it was anti-Catholic.

This also helped to make Britain more of an Atlantic than a European power, and a state that was rapidly generating its own theory of self. In particular, the works of Thomas Hobbes and John Locke helped develop an ideology of Britain where it seemed that the great traditions of European civilisation were less salient than Britain's particular political experience. Just as Rome eventually moved out of the intellectual shadow of Greece and perceived its own vast imperial mission, so Britain began to sense its global destiny. Eventually, after much refinement, this mission was encapsulated in the rule of law and parliamentary government. After Athens, Westminster became the most potent democratic space on earth.

Unsurprisingly, Britons took a great pride in the success of their political institutions, a pride that survived the rapid decline of the British Empire and the evaporation of its imperial mission. To some extent the Second World War provided a fillip to Britain's sense of moral destiny. Britain was the only democratic European state not to be shattered by a Nazi invasion or its threat, and this inevitably renewed the sense of confidence Britons had in their institutions. While the idolisation of Westminster as the 'mother' of parliaments was no doubt overdone, it reflected a view that Britain was in a profound way a righteous nation and an example to other, less successful, states.

The Cold War, the moral regeneration of Germany, and the political ascendancy of the USA, together with developments like the EU, have eroded Britain's sense of distinctiveness and mission. However, this merely changes the nature of Britishness and does not question its very feasibility. It is time to think about another useful example Britain could provide in a most uncertain world. Should Britain remain intact as a multinational state it could help the world avoid fragmentation into many hundreds of sovereign nation states. There would be another option, a more coherent alternative, for those intent on defending and propagating liberal values.

Serendipity added to Britain's growing sense of distinctiveness. Britain's profound geographical integrity started to produce powerful social and economic forces in the 17th Century. In time they created an English-speaking 'world' and an industrial society that made much of modern life possible. To be British is to speak English and to be part of the cultural world it generates. At the eve of the Reformation, when the discovery of the Americas was astonishing what were still in essence medieval minds, no one could have predicted the growth of English into a universal language. In 1590 barely two-thirds of the population of the British Isles could speak it and in total there were some six million English speakers world-wide. By the mid 20th Century this figure had increased fifty-fold, and most native English speakers lived outside Britain.[39] This process created a continent of the mind every bit as real as the physical continent of Europe.

While the growth of English into the world's most adaptable and common conduit of culture has brought Britain enormous intellectual strength and influence, in Wales the blessing has been mixed. Welsh may be the language of heaven, but the world of Victorian business used English and this encouraged many in Wales to bite their own tongue and so Britain's oldest language was stifled. Yet, as our common language, English remains at the heart of British national life. As Trevor Phillips put it when head of the Commission for Racial Equality, we must value 'the common currency of the English language'.[40]

The Prime Minister, Gordon Brown, believes that a kind of mission lingers in the responsibility Britain has to further English as the world's language. He asserts, 'I want Britain to make a gift to the world – pledging to help support anyone, whatever their circumstances, to have access to the tools they need to learn or to teach English'.[41] At home and abroad the BBC is the supreme and benign agent of the English language. Should the British state ever fragment, the cultural power of the English language would be little diminished and it would continue to create close bonds between the populations of the successor states.

The world's world of work has been shaped by British economic experience. Britain did not participate in a European industrial revolution but sparked the process itself. This brought great wealth and power and reinforced the belief that Britain had a manifest and rather non-European destiny. In 1707 what most attracted the Scottish élite to the Union was the prospect of access to Europe's largest free market. The economic forces unleashed by free trade helped transform the Scottish nation and inspired one of Europe's brightest intellectual enlightenments. In Adam Smith Scotland produced a thinker of global significance. *The Wealth of Nations* was as significant in the 18th Century as Charles Darwin's *The Origin of Species* in the 19th Century. Both helped shape the mind of modern man.

In sparking the industrial revolution Britain became the world's exemplar state and economy. To be British was to be in the vanguard of mankind's march to prosperity and civilised life. Even the great political shocks of the late 18th Century, the American and French revolutions, did little to undermine Britain's sense of destiny. The period 1815-1914 became what many commentators call Britain's 'century' such was the global reach of British political and economic power. Britain had competitors of course, but no serious match. This situation was itself exceptional and it was not repeated until the end of the Cold War established the USA as the world's pre-eminent power.

The Conservative politician, Lord Baker, has called for a museum of British history to be established as he believes that British history is all too often neglected. We have a stirring national story: in many places great, in some places disturbing, and nearly everywhere carrying influence well beyond our shores. Lord Baker's proposal is a nation-building project of the most classic kind, and one I enthusiastically welcome.

However, it remains the fact that a British identity has not been historically determined for us nor stands fixed as something we cannot much alter. Britishness became an instinctive identity relatively late, in fact only sometime in the 18th Century. Even so, it was uncommonly powerful. Now that Britishness is not so instinctively felt it is natural to search for a reassuring list of virtues or values that demonstrate its continuing vitality. Parliamentary democracy and the rule of law are sound historical achievements, but they have long passed into the common ownership of liberal states all over the world and are no longer uniquely British. All national identities corrode under forensic analysis. When broken down into specific principles or values any national identity becomes a less convincing image. The question is not can I *prove* that I am British? Rather, do I *want* to be British?

ARISE FEDERAL BRITAIN!

It is now time to consider what a federal Britain might look like. This is conjecture indeed, but without some prediction these deliberations will remain too abstract. Conjecture runs the risk of ridicule and even those political giants Hamilton, Madison and Jay were accused of making harebrained prescriptions in the 1780s when urging America to federate. Alas, I have little of their skill but their example is both instructive and inspirational.

They realised that the great gains of American independence and the principles that inspired it, would remain unsecured unless a strong and stable federal constitution was adopted. *The Federalist Papers* proposed a constitution that was not new in a revolutionary sense, but a more complete institutional expression of American political experience. And so, when proposing a federal constitution for the UK, the aim is not to overturn our political traditions but to give them new vigour.

There appear to be two options for a federal Britain, one involving a full federation, the other just partial. But both would contain the essential premise of federalism, the division of sovereignty. Federal and unitary constitutions can successfully embody the traditions of British parliamentary democracy, and do so in Canada, Australia and New Zealand. This is why we can confidently predict that Britain's political life would not be radically disturbed by federalism. And federalism would bring the great benefit of preventing Britain from stumbling towards fragmentation through the muddle of devolution. Federalism would require preparation and careful planning. This might be done in a wide-ranging and inclusive constitutional convention. In itself this would give the electorate an opportunity to affirm their desire for a British state, or – to put it more passionately – their determination to remain British!

Britain as a Full Federation

The people of Britain would still look on Westminster as the heart of political life. Westminster would become Britain's federal parliament, the embodiment of Britain's democratic traditions and the most authoritative institution in the state. The United Kingdom government would be responsible to Westminster in accordance with the British parliamentary tradition. However, the fiction of absolute parliamentary sovereignty would end and be replaced by sovereignty over only those areas set out in the constitution and necessary for the effective functioning of the British state. These functions would include macro-economic policy, most taxation, immigration and citizenship, defence, and foreign affairs. Sovereignty over what may be termed domestic issues (such as health, education, economic development, transport, housing and planning) would lie with the national parliaments in Wales, England, Scotland and Northern Ireland. It is possible, but initially unlikely, that England might be divided into several units. The federation might also include the crown dependencies of the Isle of Man and the Channel Islands.

Westminster would probably remain a bicameral parliament. The House of Commons would contain perhaps 300 MPs and all members would have equal rights and represent electorates of similar size. The UK government and its ministers would be drawn from and be responsible to Westminster. Party politics would operate much as it does today. The revising chamber, the House of Lords (or Senators?) could be structured to reflect the federation's multinational character. A disproportionate method could be used to elect or nominate, say 100, members. For example, each Home Nation could be guaranteed a minimum of 15 members in a chamber of 100. This would promote the principle of equality between the federation's member nations. A revising chamber constituted in this manner would not find itself in direct democratic competition with the House of Commons.

A written constitution would set out the formal division of sovereignty and the respective rights and responsibilities of the federal and national governments. Unforeseen problems and areas of constitutional ambiguity, together with disputes between jurisdictions, would be settled by a Constitutional Court. The position of the Queen and her successors as Head of State would be unchanged. However, it is likely that the customs and practices of the monarchy would adapt over time to reflect Britain's federal character.

Britain as a Partial Federation.

Even after a long national 'conversation' (as the Green Paper *The Governance of Britain* puts it) it might still not be possible to adopt a fully federal constitution. The people of England, so long left out of discussion about devolution and its likely consequences, might consider federalism too great a disruption to meet the constitutional demands of Britain's multinationalism. Nevertheless, there may still be pressure in England to address the central anomaly of devolution whereby English domestic policies are determined by the United Kingdom parliament (which includes Welsh and Scottish members) but such issues are the sole preserve of the devolved institutions in Wales, Scotland and Northern Ireland. Worse, it is possible that a United Kingdom government would one day find itself responsible for English domestic policies despite lacking a majority of English MPs.

A partial or quasi-federal agreement might meet the legitimate concerns of the English electorate and increase the authority both of Westminster and the devolved institutions. Westminster would make an historic declaration affirming the sovereignty of the devolved institutions over those matters under their jurisdiction. This would be a federal action, even if merely contained in a convention rather than a written constitution. Westminster would operate in two distinct modes: one for English affairs (in which only English MPs would participate), the other for UK matters. This would create an English legislative process *within* Westminster rather than in a separate English Parliament.

This solution has a cost in that MPs from England, Wales, Scotland and Northern Ireland would not have equal rights, and this would be untidy. However, it is a compromise that could work as the non-English members would specialise in UK and foreign affairs rather as if they were in a federal parliament. The danger that would still lurk in this solution is that one day Westminster could find itself with two governments responsible to it. On United Kingdom issues there would be the United Kingdom government headed by Britain's Prime Minister. But this government may lack a majority of English MPs and so decide not to govern for England. An additional government would then have to be speedily created to avoid a constitutional crisis.

Happily this is a rather fanciful scenario. A United Kingdom government in this predicament would have other options. It might simply form a coalition to secure a majority of MPs in England, surely the most likely course of action. Alternatively, it could seek to govern England as a minority administration but only after securing agreement on a policy platform agreeable to English MPs. Nevertheless, as we consider some of the practical issues a quasi-federal system might have to face, it appears a more convoluted approach than a full federation. However, the revising chamber could be much the same as it would be in a full federation, and this would strengthen the federal principle considerably.

Although clearly a compromise, a quasi-federal agreement might be seen as a useful interim solution to Britain's constitutional challenges. It would be much more stable and balanced than the current system of devolution because it would have largely addressed the English anomaly, sometimes called the 'West Lothian' question. In time it might evolve into a full federation, but from the start it would divide sovereignty between the Home Nations and the British state.

References

1. K.C. Wheare, *Federal Government* (Oxford 1946) p. 52.
2. *The Governance of Britain*, CM7170 (July 2007) para. 143.
3. *Choosing Scotland's Future*, Scottish Executive (August 2007) para 1.11.
4. Jacob T. Levy, *Federalism, Liberalism, and the Separation of Loyalties* American Political Science Review, Vol. 101 No. 3 August 2007, p. 465.
5. A point developed particularly in Federalist Paper No. 25.
6. Lord Acton, essay on 'Nationality' in *The History of Freedom and Other Essays* (London 1907).
7. Wayne Norman, 'Towards a Philosophy of Federalism' in Judith Baker (ed) *Group Rights* (Toronto 1994).
8. John Kendle, *Federal Britain* (London 1997) p. 77.
9. John Barnes, *Federal Britain: No Longer Unthinkable?*, Centre for Policy Studies (1998) in the unnumbered preface termed 'The Argument'.
10. *The Governance of Britain*, compare paras. 57-66 to paras. 141-144.
11. Ibid, para. 195.
12. Ibid, para. 211.
13. Tom Nairn, *Gordon Brown: Bard of Britishness*, Institute of Welsh Affairs (2006) p. 11.
14. *The Governance of Britain*, p. 5, *Choosing Scotland's Future*, p. v.
15. Michael Keating, 'So many nations, so few states: territory and nationalism in the global era' in Gagnon and Tully above.
16. Barnes, p. 44.
17. Lord Hailsham, *The Dilemma of Democracy* (London 1978) p. 167.
18. Helen Mary Jones AM, *Western Mail* 5 August 2008.
19. Norman in Baker above, p. 82.
20. Lord Dafydd Elis Thomas, *e.politix* 16 September 2004.
21. Rhodri Glyn Thomas AM, *The Role of Plaid Cymru over the next 10 years*, speech delivered at the Temple of Peace, Cardiff 19 November 2003.
22. Cynog Davis, *Western Mail* 11 August 2008.
23. Michael Oakeshott, *On Human Conduct* (Oxford 1975) p. 188.
24. *Choosing Scotland's Future* para. 3.4.
25. Allen Buchanan, *Secession: The Morality of Political Divorce from Fort Sumter to Lithuania and Quebec* (Boulder, USA 1991) p. 88.
26. Ibid.
27. *Scotland in the Union*, Cmnd. 2225 (March 1993) p.5.
28. Ibid, para. 10.3, p.38.
29. *The Governance of Britain*, para. 9, p.11.
30. Ibid, para. 10, p.11.
31. *Choosing Scotland's Future*, particularly paras. 3.2-3.6.

32. R.R. Davies, *The First English Empire* (Oxford 2000) p. 35.
33. Most notably, Michael Hechter, *Internal Colonialism*, (London 1975).
34. Quoted in, Peter Ackroyd, *The Life of Thomas More*, (London 1998) p. 386.
35. Tom Nairn, above, pp. 27-8.
36. *The Governance of Britain*, para. 122, p.40.
37. *Choosing Scotland's Future*, para. 3.4, p.19.
38. Linda Colley, *Britons: Forging the Nation 1707 – 1837* (London 2003) p. 54.
39. *The Cambridge Encyclopaedia of the English Language* (Cambridge 1995) p. 92.
40. *The Times*, 3 April 2004.
41. *Gallery News*, 17 January 2008.

Epilogue

William V, King of Great Britain, England and Scotland, Prince of Wales, Duke of Belfast, received the final briefing for the celebrations of federal Britain's silver jubilee while flying back from his state visit to the USA. His Majesty's hosts had been particularly fulsome in their praise of Britain's achievement in turning itself into a federal state. The President had quipped 'we are even closer cousins now, your Majesty – perhaps you might get the 13 colonies back!'

Despite dire predictions, federalism had not been the halfway house to disintegration but the means to re-build the constitutional foundations of the UK. The referendum on the new federal constitution had produced strong 'Yes' votes in each of the Home Nations. Britain had revived itself and set an example to the world on how to accommodate the liberal demands of nationalism.